Julius
★Pam★

Beyond Reason

Contents

The author, 1970

All these top acts needed supporting artists. That's where the small groups came in, rubbing shoulders with the famous and hoping they might make it themselves.
Ray Broome

Foreword

I AM DELIGHTED to write this foreword as Andy, a fellow guitarist, has been a friend of mine for over fifty years. I first met him as a frequent visitor to the local music shop, which I managed in the mid 1960s and early 1970s, equipping him (and many other young aspiring musicians) with the necessary 'tools of the trade' to form groups of various musical persuasions – Rock/Pop/Country & Western, etc. I was well known in local musical circles as I had had my own band since the early sixties, quite a successful outfit playing mostly cover versions of current hits.

His book presents a real snapshot of those times – completely unimaginable to anyone born once use of the internet was established and changed the pattern of our daily lives forever. For example, in the sixties social media had not yet been invented. No one felt the need (or had the ability) to be in contact with everybody and anybody at all times via mobile phones, sharing the minutiae of their daily life. For the less well off, the standard of motor transport was laughable – they drove old 'bangers', both cars and vans, which today would no longer be allowed on the highway, but in the sixties and seventies were commonplace. Top musical acts played ordinary venues in the provinces, not just huge stadia like the O2 in London – there were comparatively few of those at the time anyway. The Beatles, for example, played Ipswich Gaumont Theatre in the early days of their fame – something that would be unheard of for any chart-topping band now. All these top acts needed supporting artists. That's where the small groups came in, rubbing shoulders with the famous and hoping they might make it themselves. Some did – most of us didn't.

This is the story of just such a group – one of many thousands up and down the country with similar aspirations, all of whom would have stories to tell. The book recounts very accurately how young musicians (I use the term loosely) enjoyed themselves making music for the love of it and gaining invaluable life experiences while doing so, not least from their encounters with the music agents, who were also looking for the 'next big thing' and overnight success. For many groups, their music-making days were short-lived – even the really successful ones – but I am certain that in later life all of them retain, or retained, fond memories of a much simpler time when they were privileged to play the great music of an era that will always be remembered.

Ray Broome

It was dark and overcast that Monday morning, I was rummaging through the under stairs cupboard and the torch batteries were fading fast. Like most everything within they were beyond redemption. A box of diaries, envelopes, posters, and general rubbish surfaced from under the twenty thousand shoes my woman had collected over the last 38 years. One large envelope opened intrigue and as its contents emerged from the gloom I could just make out a photograph of four young men. Up off my knees the increasing light revealed the true image; my memory flashed back and back again as my eyes welled. Forty five years had passed since I had seen or spoken to the three young men in the photograph with me. So much was stimulating my memory. I was drifting back to a completely forgotten time...

Julius Pam, 1970

Beg your pardon, sir,' said Sam, suddenly breaking off his loquaciuos discourse. "Is this Bury St Edmunds." "It is," replied Mr. Pickwick.
Charles Dickens,
The Pickwick Papers

Prologue
Bury St Edmunds
July 1970

BURY ST EDMUNDS back then was a sleepy old Suffolk market town surrounded by farming. Not the most vibrant place; hardly renowned for its wild parties, rave ups, orgies, music venues – or night life come to think of it.

The liveliest attraction was probably Wednesdays livestock and cattle market; the most likely place to find entertainment in the evenings, the town's many pubs. For over two hundred years they had been serving the locals ales produced in the towns brewery, a legacy from the monks of the Abbey of St Edmund, and they were not known for their outlandish behaviour, either. Some locals hadn't yet come to terms with long hair down to the shoulders supported by the male species. Fancy a drink gorgeous, or give us a kiss, were still vocal innuendos as long haired loafers had the audacity to wander the streets.

Sleepy is an understatement when it came to the pop world. The Corn Exchange and surrounding village halls were often filled with the sound of Country & Western music, the Athenaeum and hotels hosted dance bands catering for the middle-aged and well-to-do. Pop dances had become a rarity. Not much, then, to appeal to the music-loving young locally, to broaden their experience and open their minds to the wider world.

This historic town had spawned a number of groups that quickly came and went during the sixties music phenomenon, only a few surviving by July 1970. On the odd night, quiet, dimly lit Mill Road and Brentgovel Street were barely hanging on to the echo of a group rehearsing for a couple of hours at The Cricketers or White Lion.

In Risbygate Street, however, there was a light still shining brightly. So, what of Risbygate Street? Well, on the outside, nothing out of the ordinary. The busy A45 trunk road from east to west, often with wall to wall traffic backed up to the red, and sometimes green, lights on the St Andrews Street junction. The access road to the cattle market halfway down the street, the well-established jewellers shop, Jolly's Café, Bowers – stacked up outside with motorcycles of every vintage. Along with the old Co-op and Dance Hall, in grand tradition, there were two classic examples of English pubs, the Rising

Sun and Market Tavern, where every Wednesday local farmers gathered in droves to down numerous pints, often staggering out to find their way home – or not, maybe? Oh, and not to forget the odd escaping cow frantically followed by a gaggle of cattle market porters.

And then there was that shining light, Albert Balaam's Music Centre, still the centre of the universe for those fading numbers of budding musicians with dreams of pop stardom. Albert Balaam, the owner, was a large, portly, Dickensian figure with baritone qualities, moving in classical circles. Catering for the orchestral and traditional market, Mr Balaam, as he would be respectfully known, nevertheless did reluctantly recognise potential in the pop music world during the 1960s, employing Ray Broome, a talented musician and member of a local group since 1961, to harness potential sales to young musicians. However, Mr Balaam would always have profound reservations about long haired layabouts invading the shop and lowering the tone. Ray was a popular, likeable character with a lively sense of humour, modern thinking, full of life and highly experienced in the music scene. With one hand tied and limited space, he successfully built a healthy level of interest and trade, which culminated on Saturday mornings, young musicians descending on the shop to talk and socialise, regaling their recent experiences and conquests. All this was interrupted around 11.00 a.m. by Mr Balaam, who would purposefully stride through the door, his loud baritone voice hailing one of his assistants, the 'delinquent' youths scattering headlong for the exit and the showroom falling silent, awaiting the elusive 'suitable' customer.

So in July 1970 where was there to excite the outward looking, upwardly mobile, music loving young from Bury St Edmunds? Cambridge, maybe, with its majestic university, extensive student population and scattered night spots catering for the young and imaginative? Where else? North and East Norfolk. North and East Norfolk! you may ask. Never! – surely they were populated by more farmers than Suffolk! But there was Norwich and its University of East Anglia and a vibrant and successful entertainment scene, many well-known and famed groups appearing frequently at night spots and clubs around the city. And in Oak Street were the offices of Norwich Artistes, an established entertainment agency.

The long and at times windy road to Norwich, weaving through numerous small towns and villages, to some, may have appeared an unattractive and lonely journey from Bury St Edmunds. A few adventurous young did find their way and discovered the beauty of this wonderful historic city and its night life.

Oh, and who could possibly overlook Cromer, on the North Norfolk coast, a further twenty four miles north of Norwich. Here in this peaceful old Victorian seaside town, totally out of character, was the Royal Links Pavilion, a jewel of entertainment, which on every Saturday night throughout the year electrified the surrounding countryside with the sound of groups, current: up–and–coming and fading stars and many talented acts in support.

Since 1964 hundreds of music lovers had flocked there every weekend from far and wide to see such iconic names as The Who, David Bowie, Jeff Beck, Ten Years After, John

Mayall, Edwin Starr, The Move, Slade, Manfred Mann –
to name but a few.

So the scene is set. The shocking sixties came, and
were gone, the pop world was in limbo, not sure of the
way forward, but a new pop movement was soon to be
conceived...

The thing the sixties did was to show us the possibilities and the responsibility that we all had. It wasn't the answer. It just gave us a glimpse of the possibility.
John Lennon (1940-1980)

Chapter 1
Beyond Bertha

A TALL, DARK figure with shoulder-length hair, dressed in an army trench coat and standing behind a solitary bass drum, was stamping out the slow thud, thud, thud in my head. A laughing unicorn and leaping hare were singing in the clear blue sky. The image faded as my eyes opened to a ray of sunshine through the open window. That constant dull thud changed to the sound of metal on metal, ending abruptly with a single muted thump.

"Arrrrrrgh!!" After that his expletives were mind numbing.

A peaceful calm floated through the window.

I drifted off again, that dream replaced by an endless staircase and an angel holding a duster floating up towards me. She gently touched my forehead.

"Are you getting up?" Mum was standing over me.
"Ow, what time is it?"
"It's gone eleven and it's a lovely day. You need to find some work or go to the dole office at least. No good lying in bed half the day."

I fell out of bed, cleaned up, dressed, pulling on my black T-shirt, slightly washed blue jeans, white socks and black moccasin shoes. Then it was the usual stagger downstairs to the waiting bowl of cereal, glass of water and a promise of revival.

"What's happening with the group?"
"Oh, nothing to worry about, Mum."
"Look after yourself," she said and kissed my cheek. Walking out into the warm sunshine, I looked back at her watching me leave with that familiar, sensitive expression, full of concern.
Pulling back the handle, the sliding door opened to the aroma of worn 1950s luxury leather seats warmed by the summer sunshine caressing my senses. *Christ, I hope she starts,* I thought, looking down at the fuel gauge as the ignition key turned. The gauge didn't register. Empty again. Oh well, just got to hope. Four miles felt like an impossibility. *If she gets me to Newmarket Road I'll be lucky.*

To my euphoric surprise she started on the first press, and after struggling to find first gear I set off, wondering how far I would have to walk. Ahead on the pavement a neighbour meandered down the road with a gargantuan bandage wrapped around his thumb.

Then out into the countryside, the door half open, a warm breeze, sunshine on my face, Mott's 'At the Crossroads' playing in my head, and a vision across fields to an endless goods train running lazily silent along the embankment. All appeared so wonderfully tranquil as I summoned memories of Bertha Dorn, the euphoria of some successful performances and our name appearing in that 'Move to Laney' promotion in *Beat Instrumental* alongside Black Sabbath.

Those good vibrations quickly subsided when thoughts returned to the day before: the group breaking up and the daunting prospect of debts to be settled; the promise I made to my parents I would work hard to pay back all of the HP my father had taken out for me; the money I had borrowed from a work mate for the deposit on the equipment; the £50 for the Fender Strat still unpaid, and monies borrowed from a friend to pay some of the monthly HP instalments. And I hadn't a penny to my name!

"Never once did we ever walk alone," I said with monumental relief as she drifted across Risbygate Street car park, engine silent, into an awaiting parking space. I sat for a while, wondering how I would approach Ray with the news. Clueless, came to mind. There was no need to lock the doors, none of the locks worked. I jumped over the low car park wall into Risbygate Street and wandered up toward the town centre.

The street was busy with traffic backed up to the traffic lights. Large lorries, engines throbbing, waiting in the queue. On my side of the road, a frail, petite old lady, wearing a black dress and hat, stood resigned on the edge of the kerb. Lady in distress, long-haired unemployed teenager to the rescue… sounded good to me. I offered help, feeling chivalrous.

"Take my arm, we'll cross together."
Without hesitation or reply she took my arm. A London Brick lorry driver beckoned us across through his open window. Slow and gently, we reached the pavement.

"Will you be OK now?" I asked sympathetically.

Carrying worn and weathered features, looking up she stared in silence for a while. "You need a haircut!" she demanded. Brandishing her basket she toddled down the street without falter, taking a right turn, straight into The Rising Sun pub.

I was momentarily floored. *Great, old lady dressed in black, haircut… Was this a bad omen?* Soberly, I walked on ahead as two members of the pro group drifted down the street toward me. Immaculately dressed in tight flared trousers, both with shoulder length hair, they displayed that perfect rock musician look.

"Hello" I said. They immediately looked the other way. Hell, why do I always fall for that one!

As I reached the heavy glazed door where so many times in the past I'd entered with inspiration, I paused for thought. The dream world I lived had been filled with the haunting and majestic sounds of Page, Iommi, Clapton, and all that followed my journey out of the sixties pop wonder world and into the underground. That fantasy was about to end as reality thundered through my brain.

Head down, apprehensively I pushed the door open, the lazy click of the latch breaking the silence in the showroom, the busy street falling silent as the door closed. I negotiated my way through the crowded room filled with keyboards of all kinds, brass and woodwind, new and not so new, musical instruments of all shapes and sizes, to the long high counter and the old till, almost indiscernible under the weight of cards offering all manner of entertainment, large or small. The shelves and drawers behind the counter were overloaded with strings, reeds, recorders, sheet music, spares and extras of every denomination. The silence was only broken, occasionally, by the sound of Ron Ely, master of repairs, in his workshop just off the showroom, tinkering with a violin or some other classical instrument, and Ray's occasionally interrupted telephone conversation in the office. I peered into the modest alcove at the back of the room, packed with amplifiers, guitars, drums, new and not so new. Not tempted to go look, I waited for attention.

The telephone conversation ended. Ray sprang from the office with his usual bright and enthusiastic greeting.

"Hello Andy, how's things? Haven't seen you lately."

That's because there'd been no repayments made lately. He'll know that. Was this a hint, I thought? I was on the back foot.
"Err, I'm OK."
I paused awkwardly. Ray looked puzzled.

"The group has split and I need to bring all the equipment back," I said hesitantly.

"Oh, what's happened then?"

"Um, we just couldn't get enough work to sustain the repayments."

Ray looked on thoughtfully. "There's not much demand for heavy groups locally. You need a good agent with faith, from further afield, to promote and work with you."

"Well, we hadn't a clue where to start really, and it's too late now. It'll all have to come back," I said with a little more confidence.

"Don't be too hasty. Why don't you try pop music? There should be plenty of work around for a good pop group."

Must be more forthright. "I don't know if I want to go back to that. Rick and Brian would never lower themselves to play pop. Anyway, they've finished with it all, and besides there's the eight hundred pounds of HP debt, the payments are well overdue, and there's no money."

Ray replied with a level of diplomacy, "Even if you brought it all back, what we would take it in for wouldn't cover the amount still outstanding, so there would be a fair amount still to pay."

I was totally at a loss for an answer.

"Have a think about it. Don't worry about the repayments just yet, see if you can put a pop group together."

"I've no idea where to start, who to ask, where to get bookings from." But in my mind the little breathing space would be a blessing.

"Let me know in a week or two. If no luck we can have another look again then."

I had always trusted Ray and knew he would try to help if he could. "OK, I'll see what I can do," I said reluctantly. Well, that hadn't gone as I'd hoped.

Out into the traffic laden street, past Jolly's Café, the jewellers' shop across the road, the queue outside Dixons the butcher, left down St Andrews Street… the world hadn't ended but I wasn't thinking seriously about how to resolve the situation, having concluded it was an impossible task. I wasn't very worldly wise, didn't move in the right circles, despite having played in two groups. My immediate priority was petrol to get home as I approached the modern government building, Triton House.

Walking into the clinical, intimidating dole office, the prospect of having to queue up for a hand out induced a feeling of small and humble. There were five people waiting in front of the payment window. At the end of the line, standing quite still, a slim young man with dark, well groomed hair, down beyond his shoulders. Didn't he once play in a group? I felt sure I had never spoken to him before. Awkwardly, I tapped his shoulder, immediately thinking, *not the best way to introduce yourself!*

"WHOT!!" was the retort, as he turned to see who had so rudely summonsed him. I was   instantly taken aback by his remarkable good looks, even with that fierce frown.

I hesitated, taking in that look. "Didn't you play bass in Purple Haze?"
"Yeah! So what?" was his terse reply.

He turned away.

Heck, this is not going very well. Perhaps I should leave it. Oh, what the hell? I'll give it one more try.

"Have you still got your guitar?" I said nervously.

He didn't bother turning this time, replying, "YEAH, SO WHOT?"

Hell this is impossible! "Do you want to join a pop group?" I blurted, thinking, *he's not going to land one on me, is he?*

At last, I had his full attention. As he turned, this time his face came fully into view, his almost feminine features peering through the thick mousy hair framing his face.

Staring at me curiously, "Well, I haven't got anything else better to do," was his abrupt response.

Well that's pretty obvious, isn't it, otherwise he wouldn't be here! Would he?

"I'm Andy."

"Dave," he said, with the hint of a smile. We shook hands. I was intrigued. There was something about him…

"I've a van full of equipment and need at least four to complete a line up."

"Well you're half way there then!" said Dave.

By this time we were at the front of the queue. Dave collected his dole and waited as I applied for my hand out, the counter clerk almost scowling as he grudgingly passed me £3 10s.

"The van and all the equipment is in Risbygate Street car park."

"I'll come back with you if you like," said Dave,

enthusiastically flicking his hair back and holding the door open obligingly.

As we were walking up St Andrews Street, "Just gonna pop to Williams in Brentgovel Street, won't be a minute," he said. I followed.

Serving behind the counter was a very pretty young lady whose eyes lit up at the sight of her next customer. There was instantaneous, infectious chemistry between them. *Any minute now they'll be making mad passionate love on the counter...*

"A packet of Spangles — Old English," said Dave.

"That'll be tuppence. Anything else?" she said, with that 'are you going to make love to me now?' reply.

"No. Not now, maybe later."

The walk to the van was filled with meaningful interaction; the conversation was endless. Jumping over that car park wall, Dave's optimism subsided.

"This is the van?!" he said in scornful voice.

"Yep, 1962 vintage. She looks a little forlorn and uncared for, a bit stubborn in the mornings and draughty in the winter, but underneath has a heart of gold. Never lets me down, only when I don't feed her. We've had a love affair since 1968. Oh, and there's a hole in the floor."

"I like the large leather seats," Dave said, peering through the window, "and a bench seat in the back!"

"Yes, and all the equipment is in the back there: two hundred-watt twin cabinet Laney Supergroup stacks and a hundred-watt twin column Laney PA system. Mics, stands, all about nine months old, and Rick's complete drum kit, which I'll need to take back to him."

Impressed, Dave had never enjoyed the luxury of playing in a group with such a complete set of up-to-date equipment.

"Oh, and course eight hundred pounds of HP debt," I said quietly.

"How much! Who's responsible for all of that?"

"Errr, at the moment, me."

"I've got to go up town right now," he said.

My mood dropped. Had he just opened the escape hatch?

"I can meet you in Jolly's for a drink in half an hour, if you like?"

Panic subsided. "Never been in there."

"Groups often meet up there!" Dave was probably wondering, *where has he been?!*

"It'll be a first for me. What's the tea like?"

"Like nothing you have ever tasted before, perhaps."

"Erm.. I've, err, got to get some petrol first for the van. She ran out as we came into the car park. Can's in the back," I voiced with some embarrassment.

"What!! I'll buy the drinks. Sounds as though you need some charity!"

I walked to the Chevron garage on the other side of the street to Albert Balaam's. The attendant filled the can with a gallon of two star. "Six shillings and thruppence, please," came from my hand out money and I wandered back to empty the can into the fuel tank, thinking *that should take us around twenty five miles with a bit of luck and a following wind, old girl.*

Dave and I met at one o'clock outside Jolly's Café, a two

storey Georgian terraced townhouse. We walked up the steps and through the door to the passage, turning right into the small, sparsely decorated former reception room, still with its graceful Georgian fireplace. The room seated around twenty at a squeeze.

"My treat. What's your poison?" my host offered.

"You've put me off the tea."

"They do a very nice Welsh Rarebit!"

"No, as you're paying I'll have a Vimto, three ham sandwiches, a tea cake and a bar of chocolate, please!"

"Crikey, I'll get you the Vimto and you get the rest on HP."

The café owner, Bill Bayliss, much in the image of a previous generation, a short, thin man with combed back Brylcreemed hair, served us. His son was a boxer. "That'll be one and six".

Dave dug deep into his pockets. "You look as though you need some help. My charity is flushed at the moment." *Where's the dole money he collected earlier?* I thought.

"No, I'll get it. I'm not always this generous, so make the most of it." He unearthed the last sixpence from his back pocket.

We sat at the table by the window on bench seats facing each other.

"Well, what do you think?" said Dave.

"Well, I like the hair."

"No, I mean, what do you think about getting two other members for the group?"

"We'll be lucky to get another hairstyle like that… need a drummer, of course, and I was thinking earlier it would be good to try for an organist."

"Right, well, I know someone who might be interested. He used to play in that wild bunch, Little Sidney."

"They weren't bad."

"He works in the jewellers' across the road."

"I hope he hasn't got expensive tastes! Or maybe that could be a good thing. Perhaps he has a Hammond. Has he still got a keyboard?"

"Dunno," said Dave. "We could go over there now and ask him, if you like?"

"Well, I haven't got anything else better to do!" The drinks were massacred and we meandered across the street to the jewellers'.

Entering the shop, Dave asked, "Is John here?" The pretty young assistant, almost swooning at his good looks and cheeky smile, replied, blushing, "I'll fetch him. Who's asking?"

"Dave."

"Dave who?" the voice enquired from above.

She returned, still blushing. He's just coming."

My mind was loaded. This counter looked to be in danger of serious misuse, the same as the last one.

John entered the shop front through the back door.

"Oh Dave, good to see you. Must be six months."

"I'm hermitized, no money," replied Dave. "This is Andy, we've just met. He's trying to put a pop group together and wondered if you were interested in joining."

I was already preoccupied. Jet black hair, jewel-like eyes, that handsome look again. *This is getting better all the time.*

We shook hands. "Hello, John, pleased to meet you." Distracted by that look, thoughts rushed through my mind, these two together, very photogenic, The Pretty Things perhaps. Damn, why are all the best group names already taken?

"Pleased to meet you, Andy. Sounds interesting, who else have you got?"

"Well, only me and Dave at the moment. Trying to get

four, so if you join us, just a drummer needed. Have you still got your Hammond?"

"Never had a Hammond, I still have the Vox Continental, and the Farfisa in need of repair."

"Does the Vox still work?"

"Think so, I haven't tried it lately."

"That'll do," Dave said loosely, his attention firmly fixed on the young assistant who's eyes sparkled like the jewellery on display under the glass-topped counter.

We exchanged telephone numbers. "Let me know when you get things together, happy to rehearse when you're ready," said John.

Dave looked back smiling at his new-found love interest as we were leaving.

"Do you have that effect on all the girls you happen to bump into?"

"Often," he replied.

"Christ, will you have time to play in this group!"

The infectious approach and instantaneous effect he seemed to have on young women made me wonder if he was some sort of sex god. Surely not?

We walked down Risbygate Street, toward the car park.

"I'll give you a lift home, Dave, the least I can do."

"OK, thanks. Incidentally, are you any good at playing that Fender Strat of yours?" he replied.

"It's too late now, you're signed up. Anyway, I've still got Burt Weedon's *Play in a Day* to refer to! What about you, are you any good?"

"Fair, I suppose. Play with one finger. Can't sing, won't dance."

"Well, if you are as good as you are at attracting the girls, that'll be fine."

We reached the van. "Hop in."

"Aren't you going to unlock it?"

"It doesn't lock."

"Profanity! What other surprises are you going to spring on me?"

"It won't start straight off because the engine needs to turn over for about an hour to bring the petrol up from the tank, but the battery might go flat before it sparks into life."

Dave sat with head in hands, me with a wicked smile. I pressed the starter button and held it down with fingers crossed; the battery started to fade. Just as I said, 'We'll have to push her down the hill' she came to life.

"She never lets me down," I said with absolute confidence.

"Thank god for that," mumbled Dave.

"Don't get too optimistic."

I was struggling to find first gear again, yanking at the column gear change.

"Hell, where did you learn to drive!"

"'Don't panic, Mr Mainwaring…' It's the linkages, they're worn to hell. 'They don't like it up 'em, you know.' I'll find it in a minute but you may need to walk in front with a red flag."

I dropped Dave off at his home in Tollgate Lane, saying "See you tomorrow at Jolly's around one."

Reflecting on the last four hours as I drove home, my whole demeanour had changed. Perhaps the old lady in black wasn't a bad omen after all, more like a good luck charm.

So, onward, my focus turned to the search for a drummer.

What I didn't know was how much this day would change my experience of life, and how much it would contribute to shaping my future.

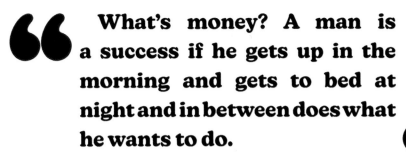

> **What's money? A man is a success if he gets up in the morning and gets to bed at night and in between does what he wants to do.**
> Bob Dylan

Chapter 2
Jolly Good, Lovely Weather

SO, WHAT ABOUT Clive? Well, he was very laid back, very very laid back, in fact nearly horizontal, a leftover hippy and he was still only seventeen. Enhanced by long straight hair and emblazoned with a jacket of strawberry pink with black and white stripes over scarlet velvet trousers, he carried a droll sense of humour and was nearly always straight to the point.

His father was a former drummer. Clive never professed to be any good at it, although he could occasionally hit the drums with a bit of guidance. But he usually missed. I became friends with Clive, and his friend Keith, in January 1969, during Bertha Dorn's totally underground, heavy-leaning performance in the assembly hall at the Silver Jubilee School. Nirvana for Clive.

That morning, the day after meeting Dave and John, I was up early, a quarter to ten. Mum was outside hanging the washing, it was another warm summer's day. Plenty of time, I thought, not seeing Dave until one, could call in to see Clive on the way in. I had my usual breakfast, checked the image in the mirror and ambled down the garden to say goodbye to Mum.

"I'm just off out."

"Say hello to Mrs Bettson for me."

"What!"

"Well, you and Clive are cleaning her windows this morning at eleven, I thought?"

There was a constant vacant space in my memory which should have been occupied by a vast number of important assignments that had been conveniently forgotten. This was one of them.

Steaming hysteria!

The casual walk down the path mutated into a rush and a frantic hurl of ladders. *Will the van start?* Two-and-a-half turns and she leapt to the rescue. *She never lets me down when I need her most!*

On the way into town, premonition darkened the horizon. Clive will never be ready, he never is, he's worse than me. The time was twenty past eleven as I turned into Oliver Road. Bewilderment and shock! Clive was standing outside his home waiting, buckets and stuff in hand. I drove up alongside and pulled back the sliding door.

"You're early," said Clive, "we were supposed to be at Mrs Bettson's at eleven. I've been ready for at least five minutes."

"Heavy Hurtle Mertle." The enigmatic response.

Outside Mrs Bettson's house we surveyed the numerous large windows. The trauma inspired a desperate need to have a break.

"How long is it going to take to do that lot!" said Clive. "And how much are we getting paid?"

"Four shillings."

"What – each?"

"No."

"You're joking!"

This was the first job in our new so-called business partnership in an attempt to avoid bankruptcy. We hadn't given any serious thought to the tools needed for the job, other than a couple of buckets and cloths borrowed from Clive's mum and a heavy wooden extending ladder and steps borrowed from my uncle Bob. Not that you need any serious tools for cleaning windows, do you?

Mrs Bettson, a well-to-do and immaculately dressed lady, answered the door.

"Sorry we're late. Andy got to mine early, about twenty past eleven, and I was ready about five minutes earlier, and we left about ten minutes ago," announced Clive.

"Jolly good, lovely weather," she replied.

Whilst we were working, kind of working, well, not working at all for most of the time, and during our numerous breaks, I filled Clive in on the events of yesterday and the visit to Jolly's at one o'clock.

"Going around with a pop group, I'll never live it down," cursed Clive.

By lunch time there was still a distinct lack of enthusiasm. Two windows were clean, but they were small ones.

"We're just off to see a man about a horse," Clive declared to Mrs Bettson as we were leaving. "Back later."

"Jolly good, lovely weather," she replied.

"Last time I saw that rocking horse it was a donkey!" was the inexplicable counterattack on our way into town.

We arrived at Jolly's quarter of an hour late. There was an air of optimism floating between my eyes as we walked in. John was sitting with Dave at the table by the window. "John! Good to see you, and thanks for coming," I said, trying to disguise the over-the-top salesman rhetoric. Turned out he had already been there when Dave arrived; apparently it was his irregular regular at lunch times.

"We've gotta big contract on the go and it was a bit of a job to tear ourselves away. That's why we're late." I sounded convincing.

"You'll get used to it. He couldn't possibly be on time, it would damage his reputation," pronounced Clive.

"And this is Clive." He shook hands with John and Dave.

"So what do you do?" asked Dave, inquisitively.

"As little as possible," Clive replied candidly. "Roadie was my last title."

We got drinks and sat down. Clive, obsessed, loaded his sandwich with free tomato ketchup. It was nearly two inches thick by the time he took the first bite. I had experienced the blast after the squelch before, so, aware of the dangers of sitting beside him, I retreated to the edge of the bench seat.

John asked curiously, "so what do you do, Andy?" I had no idea what the expectation was so I decided on the plain unvarnished truth.

"Well, I'm out of work, apparently unemployable, a former apprentice electrician who got the sack for turning up late on three occasions, the last time not getting into work until ten thirty, the works van leaving for site at eight. Sacked from my last job with landscape contractors a week ago for burning out the clutch on a site lorry… twice. I've played in two groups as lead guitar and singer. Before that I was in the church choir until I got my marching orders at the age of twelve for falling asleep flat out on a pew, at the back."

"That sounds, well, excellent, then." stuttered Dave.

"Oh don't worry," Clive added with total confidence. "When he's on stage it's the only time he's fully awake."

John looked apprehensive, perhaps unsure about this band of not-so-hopefuls.

I got to know Dave very quickly. He was easy to get to know, accommodating, you could say. I felt it may take a little time to get to know John. He appeared naturally guarded, thoughtful, careful about what he said, and perhaps more considered in whom he chose as friends.

"What about you, John? What's your organ playing like?" I asked awkwardly, wishing I could delete that clumsy overture and start again.

Dave interrupted. "He can't be any worse than we are."

Christ Dave! I thought. *I'm glad you know John better than I do.*

John choked on his drink momentarily, and then there was harmonious laughter.

I was again taken by the image of these two as they sat

together, whilst reminding myself it was by pure chance they were sitting there in front of me. Image in whatever form was something that didn't need serious consideration in the last group I'd played in; this time as a pop group it seemed more important.

So, from this sleepy Suffolk market town, who had I gathered together so far? A seventeen-year-old, near-horizontal former hippy, mad on the underground scene; what appeared to be an unemployed sex god, compelled to pursue any shapely form he encountered; an unemployable and wayward over-sleeper who was both broke and deeply in debt; and a level-headed, reserved and grounded jeweller, formally in a notoriously madcap group. Perfect!

"What about a drummer?" said Clive. "And before you ask, no, you're not getting me to do it."

"I've given that some thought," I said. "Mick Howlett, the former drummer with Village Green, lives in Long Melford. As far as I know he's not in a group at the moment. When I last saw him he still had his kit. I'll see if I can contact him."
"Or we could advertise," said John, "maybe place an ad in the Music Centre." A high quality, well designed notice was duly written in pencil on a piece of scrap paper covered in classic café stains Bill had loaned us and insisted we return after use.

Drummer Wanted for Pop Group
Contact Andy on Barrow 206
Must Be Handsome

As we left Jolly's, Dave and John took a left turn, I had no doubt because Dave wanted to check out one of those sales assistants again. Clive and I took a right turn into next door to ask Ray if we could display the ad on the till.

As we entered, a morbid sense of regret completely overpowered my existence. Mr Balaam came from the office to serve us, personally!

"Hello, Andy," was the ominous greeting in that deep commanding tone. I knew the danger of going into the shop at this time, the possibility of being served by Mr Balaam, and fully aware he would be perfectly within his rights to address the HP arrears. After all, he had been accommodating so far, to say the least.

"Err, is Ray here?" I said with unease.

"No, he's at lunch."

"OK, we'll pop back later," I said quicker than quick.

"Just a minute!" Mr Balaam demanded as we turned to leave. "So you haven't come in to pay the outstanding arrears on your equipment then?"

Prophet of doom. I hadn't prepared for this!

"Sorry, no."

"You do realise you are nearly three months in arrears?"

"Err, yeah, but it's just… haven't got any money at the moment," I said with a twitch, dreading his response.

"Well, at the beginning of next month you'll be a hundred and thirty-five pounds in arrears and I'm not prepared to let that go on for much longer. I expect to see at least some of that paid back within the next week!"

Blacken my vocal chords, where was I going to get that much money from!

"Well, I can't promise anything but I'll see what I can do," I said, with an absolute lack of conviction.

Clive cringed at that statement. The two shillings each

we'd get after completing the window job would barely cover a double bacon sandwich and a Vimto. And there was no guarantee we would finish the job!

"Don't leave it too long or we may reclaim the equipment and see what's outstanding after we take it all back!"

I had to censor my spontaneous silent reaction to that. Now what!

"OK Mr Balaam. I'll do what I can and see Ray later," I replied, trying but failing to sound sincere.

After all the positives of yesterday and today, that fiasco fabricated a rapid plunge downward toward an earth-shattering crash. In reality there was no way I was going to find that sort of money, even if I found full time employment for several months. Perhaps all this was a brainless idea, and I should take it all back and try to deal with the outstanding amount somehow. At least it won't be nowhere near eight hundred pounds. Surely?

We returned to Mrs Bettson's and finished the job about 5.30 p.m. I was ready for bed, and Clive looked shattered. Our patron paid us the four shillings.

"Well done, boys! I'll let your mum know, Andy, when they need doing again."

"There's no way I'm doing that again," grumbled Clive. "Two shillings a day." I didn't see any fortune in it either, even if we charged more and worked harder. It was cheaper to stay in bed, I decided.

"See you tomorrow?" I suggested.

"Don't make it too early, I'm having a lie in."

"I'll bring the latest edition of Mayfair. Perhaps that will stir your inner sanctum."

"Mother's little helper would be much more potent."

Back at home, my first and only priority was the arrears. Hell, what was I going to do about that? I sat slumped in the armchair for quite some time. I couldn't ask the others to get involved in this hangover from Bertha Dorn. They didn't have the means anyway. I had to try to resolve this myself somehow.

"You look a bit distant – anything wrong?" my mother observed.

"Oh, it's OK, nothing to worry about, Mum."

"Are you sure?"

"Just a bit tired, that's all."

"How did things go at Mrs Bettson's?"

"Fine. She was happy, I think."

"Have you got any more jobs?"

"No, don't think we'll do this, it's not what I want to be doing."

"You need to take the ladders back to your uncle then."

"Yeah, OK, I'll do that in the morning."

I lumbered up the stairs in meditation. What could I sell to raise some money? After lying on the bed for around thirty minutes I opened the bedroom cupboard and fumbled through my childhood. There were boxes I so treasured, most of them from my brother Cliff's collection that were handed down to me, and really old toys going back to my father's and grandfather's childhood. Could I bring myself to sell these? I wouldn't get much for them anyway. Closing the doors, I decided to sleep on it.

> **I tried several things and this was the only one I enjoyed doing.**
> Keith Moon

Chapter 3
Mr Matheson
Saviour of Sanity

THE NEXT MORNING I telephoned The Music Centre.

Ray's response, "How's things?" Again!

"Well, not so good. I came in yesterday and Albert was there. He read the Riot Act about the HP arrears."

"Yes, he did mention it. I hadn't had a chance to talk to him about our conversation on Tuesday. I explained what we spoke about, but he was insistent, wanting to see some of the outstanding amount within the next ten days, at least."

"Well, you can't blame him. At the moment I have no means to meet that deadline, but I will try to find a way, or maybe rob a bank. I'll let you know by this time next week if I've had any luck or I'm in police custody. Actually, I called in yesterday to ask if you would place an ad on the till for a drummer. Purely by chance, I think I have a bass player and keyboard player, just need a drummer. If I read out the detail of our ad, could you write it out and put it on the till? I don't really want to come into town today, trying to preserve the level of my bankrupt status."

"Of course. Andy. That was quick – you must be on 'a Mars a Day'! If it works out, I may be able to introduce you to an agency."

"That would be a blessing." Or a miracle, given my track record.

Mum returned.

"Got to go now!"

The call ended, and when the all clear sounded I covertly dialled Clive. His mum answered. It was 10.15.

"Is Clive up and about?"

"No, he's still in bed."

"Could you give him a message? I won't be round today, got to see a parrot about a rhinoceros, he'll understand – will give him a call at the weekend perhaps."

I couldn't focus on anything other than the debt mountain; the search for a drummer would have to wait. How could I raise at least half of the arrears in such a short space of time? I really only had two options: the boxes of old toys upstairs – I had no idea how much they might be worth, if anything – or take all the equipment back. If I chose the second option, how much would still be outstanding? It could be, say, half the current total? On top of that there was the £50 still owing on the Strat, the £41 outstanding from the £50 borrowed from a workmate for the deposit, and the £30 borrowed from a friend to pay for two of the earlier monthly HP repayments. What a mess! I hadn't seen this coming, so preoccupied with playing in a group I loved, alongside two very inventive musicians, that I lost all sense of reality. Anyway, too late now.

But there was something distinctly promising about the recent chance encounters that had brought me in touch with Dave and John so effortlessly… and so many 'what ifs' still running through my mind. Did I really want to go back to the manual work I found so unrewarding and unchallenging? Besides, I would almost certainly have difficulty in getting a regular job with my employment record, having got the sack from two in the last twelve months. Not to mention how I would miss the adrenaline rush when walking out on stage, the simple joy of playing in a group and all that went with that: the nervous anticipation on the way to bookings, the euphoria when everything came together live.

It had to be the toys then, though I'd need to hide the emotional attachment I had to some of them and seek approval for the sale from a higher authority, particularly as nearly all of them came from earlier generations. Mum was bound to ask why I wanted to part with them. I wouldn't mention anything until I had found a potential buyer.

So who would want to buy several boxes of old toys? There were former classmates who had been bonkers on anything from Rogers' or Townsend's toy shops, but I couldn't imagine any of them would be even vaguely interested in any of these old things now. Oh, yes, there was that busy lad who was always buying and selling things and asking if I had any antiques to sell. He once bought some old coins my great-grandmother gave me. I knew where he lived. I'd have to break today's petrol prudence rule and drive into town this evening. Hopefully he'd be at home.

I arrived at 7.30 that evening; he was in but wasn't interested, he didn't buy antiques any more, had a 'proper job'. But he did give me an address for someone who might be, an old gentleman living about four miles outside Bury. I'd go the next day, I decided.

I was up early for once, 9.15.

"Mum, I'm going to try and sell all the toys from upstairs," I announced.

"Why? What do you need the money for?' She knew I'd no job and the HP payments must be due.

"I can't tell you right now but I need to do this. Besides, I may not be able to sell them."

"Don't part with them too cheaply then. Remember, there's Cliff's old toys amongst those."

I departed, slowly, down the road in the loaded van. It was raining heavily and very overcast, the wipers about as effective as a feather in a force-nine gale. Petrol... I'd better get some and spend more of that precious hand out money. The White Horse petrol shed on the A45 stood just outside the village. Bett Crouch emerged from within to serve me, dressed in his heavy raincoat and trilby hat.

"Hello, Andy, what can I do you for today?"

"Half a gallon of two-star, please, Bett."

He wound the dial back to twelve o'clock with the handle, switched on the pump and started to fill.

"Not far to go today then, Andy?"

"Err, can't really afford it but needs must. Gotta go to London," I said seriously.

"That's one of your jokes again, I suppose. That'll be three shillings and tuppence."

We were wet, the van and me that is, and ready to go.

I found the entrance to the secluded property quite easily but began to wonder if I was in the right place. The drive was long, lined with trees and meadows to each side. It was very overcast; the rain was still pouring down and reminded me of Black Sabbath's intro to Black Sabbath. As the avenue ended the landscape opened, and, '*What is this that stands before me…*' a wonderful old country house partially covered with ivy. I sat for a moment in thought. Would there be anybody here interested in what I had to sell? The lion's head brass door knocker was heavier than Ozzy Osbourne. I knocked twice. No answer. Tried again. After a few seconds the door opened slowly, and there before me, an incredibly good-looking young woman with long blonde hair and hazel eyes, wearing a short skirt and high heels.

"Is Mr Matheson in?"

"Who's asking?" she said with a mindful voice.

"Um…. Mr Garrard suggested I should see him."

"Just a minute." She closed the door. I was abandoned to the rain and getting soaked.

About sixty seconds later the door opened and she reappeared. "Come in, Mr Matheson will see you."

Dripping, I stepped into the entrance hall as she closed the heavy door behind me. High ceiling, oak panelled walls, furniture from a different century… I was in awe.

"This way, please."

I couldn't take my eyes off her wonderful form as she led the way down a passage into a back room where Mr Matheson was sitting at a trestle table, tinkering with an oil lamp. He looked to be in his seventies, quite tall, grey hair, wearing an old jumper and corduroy trousers. He stood up to politely greet me.

"What can I do for you?"

"Mr Garrard suggested you may be interested in some old toys I have."

"Oh," he said after a thoughtful delay. "Why are you selling them?" The query was tinged with a subtle level of suspicion.

What do I tell him? Best to be honest, I decided.

"I have some outstanding HP debt I need to resolve and these are the only option open to me at the moment."

"I see." He paused, looking at me with curious expression. "Very well young man, bring them in," he said, almost kindly.

After several journeys out into the rain, the boxes were lined up on the trestle table. I started to unpack them.

"No! Please, allow me," he declared, carefully selecting an old clockwork locomotive from one of the boxes.

I watched, standing, as he inspected each item, slowly, one by one, like a curious child.

I could be here for a while, I thought. A drink would be welcome.

After the first two boxes he asked. "Where did they all come from?"

"They're mainly hand-me-downs from my brother, father and grandfathers."

"Would you like a cup of tea?"

"A glass of water, please."

"Emily, get that for this young man, would you, and a

whisky for me."

He continued to unpack, slower than slow, examining each object intensely. *I could be here all day*, flashed through my mind. *I wonder if there's anything to eat on offer.*

Emily returned with a glass of water and that tumbler of whisky, served up on a blue-and-white china tray. When all the boxes were emptied and all were laid out, overflowing onto another table set against the wall, he studied me again, thoughtfully.

"Would you like something to eat, a sandwich perhaps?"

He's reading my mind – must be careful what I'm thinking! I mused. "Yes, very much, thank you."

"Emily," he called, "could you bring us some sandwiches?" His focus returned: "So you're looking to sell these to meet an HP debt?"

"Yes, I'm afraid so."

"And how much are you hoping to get for them?"

I had no idea what they were worth, if anything, or how much I should ask. I needed £135, urgently. He appeared to be very interested in them. Should I try for this amount, or would that put him off? *Be bold*, I thought, *you can always come down to £20.*

"Well, I was thinking a hundred and thirty-five pounds," I replied, filled with pessimism and without any conviction.

"Really?" he said, looking me straight in the eye.

Oh, well, obviously that's far too much.

Emily returned with the sandwiches, a welcome intervention at a very tense moment. We paused, he took another sip of his whisky. My ham and cucumber sandwich was a delight. By this time I had been there for nearly an hour.

"So what is the outstanding HP for?"

I searched for a reply. What do I tell him? I'm an out-of-work delinquent guitar player who's trying to get a group together? No, that would be a disaster. "Well, to be honest, I'm an out-of-work delinquent guitar player who's trying to get a group together."

"Really!" He smiled properly for the first time and in animated tone asked, "Tell me more." He appeared truly interested. I launched headlong into the full story of how I'd arrived at his door, and by the time I'd finished, all the sandwiches had disappeared and the whisky tumbler was empty.

"How intriguing."

He looked me in the eye once again. "I'll take them all… a hundred and thirty-five, you said?"

Tears nearly came to my eyes. I could hardly find the words. "Thank you," I said, barely audible.

"I'll just go and get you the money."

Emily was still in the room. "What's the name of your group then?" she enquired in a sensual and captivating tone.

"We haven't decided on a name yet. Emily sounds good, don't you think?"

She blushed. I was delighted. I'd never achieved that kind of reaction from the opposite sex before.

Mr Matheson returned. "Here you go, young man, I'll count it out," he said. So significant was this moment it seemed an eternity before he finally came to, "And that's one hundred and thirty-five." Good luck to you… what's your name again?"

"Andy."

"Good luck with your group, Andy, and keep me updated with how you get on."

"I certainly will, sir, and thank you again," I said with

true meaning. We shook hands. As I left, I could almost have hugged him. I certainly could have hugged Emily. "I will return to let you know how things are going," I promised.

Walking onto the drive, the rain had stopped, but it was still overcast and wet.

The elation was immeasurable, I couldn't have imagined this outcome in my most fanciful daydreams.

Albert Balaam's was to be my next pressing call, and on the way there I began to wonder why Mr Matheson had been so generous. Was it because he was sympathetic to my predicament? Was it the old toys, were they worth that much? Surely not. I think he was most likely a very generous man with a kind heart. Whatever the reason, a huge weight had been lifted from my shoulders for the time being.

It was early afternoon, the Risbygate Street car park wall was having a positive effect on my hurdling skills and I decided to keep £15 to pay off part of the £50 debt on the Strat. As I was about to turn into Balaam's, and looking up the street, in the distance walking toward me came the Old Lady in Black with basket over her arm. *This is surreal,* I thought. *What power does she hold over me?*

The stride to the counter was full of confidence. High drama: Once again Mr Balaam himself came from the office to serve me. I could hear Ray on the telephone.

"Yes, Andy!" His familiar forthright greeting.

"I'd like to see Ray, please." I wouldn't give the proprietor the pleasure of taking my money after the drubbing he'd given me yesterday, even if it was deserved.

"You'll have to wait, he's on the phone!"

"OK, I'll wait."

Ron emerged from his workshop, walking past us.

"Hello Andy, how's things?" Obviously a Music Centre catchphrase.

"Fine, Ron, thanks."

Ray then sprinted from the office. "Hello Andy, how's things?" My thought processor was paralysed.

Mr Balaam made his presence felt, observing in silence behind the counter.

"I have a hundred and twenty towards the HP payments." I announced with fortitude.

Ray signed off the HP cards. In a statement to Ray but clearly aimed at Mr Balaam, "That brings everything up to date and slightly in advance, leaving only fifteen to pay on the first of August."

"Thank you, Andy," said Mr Balaam in that persistent, authoritarian tone. That took me by surprise!

"Thank *you* for the extended credit, I did appreciate it."

Mr Balaam returned to the office. Ray walked with me to the door. "So how *did* you manage this?" he murmured.

"Well, I didn't rob a bank, I've never bet on the horses – or the dogs, come to that. Let's say I've been blessed with a one-off benefactor I don't have to repay. Divine intervention perhaps. But this only plugs the gap temporarily. My main concern is finding a drummer and getting some rehearsals going."

"I think you should be ok now for at least five or six weeks. Keep me updated."

I turned left out of the shop, walked on high to St Andrews Street and across the road into Ron's Café. I was greeted by Ralph, a tallish, well-built, late-teenager with an unusually solemn air. The numerous gaming and slot machines were buzzing and ringing as I paid him the £15, giving him the unpaid Bill of Sale written on a scrap piece of paper dated 2 3 70. It read: *One Fender Stratacaster (misspelt) £50*. He signed it off: *paid £15.00, Balance £35.00 remaining*. I had had my, or should I say his, treasured Strat since December' 69, initially on approval and then unpaid since March, this the first payment I had made to him.

On the return home my self-esteem was higher than high. I focused on the need to find a drummer without the thought of returning all the equipment occupying the recesses of my mind, at least for the time being.

When I announced how much the old gentleman had paid for the toys, surprised and delighted, Mum advised, "don't waste the money." After explaining I had already spent it all, there was a second sharp reminder I still needed to take the ladders back to my uncle!

That evening, after finding the telephone number in my old 1968 pocket diary, I called Mick Howlett, an old tech college friend of mine and formerly the drummer with Village Green. His father, a policeman, answered the phone: "He's not at home at the moment." I left a message and Mick called me later that evening. "I have an apprenticeship to consider and don't want to jeopardise that in any way. But thanks for the offer."

But, the hunt was about to take a hip turn.

Moon dust in your lungs, stars in your eyes, you are a child of the cosmos, a ruler of the skies.

Anon

Chapter 4
An American
Linguistic Madhouse

THREE OF US met socially that weekend on the Sunday. The festival marking the 1000th anniversary of the Martyrdom of St Edmund, held in the Abbey Gardens from 6th–25th July, had ended the day before. As we wandered around this ancient place, so steeped in history, the scene was of clearing up after a significant three week event. One topic of conversation surrounded the group: possible names were being given airtime. My suggestion of Emily completely dismissed before the list was drawn up, even after I'd thrown in a totally spurious reference to Pink Floyd. ICEICLE, frozen out, too cold. DAVE (his suggestion), definitely not! ST EDMUND, not bad. BALD TYRES – that reminds me! SEXTION – great! BROKE, pass. ANDY DAVE JOHN & (Drummer?), crap. THE BEAUTIFUL – brilliant. As we passed a heap of discarded pageant ephemera, Clive turned.

"Hang on a minute," he said as he wandered over to the pile. "What about this for a name?"

In amongst the debris were printed black on white background 'EXIT' signs.

The agreement was unanimous, particularly as they appeared to be the ideal size for the two back door windows of the van.

"That's settled then. Painless," said Dave.

One of the groundsmen, clearing up, appeared with some more signs. "'Elp yerself mate, they're bein' frown away," he offered. We extracted three, one extra for the bass drum, made a beeline for the van at pace. The fit behind the glass was perfection.

"Stupendous!"

"That's it then."

"Well at least we'll know the way out."

"Far out," replied Clive, predictably.

On limited funds, a collective splash out at the Wimpy in Abbeygate Street completely obliterated any chance of 'A Shanty and Chips, no Tartare sauce, please', and resulted in one large drink with three straws which lasted for two hours. The search for a drummer was the centre of attention. I explained the no-go with Mick Howlett and suggested perhaps we should try Rick, drummer from my previous progressive cum heavy group, Bertha Dorn.

For me Rick was a joy to perform with. His heavy, full on

drumming and solos, modelled on his idol Ginger Baker, making use of every part of his double drum kit including the shells, added impact to our three piece line up. I had no doubt his talent would be a true asset to any group. The major stumbling block would be, without doubt, one of the added reasons for Bertha Dorn's break up. Rick's girlfriend, met at a booking when we were in support to Ace Kefford, Terry Reid and Bill Bonham, was pregnant, and they were to be married. But there was hope he would come in initially, to get things going, and if we were successful at finding work this might persuade him to stay.

The friendship with Dave was thriving and we agreed to meet up again on Tuesday.

Monday 27th July

"It's Ray on the telephone!" came a call from the bottom of the stairs at 9.10 a.m. I stumbled down to the hallway in my pyjama bottoms; over-exposure was threatening.

"How's things, Ray?" I yawned.

"Fine, Andy. Is that the title of your new song?"

"I'd need to check copyright from you on that, I think."

"A chap came in on Saturday and saw your ad, gave me his telephone number saying he would be in all day today. He's American, living in Cambridge. Name's Dave."

"Many thanks, Ray, I'll call him as soon as I've made myself decent."

"Good luck with that one! Let me know how you get on."

Another Dave. Impossible he could be as good-looking as Dave1, surely. Completely out of character, I had a hurried breakfast and with great optimism telephoned the Cambridge number.

"Hi, iss is Dave, wassup?" he answered in broad American and sharp delivery.

Crikey, I'd never spoken to a bona fide citizen of the USA before. "How do you do?" I began nervously. Where did *that* come from! "Ray from the Music Centre gave me your telephone number re. our ad for a drummer."

"Hey, man, how do you do?" With a disconcerting upturn on the last word.

"Err, yes, very good, thanks."

"Yeah, man, I'm lookin' to jam with a band."

Jam and band? I thought jam came on bread? "Have you played in a group before?"

"Yeah, done it all man. Grooved everywhere, rock 'n' roll – no sweat."

"This is a POP GROUP!"

"Yee–ha, dig it dude, far out."

Hell, I didn't think I'd understand him most of the time. Was this Ray winding me up? He hadn't warned me… no wonder he'd wished me luck! *I'll give it a miss,* I decided. *Oh, I don't know, still not sure about Rick.*

It was no good asking him to come to an audition, the group hadn't even rehearsed, yet.

"Can I come out to see you?

"Ow yeah man, ass cool, got all my kit here."

"What about this afternoon?"

"Hey? Wha' about it?"

"Well, can I see you this afternoon?"

"Man, had a change a plan. I'm groovin' in Bedford. Yeah!"

What the heck does that mean?

"Wednesday's right o-n-n-n fer me, man," he said.

Right on-n-n-n fer me man?!! I assumed this meant something along the lines of 'I'm at home all day Wednesday, what time would you like to come? I'll put the kettle on, would you like a cup of tea and some scones?'

"Yeah, that's cool man," I replied. He'd got me at it!

"About eleven?"

"Assa a gas."

Gas???? What the hells he going to use that for? "Err, hang on, where do you live?"

He gave me his address but I had a feeling it could be in San Francisco. (Let's go). "Toodle pip," I said as the conversation ended.

Dread! What had I let myself in for? Anyway, Wednesday had to be better, my hand-out money had almost evaporated and the petrol gauge on the van was screaming nearly empty again. Tomorrow was shame-at-the-dole-office day again so I would at least be able to buy another gallon. If I had gone today I may have got there but possibly had to walk back home, ask him for a lift – embarrassing, or, even worse, borrow some money from him to get some petrol. What a thought! I almost hoped he would be ideal as this could be a lot of fun, once he came to know and understand us, and we had purchased a book of translation. Now I knew where Clive got 'far out' from.

The next day Dave, Clive and I made our weekly cringeworthy visit to Triton House – I'm sure that dole office clerk was on a bonus to be as mean as he possible could – and then onto Jolly's.

"Thought you'd be here on Tuesday. I hear you're all helping to create employment at Triton House. Highly commendable," said John.

"Thanks. We aim to please, you know. In fact I'm going to ask for more money next week," replied Clive.

"I suppose I'd better get the drinks in this week," I said with excruciating monetary regret.

"I'll have three double bacon sandwiches, a large slice of

angel cake, fourteen sausage rolls and an extra-large cup of coffee," ordered Dave.

"Is that all? Lend me some money can you."

The two holier-than-thou pro 'rock musicians' were sitting at the table next to ours. As I returned, I politely said "Hello." Their response: ZERO. An icy gale was blowing in my direction. Would you believe it, I'd fallen for that one. Again! Would I ever learn?

I was curious to hear more about John's former group.

"So tell us… Little Sidney. What exactly did you lot get up to?"

John hesitated before he replied. "Nothing much to tell really. Lasted about a year or so. We used to set fire to the stage during our performance of Arthur Brown's 'Fire', had to call the Brigade out on one occasion, and placed an old mortar bomb we'd found in a shed in front of the bass drum for four months, until we realised it was live."

"Really!" I replied, shocked. I thought he was very grounded, but perhaps he had a wild side he'd not as yet revealed. Great!

I explained the conversation of American confusion and my visit there on Wednesday.

"I'll come," said Clive.

"That's cool man! You seem to know the lingo, you can be the interpreter."

"Funky," he replied. "If he passes the 'audition' perhaps we can rehearse on Sunday."

There was a kind of semi-enthusiastic agreement. John at this point was not so socially involved but I warmed to his common sense approach and his growing understanding of our knockabout humour. Already there was a feeling of being glad to be associated with Dave and John now I knew them better. There were no airs and graces. In our parting conversation I arranged to telephone and let them know how goes tomorrow.

On our way to Cambridge we practised at cool, Clive giving me the low down on how to sound 'far out'. After circling the block three times we arrived. Dave2's house wasn't what I'd expected: small with a bright yellow door, which he threw open before we had a chance to knock. "Wow, outta sight! This is my pad, guys, come on in."

The room was small, packed with Marshall and Sound City group equipment, most unrelated to drumming and probably more there than when Cream played at the Albert Hall. An extensive drum kit was set up in one corner and there was barely room to manoeuvre. We shook hands and I introduced Clive. Dave2 didn't introduce his stunning girlfriend, but instead hurtled into overdrive running through all the pieces of kit, none of which had anything to do with the drums. By the time he had ran out of breath my mind was frazzled. I'd barely understood a thing and knew less than when he'd started.

"Can we hear you on the drums then, Dave?" I calmly requested.

"Sure man. Check it out," and he thrashed out a good rendition of ad-lib drumming. *That'll do*, I thought, looking at Clive. He shrugged his shoulders in *don't-ask-me* style.

"We'll let you know, got to go talk to another chap later today," I said, thinking about Rick. "Could you make a rehearsal on Sunday if we decided to go with it?"

"Thass baaaad, man," he replied.

Oh, hell, he's not happy about that!

"Come in my Slug Bug and shades, you dig."

I summoned Clive for translation, but, he was totally mesmerized by Dave2's dazzling girlfriend. I looked out the window, couldn't see a garden! *Surely he hasn't got problems with slugs and if he has why does he need to wear sun glasses? And I didn't bring a spade.*

Clive could see my brain was overheating, eyes dilated, and hair turning green. "He means Sunday's OK."

"OK, man, that's far out, catch yer later on the blower," I said, thinking he'll never know what blower means.

"Yeah, man, thass cool. Ring anytime, I'm chillin' out today."

Christ, has he got a refrigerator as well?

"Hey, man, before yer split – wass the bread like*?" How did he know I'd brought my own sandwiches?*

"Yeah man, very tasty."

We departed with brain dysfunction.

On our way back Clive gave me the low down on some of the terminology, and I asked for a rundown on Slug Bug. He hadn't got a clue what he was on about. Although Dave2 appeared to be a good drummer and the American thing was great, all that technical stuff was over the top and I wondered how much this could overflow into rehearsals. Rick, on the other hand, shared my sense of humour and I was very familiar with his standard of drumming. He was down to earth and easy going. I decided to telephone him that evening with reserved hope.

We had a long conversation after I explained what was happening and the reason for my call. To my surprise he was happy to come along and help with rehearsals whenever he could, but not so sure about coming in permanently. This was OK, I thought, at least it would see us up and running, I knew what to expect and his drum kit was still in the van. We arranged to meet outside his home on Sunday afternoon at 2.30.

So in just eight days, from oblivion to a complete line up… for rehearsals at least. But this was only the beginning. First, rehearsals, then a full set of numbers, the all-important bookings, and would we be good enough? Sunday could be Judgement Day.

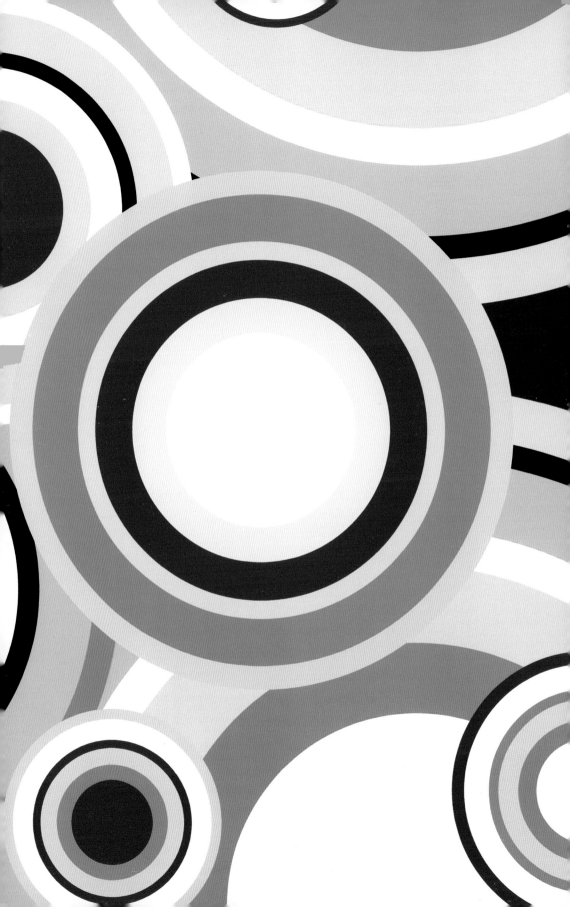

Assa hekofuh raynun owtsyde, oye reckun ut'll be wholly wet afore us droy.

Rissoles,
Flempton Road, 1970.

Chapter 5
Midnight Mint Provokes an Enchanting Chorus

THREE OF US, Dave Clive and I, met up a couple of times socially in the evenings that week, Dave calling to see John in the shop to let him know about Sunday's two-hour rehearsal at the village hall. Cash and the fuel gauge were always an issue. Never sure of getting to where we were going or getting home again, we had to improvise at times with inventive ideas including pushing or praying, and other not so religious cures.

Up until then my friends hadn't taken too much of

this seriously, adopting an it's-purely-for-fun approach whilst staying connected to see what evolved. That loose commitment was about to be challenged.

Sunday the 2nd of August, a huge day. I was up earlier than the last time I got up early, wondering would it all come together or be an unmitigated disaster, when a voice from the kitchen called out: "When are you taking those ladders back to your uncle!!"

A sunny afternoon followed another beautiful summer morning. I was supremely confident she'd (the van that is) would never let me down on the big occasion – fingers crossed. With the fuel gauge radiant, showing nearly empty, I set off with Art's 'What's That Sound?' (Supernatural Fairy Tales) filling my head, feeling cool and 'outta sight', whatever that meant. Rick was ready and waiting outside his home in Norton, drumsticks in hand. We drove to town, picked up John, Clive and then Dave. There was no need for prolonged introductions. As ex-roadie for Bertha Dorn, Clive already knew Rick. Dave and John had had an introduction of sorts via my ramblings about our former group.

As we approached the hall there was an air of quiet apprehension. I think we were all of the same mind, hoping but not sure, except for Clive, of course, who was, as ever, laid back as far as possible. We passed the red telephone box that was regularly subjected to vandalism, a number of glass panes shattered, the police under pressure to find the offenders. As the van came to rest beside the steps up to the hall, a group of girls were walking past. Dave's focus instantly changed from rehearsal to the opposite sex. "Hello, girls," he called as we exited the van, their almost shy "hello" reply delivered simultaneously. We had difficulty dragging him away.

Risby village hall was built in 1923, with its cast iron heating stove, metal flue extending upward through the vaulted roof, no stage and bare floorboards. It was plain in decoration but quite intimate, largely unchanged from when it was built. We set up the equipment beneath the Latin-inscribed wood panel running the length of the back wall which read, GRATO ANIMO DEDIMUS NOSTRIS IN ENNTIBUS ANLAM.

"Impressive," said John as he stood back, ignoring the inscription and admiring the set-up. There were several minutes of tuning, Dave and John getting to know the equipment, Rick running his sticks around the kit, and the air of apprehension was more pronounced than earlier. Clive sat at the back of the hall eating a Midnight Mint he had risked his life chasing when he heard the familiar Greensleeves tune jingling from a passing ice cream van.

"Pop music, this is going to be boring," Clive sighed. "I'm gonna have a nap."

I hadn't prepared well, thinking *let's just see what happens,* other than choosing one song, as pop and simple as I could summon, that had charted earlier in the year. After everyone settled we ran through all that was needed to put the song together.

"Let's get started then." I conducted.

The perfection was instant! Faultless, enchanting, as though we'd had union for a million years. I was astounded. Could it be I was dreaming? How was it I found time to smile? This was special, and so easy, as we glided on effortlessly. Clive was actually standing! Was he in shock? A short but serene silence flooded the hall at the end of our joyous ride, a brief mystified expression shadowing our judgement.

"Bloody hell, that wasn't bad, was it?" I said.

Dave, beaming, replied: "Great!"

John, looking unmoved, commented, "Happy with that."

Surprisingly, Rick announced, "Yeah, all right, I suppose?"

And Clive ended with his own unique, pedantic and flattering verdict, "Crap song but good performance, you lot," followed by a round of applause.

The tonal sound of John's Vox keyboard made it for me, filling a void I was unaware of, having never performed alongside a keyboard player before. "Go again?"

Apprehension mutated into enthusiasm as we ran through the song for a second time. "Perfect," said Dave. "We don't need to run that again just yet, do we?"

"Definitely not!" Clive demanded.

It was just about as good as I could have expected, better in fact, and without doubt *the* best moment so far on this journey. There was a long, long way to go, but it was a beautiful beginning. I couldn't put my finger on why we gelled so quickly – maybe because all of us had experience in groups before. 'I believe everything happens for a reason' – Marilyn.

Or was it we were so bad, we had no idea what was good?

John's suggestion, matching numbers we had played in former groups, produced a few duplications. Rick, nailed to his Ginger Baker freestyling, was totally oblivious to such trivia, but it didn't matter; his talent conjured magic. We spent the next two hours rehearsing. After loading the van, I scanned the hall to make sure it was left as found and locked up on the way out. Dave was outside chatting up the girls from earlier who had hung around while we were rehearsing. A Machiavellian plan was hatched to get him into the van: John offered him a free drink.

We dropped Rick off in Norton. The earliest he could next rehearse was the following Sunday. The four of us demanded a celebratory drink at The Dog and Partridge in town, John offering to buy a round in recognition of our financial plight, and yes, the four of us were as good as broke. Maximum, a half pint each.

On the way the fuel saving device was engaged, last employed yesterday: I switched off the ignition. She freewheeled serenely down the long Rougham Hill. If all went well I shouldn't need to re-engage the engine until we reached Southgate Street, about half a mile further on. Dave and Clive had already been exposed to this out-of-body experience, as we cruised silently downward. John, with a look of disquiet, inquired, "What the…?"

Clive instantly interrupted. "This is a new Heath Robinson fuel economy system Andy masterminded – Esso have tried to buy the rights because it's bad for business. What do you think?"

John replied, "Oh, well, whatever they've offered, I would take it plus a book of Green Shield stamps."

Dave's proposal, "Free petrol for a year and a Tiger's Tail would be handy."

Clive returned fire. "I collect pink stamps!"

Another milestone passed, the next a full repertoire. If it was all as straightforward as this then we should be ready to get out there and perform in no time.

Over the next four weeks, rehearsals were held every Sunday and once mid-week. The set list increased to ten pop numbers plus two from Bertha's repertoire, Black Sabbath's 'Evil Woman' and Steppenwolf's mainstream rocker 'Born to Be Wild'– not exactly pop, well definitely not pop, but they allowed me to exercise the fuzz box and that kept Rick happy. On the occasions Rick couldn't make it, Clive stood in as drummer and knocked out a beat of sorts. Actually, he was neither bad or good, bad being good, good being bad perhaps, is that right? Totally confused, I must exorcise my brain of Dave2's 'American Cool'.

John was becoming more socially involved and we were better connected. All was going well. My only concern was Rick; as yet he hadn't given any indication of coming in permanently.

It was 30th August and the next HP payments were due in two days.

Some of my worst mistakes in life were haircuts.

Jim Morrison

Chapter 6
The Censored Phone Box

CLIVE WAS OFF hitchhiking and disappeared for a few days with the three shillings a week he had been saving to soak up the London Music Scene and to clear his head of pernicious pop. He was probably going to take in The Pink Fairies, Savoy Brown, or some other heavy progressive group at The Temple (formerly The Pink Flamingo) in Wardour Street. I made my weekly Tuesday visit to the early-Victorian grouch at the hand-out office and called into Albert Balaam's to update Ray. I hadn't visited for over a month.

The showroom was busy, Ray occupied with customers, a pre-fame Nigel Havers wandering around looking suave and just about my height and age. Ron Ely was probably sawing a Hammond organ in half in his workshop and Mike sorting through the classical sheet music. I meandered upstairs to the modest record department, an old *West Side Story* poster on the facing wall greeting me as I walked in. Lovely Linda, the sales assistant, was busy serving and Led Zeppelin's 'Dazed and Confused' was playing on the record deck. The design of Van Der Graaf Generator's *The Least We Can Do is Wave to Each Other* LP sleeve stimulated my imaginative senses as I thumbed through the one rack filled to overflowing with of-the-moment LP sleeves. Not much else, though, to fire the modern-thinking music lover, other racks full of outdated Mono LPs, some dating as far back as the 1950s, titles like *Hawaii Calls to You* and *Organ Moods*, along with the once revered names of Lester Lanin, Mantovani, Frank Pourcel, Werner Muller, to name just a few, all probably unsaleable for several years. Oh and of course the vitally important Classical section, Deutsche Grammophon and all.

Back downstairs Ray was in conversation with Nigel Havers. Ted Chapman, bass player from Smoke, was in, and we stood talking for about five minutes, Ted mentioning they were to release their single 'Dream of Dreams' on 7th November and promoting it here in the Music Centre on the same day.

Ray joined us. Ted departed.

"Andy. What's going down?"

I was gobsmacked!

"What's happened to 'How's things Ray?' Dave the American drummer must have been in recently."

"We're updating our greetings portfolio, do you like it?"

"That welcome should go down well with Albert's traditional Victorianized customers, don't you think?"

"You obviously saw the American drummer."

"Yeah, but we've asked Rick, Bertha's drummer, to come in for the time being. Hopefully he will stick with us, otherwise we'll all have to go on a university language course to study the Art of American Digabadcool."

"So you've got a drummer then!"

"Yes, and rehearsing, around twelve numbers so far, not ready yet but getting there and aware the sixty pounds HP is due. Need more time. With luck we'll to have enough material to accept bookings within the next three weeks, say."

"That'll be approaching two months' HP payments outstanding again. Sorry to have to mention that."

"Yeah, I know, Ray, very conscious of that," said I, feeling humble. "Hopefully work won't be so hard to come by this time."

"Leave that with me, I'll see what I can do."

"Thanks. Before I go, has Albert mentioned the HP payments?"

"Not as yet."

"Thank god for that!"

Traffic jammed the street as I stepped up to the kerb to cross the road. From the tailback came the blast of a car horn to my right. Blimey, it was Dave2 sitting at the wheel of a Volkswagen Beetle. He leaned across and wound down the passenger side window. As I walked up to the car, there in all its glory, a stonking great dent in the rear wing, and a piece of metal pointing skyward like Cleopatra's Needle.

"Hey Andy, whass goin' down?"

He'd definitely been in to see Ray. Heavens to

Murgatroyd, I'm going to need another exorcism after this.

"I'm good, Dave, how's things?" Dismay! Was I mutating into Music Centre mediocrity?

"Cool man, ridin' heavy in my Slug Bug. Issa gas."

What the F did that mean?!! *Has he still got problems with slugs or has he gassed them?* I wondered.

"That's very good, hope you don't get any more problems."

"Gotta gig so ca-a-n't do anythin' for ya, man."

An even louder blast came from the lorry behind. The queue ahead of Dave's VW had vanished.

"Gotta split dude, stay co-o-o-ol."

He roared off, exhaust blowing, reaching the lights. They'd turned red, he didn't stop! I wondered if I would ever meet him again. I liked him, he was hotter than cool, and what on earth was he on about "Gotta gig" at the end there.

Wandering down the street I was trying to decipher, 'ridin' heavy in my Slug Bug'. Heavy slugs, perhaps he was feeding them too much? 'Riding in my slug bug', surely he doesn't mean his car. But of course!

I didn't see him again after that. Pity.

That painful doubts syndrome had kicked my reasoning again as I reached the van. I sat for some time in thought. A similar scenario to five weeks ago was fast approaching when all was doom and gloom. I was still broke, in debt and out of work. The one positive so far, there was a group, of sorts, but no bookings and still a way to go before we're ready. Not enough rehearsal time, only once a week for certain, sometimes without Rick, and on the odd occasion on a Wednesday. Rehearsals were restricted by the cost of hiring the village hall and the limited time ten shillings provided, just two hours. Well, three for the price of two if we ignored the alarm clock, and of course we hadn't paid for any of them. But we were rehearsing again this Sunday, must try to book the hall for mid-week as well…

Clive was in London, and I hadn't seen Dave since Sunday – probably busy bird spotting. John was most likely giving a priceless diamond a manicure, or having a lunch break at Jolly's. I'd go and see. As I walked in he was sitting at the table by the door.

"John, thought you might be here, just get a drink."

Bill served me. "Hello Andy, how's things?" *What was* it with Risbygate Street?!!

"Cosmically outasight," I replied. His expression blazoned total shock, before he grinned and shook his head. He was in good form that lunchtime, classically café, and looked quite dapper. Perhaps he was on a mission.

John and Dave were aware of the HP commitment but not at that point involved. The implications of hire purchase enslavement were a browbeating nightmare without the means to support its ultimatum, as I explained.

"Need some bookings sooner than later," said John.

"That was the problem with Bertha, not knowing where to start, and not able to find many venues that suited us. The important thing is to be ready, when or if opportunity presents itself, and we're not ready, yet!"

Rehearse more and add every Wednesday or another day of the week, if the hall was available, was the suggestion. The other option, not doing it at all, find a proper job and live a normal 8 to 5 life, belt, braces, comb back and Brylcreemed haircut thrown in. The thought made me feel totally peculiar so I called to see the village hall caretaker later that day.

"Is the hall free Wednesday next week in the evening?"

"Yus oishink so, oiljus check, Andie," she replied in her South Street dialect. With diary in hand. "Yus us freee. Yew got Sundey bookt uzwewl."

"OK, we'll take that please, thanks."

"Er, jus afore yewgoo... yewdew re-erlyse er paymund furer larst sevurn tymes uz owtstandun, towtulyn freee powns un tun shilluns?"

"Um, yeah we do."

"Yew shudn't be hyrun er hawl if yew carn't paey forut, yer no. Ur tresrur wiwl moost lykely be er wrytun tew yewwiv er remyndur."

Now what? We really needed to rehearse and I needed to show willing. The only option was to use the desperately needed hand out money I'd received earlier.

"I can give you tew powns tun shilluns now if it keeps the wolf from the door?"

"Oi surpowse at'll be aweryght, Andie. Oilave ur wudwiver tresrur."

"Many thanks. We do appreciate it, I assure you."

Well, that'd torn it. With the petrol I'd put in the van earlier I was left with 'wone powns ate shilluns and forpunce' until next Tuesday!

"Ow Andie, afore yewgoo, airs bin cumplunts bout ur noyse ona Sundey arternuns frumer villige hawl. Troyta keep er vol-ume dowun, wonw't yew?"

"Yus, will tone it down a bit." This was nothing new, Bertha had the same 'cumplunts' when rehearsing.

I didn't venture out for the rest of the week, trying to preserve petrol for Sunday.

Saturday morning 10.15

"It's Ray on the phone," Dad called up the stairs.

I was in the bathroom. "There in a sec!"

I descended the stairs slowly, in thought, with just my socks on. This must be Ray ringing to tell me Albert had expressed concern about the HP.

"Hello, Ray," I said tentatively.

"Enfer sanglant," he pronounced with a chuckle. Mental road block! What did that mean?!

"Saucisses noires," I retaliated.

"A young couple came in this morning looking for a group for their wedding next Saturday, said they could afford up to twenty pounds, can you do it?"

Twenty pounds! That was huge, must be like winning the Premium Bonds. Not that I had ever won anything on my £1 Premium Bond 1958 Christmas present.

"Christ, we're not ready yet, Ray, we've only got 12 numbers. How long do they want us to play?"

"That'll be absolutely fine, I'm sure you'll manage. Seven to eleven."

"WHAT?!!! Four hours!"

"Well, you can have a break from time to time. Improvise a bit. They've been let down so would be happy to get some entertainment at least."

"Blimey, they'll have to be long breaks. Perhaps we could go home for a cup of tea half way through and go back later."

"Where is it at? Don't tell me, Aberdeen."

"No, it's beyond the wilds of Thetford forest – Brandon."

Oh, that was fine. I'd only need a gallon-and-a-half for that.

"That's great, Ray, thank you very much. We won't let them down. Will a packet of fruit pastels do, as a kind of thank you?"

"Can you afford it?" he replied. "Let me know how you get on."

Oh, hang on. I forgot to add earlier, 'pants and' before socks.

Later that evening, to my horror, Rick rang and said he couldn't make Sunday, but was OK for Wednesday when I asked.

"I'll pick you up around quarter to seven."

Another calamity… and Clive was still in London. I may have to cancel Sunday. I telephoned Clive's mum immediately. His dad answered. "He should be back late tonight. Call him in the morning – not too early, I would advise."

A quarter to nine Sunday morning was like 3 a.m. to Clive. After being summoned by his mum, to my amazement he came to the phone.

"What time do you call iss?" in a very asleep drawl.

"This is Andy Pandy, are you coming out to play?"

"Blob-a-Lob," he replied.

"OK. I'll pick you up at the usual time."

The line went dead.

I picked up Dave and John first. When we arrived at Clive's, Keith, his friend and fellow roadie from Bertha days, was there. He had been coming along to our rehearsals occasionally. We set off to the hall, and on the way I explained the hire payment blues. John and Dave chipped in ten shillings each, which injected the total relief syndrome and released some of the excruciating pressure on my overdraft – and I didn't even have a bank account.

Clive and Keith were not expected to contribute in any way. As Roadies they had never been paid, even in Bertha's days; in their words, they were our 'volunteer slaves'. The big news was the booking at Brandon on Saturday, and the main topic of conversation on the way. As we approached the hall the phone box was in its usual vandalised state with a number of glass panes shattered. The girls were there again, sitting in the veranda around the back of the hall. We set up and rehearsed a couple of new numbers, Clive doing his bit on the drums with his usual enthusiasm, although it didn't always come out the way he planned.

During rehearsal one of the girls from Bury, Dave's semi-girlfriend if you like, by that time occasionally coming around with us socially, appeared in the hall asking for a lift into town, but Dave turned down her request. She became more insistent, but after time decided to leave. Dave had decided not to continue their relationship. At the end of rehearsal, after some discussion, Clive and I persuaded the others to let her come along to town anyway. With the van loaded I followed Clive out, locking up behind us as it was my responsibility to see the hall was left tidy and to return the keys to the caretaker.

As I walked away, and looking down from the hall, I stopped. There was some stone throwing and calling out, "Are you coming with us then?" The girl at that time was inside the phone box, and in the absence of any response from her it should have been left there, but pebble-sized stones were being thrown in an attempt to attract her attention. Perhaps Dave was throwing a little more aggressively than anyone else. Although it appeared nothing more than throwing a pebble at a bedroom window to wake someone because you forgot your keys, I admit it was not our finest hour. Perhaps the honourable thing would have been for me to go to the box and ask her directly if she still wanted a lift into town. As the main reason for the group coming together, and being from the village, I perhaps should have taken responsibility for this. It was a trivial incident but it would have been better to make sure everything was OK with her. After all, she might well have been feeling uncomfortable and possibly intimidated to some degree. Clive, however, does recall going to the box, opening the door and asking her if she still wanted a lift. Apparently she was holding the receiver at the time and ignored him. I guess you couldn't blame her.

Before returning to town we called at my home, Dave, as he often did, teasing my six-year-old sister Mandy, which she loved, John chatting away to my mum about something and nothing, Clive and Keith in conversation with my dad, almost certainly about *Dad's Army*. All that was about to change. We hadn't been there more than five minutes when a knock came at the front door. Mum looked out of the kitchen window and saw a police car parked outside. Her heart sank. The last time she'd opened the door to a policeman she was given the news of a tragic accident.

Dad answered. It was the local policeman. "Is Andy here?" he asked and walked in without an invitation. Dad led him into the front room. Without a hint of delay, he told me: "I've just had a report you were all witnessed throwing stones and smashing glass at the phone box while there was a girl inside."

We were all stunned, speechless. Clive broke the silence. "Who claims to have witnessed that?"

He replied with a demanding tone. "I'm not at liberty to tell you, but I'll take down all of your names and addresses and I will be back, mark my words, when I have fully investigated this incident. You are not to make any contact with the girl while this investigation is ongoing, is that understood?" He left, as quickly as he came.

We didn't defend ourselves in any concerted way, couldn't quite believe what we'd heard. We knew for a fact the glass in the phone box was already broken and had been for many weeks. There was much discussion, theorising and speculation over the following days. Who contacted the police – was it the girl, upset because of Dave's rejection and her earlier pleas for us to take her into town being denied? Was there a less-than-impartial witness, a near neighbour to the hall who was not happy about the noise on Sunday afternoons? There was no doubt the police were under mounting pressure to catch local vandals who were smashing up phone boxes, not just in Risby. But none of us had smashed a single pane of glass in that phone box, so surely we had no case to answer.

But the police were, it appeared, on a mission to nail a conviction at any cost. Unfortunately, we were to be their prey… even if that meant their turning a blind eye to the real culprits, busy vandalising boxes regularly without being held to account.

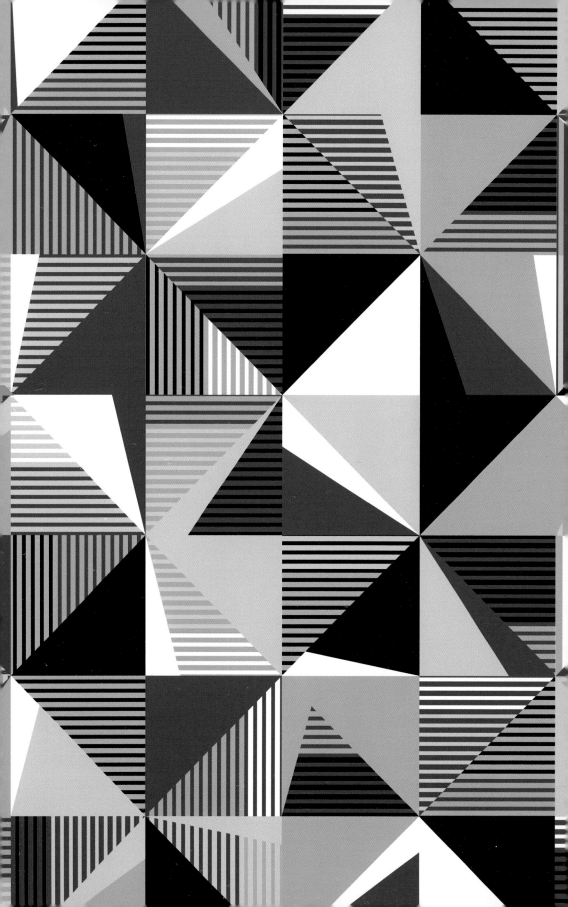

Then on into the picturesque beauty of Bury St Edmunds and its ancient charm: St Mary's, the Norman Tower, the Cathedral and the endearing Angel Hill. For the moment my troubles were lost.

Chapter 7
Beyond a Mod is a Plod

Tuesday 8th September

THE PETROL SITUATION was heading for critical again but I still had £1 left from Dave and John's hall contribution. Today was queue-up-and-grovel-for-a-hand-out day again. The debts of £30 borrowed from a friend to meet previous HP payments and £41 for the deposit on the equipment, still outstanding to a former workmate, were also on the critical list. A handwritten letter had arrived this morning from my old workmate, with a reminder the interest was building up and some payment at least was expected.

There was no employment being offered, although I was not exactly looking hard. The one job I did apply for didn't materialise. Before going into town, I called in to see Bett at the A45 shed and jettisoned twelve shillings and eightpence on two gallons.

"Going long-distance today then, Andy? Off to see Jimine Hendix on the Isle of Wight, are you?"

"That was over a week ago, in a field!"

"Owe, he's a farmer, is he?"

Clive and I lugged our begging bowl to Triton House. On the way back to the van, wandering up Risbygate Street towards us came the friend to whom I owed £30. When the heavens open it always buckets down. Dick from Barrow was very much still in the fifties rock and roll era, with drainpipe trousers, swept-back Brylcreemed hair, winkle-picker shoes, and good-looking to boot – an easy-going character, always sympathetic to the plight of others. He had lent me the money some four months before without questioning how I would repay him, but I felt I should at least make some sort of gesture towards settling the debt, particularly as I was about to bump into him. We collided outside Bowers. The street was choc-a-bloc with traffic as usual and static motorcycles were blasting in rev-it-up style. The noise. My ears were cabbage like.

"Hello, Dick, how are you?" I shouted.

"Not too bad, Andy. Still getting over the bike accident. How's the group coming along? Last time we met you were having problems finding bookings, I seem to remember?" he shouted back.

I could hardly tell him Bertha had broken up and I was out of work and deeper in debt than the last time I saw him.

"Well, it's a long story, Dick, but there's a booking coming up this weekend," I hollered back.

"Have you given any thought to the money I lent you?" he bawled. I should have been expecting that and had my answer ready!

"To be honest, only recently. I can give you three pounds and ten shillings now." That was all of my hand out for this week. "If that's OK?" I yelled.

"Well, it's a start at least," he roared.

With harrowing regret, I handed him the money. We parted with enlarged tonsils.

So there it was. I should only have offered £3 but my conscience was prodding so hard I'd had difficulty offering him as little as three pound ten.

"You'll have to enrol as a monk in the Abbey for the rest of the week," said Clive. "Give up all those luxuries."

"What, you mean spend all my time in the Abbey Gardens learning how to become a budgie fancier?"

"No, budgies don't count. Anyway you'd probably get the sack because you're too busy looking at the type of birds you really fancy."

He was completely off the mark with that one. Compared to Dave I was quite reserved when it came to approaching girls, though I did find the opposite sex extremely attractive.

So the petrol drought remained critical, the small change I had in reserve was needed for strings for the Strat before Saturday's booking and I had no money spare to top up before the rehearsal the next day. There was nothing for it but to go straight home, switch off the engine and coast at every opportunity. I was never sure if this saved petrol of any significant amount, but it concocted some probably misguided hope that I was economising. I felt confident there was enough fuel for me to collect everyone and get to the hall at least. Dave and Clive were equally as broke, John's wage at the shop was barely more than we were getting in hand outs. I was very fortunate that my parents were not expecting me to pay towards my upkeep at home.

Wednesday 9th September

That evening was the final rehearsal before our pivotal booking on Saturday. We ran through the repertoire of fourteen numbers with Rick. Leaving the hall around 10.30 p.m. I dropped everyone off in town first, after some lengthy conversations. The van was our only form of transport beyond Bury. John, Clive, Dave and Rick had no wheels other than bicycles. Rick and I arrived in Norton around 11.30.

"So you're OK for Saturday then?" I asked him.

"Yep. You're picking me up around five, yeah?" said Rick.

"Great, see you then."

Relief was abundant. At least there was only me to get home now. The petrol gauge was showing signs of the usual neglect. *Hell, I hope I can get home!* It was wing-and-a-prayer stuff. As I drove towards town the A45 was very quiet, as always at that time of night. The temperature started to drop and the fuel gauge had emigrated to the Southern Hemisphere, but she was still cruising. I had passed anxiety and reached that surreal beyond-reality state where nothing seemed to matter. Either I'd make it home or not; if not, I'd need to employ the F it hypothesis.

Around half a mile before Rougham Hill, I was plotting to engage the ingenious fuel-saving strategy I liked to think had been so successful in the past. If she got up a fair speed before hitting the top and gained speed downhill under the old railway bridge, with no traffic or obstacles to negotiate, the momentum might carry her well into Southgate Street. With a huge slice of luck she may just glide up the street, over the brow of the hill and drift down before turning left into Maynewater Lane, only then having to re-engage her engine; the agonising handicap, the sharp right turn into Southgate Street, would be a bit hairy – well, almost certainly downright scary.

But all my slide-rule calculations were about to be made redundant. The van started to cough and splutter as though she had caught a bad cold in a sandstorm. Panic stations! My reality senses had returned with a vengeance. *Keep going, old girl, better to give up in town than out here in the wilderness.* But she just couldn't find the spark. With power rapidly fading, our only good fortune was a layby looming on the left. She rolled quietly and neatly to a stop. Bugger, now what? My only option was to walk into town, leaving her at the mercy of highwaymen, unlocked, with all of our equipment on board – a tempting hoard.

Wearing just a tee shirt and jeans, I set out in the hope of hitching a lift. It was cool, dry, past midnight. The A45 was very quiet as I meandered lazily down Rougham Hill, under the old iron railway bridge and into Southgate Street. Not a potential lift in sight. Up Maynewater Lane and past the brewery… thirst, craving – sod it – all came to mind. Then on into the picturesque beauty of Bury St Edmunds and its ancient charm: St Mary's, the Norman Tower, the Cathedral and the endearing Angel Hill. For the moment my troubles were lost.

But the streets were deserted, there was no one around. I'd phone home from one of the telephone boxes at the bottom of the Buttermarket and ask the operator to reverse the charges, I decided. As I laboured up Abbeygate Street everything was serenely quiet. Approaching Plumpton's, I looked down the street before crossing the road. Careering upward at breakneck speed, decimating the silence, was a Morris 1000 Panda car. It pulled up in a blaze of glory excruciatingly close to my big toe. *It's the cops to the rescue*, I thought. Two policemen were sitting in the front seats. The passenger wound down his window.

"Where do you think you're going then?" he blurted.

"I thought you were coming to my rescue."

"That's enough of that for a start! What are you up to?"

"Well, if you must know, I'm just going over there to make a phone call."

"Oh yeah, who to?"

"My parents. You're obviously not here to help, are you?"

After Sunday my respect for the police had almost evaporated. I certainly wasn't going to allow them to dictate to me without giving a sharp, perhaps sarcastic, response.

"Right, get in the back!

"Really?"

"Yes, really!"

He got out, there were only two doors. I was coerced into the back where there was no escape route.

"So what offence have I committed now – or is this yet another stitch up?"

"Right, where are you going and why? And I want a proper answer."

"Well, maybe you can help rather than hinder. If you must know, I ran out of petrol on the A45 layby beyond Rougham Hill. The van is full of group equipment and before I was so rudely interrupted, I was going to telephone my parents for help."

"Oh, really! You play in a group, then, do you?

"Well — yeah."

They held a short discreet conversation. My hearing was none too good after rehearsal.

The driver started the Panda and drove off.

"What the hell's going on now?!" I was incensed. "Where are we going?"

"To check out your story. A45 layby beyond Rougham Hill, wasn't it?" in that 'we know you're lying, you're not going to get one over on us' tone.

"What about my phone call? Surely I can ring home before we go."

"No chance."

I was furious. After that, not a word was spoken.

JUST A MINUTE, I thought I'd recognised the driver's face. Didn't he used to be a Parka-wearing Lambretta-Mod in the sixties?

The Panda swung round across the road and droned to a halt in the layby behind the van.

"So now do you believe me?" I said.

"Black long-wheelbase CA Bedford... interesting," said the Lambretta, oops sorry, officer at the wheel. "Right, out you get!"

They wandered around the van, checking the tax disc, tyres, crisp packet on the front seat, you name it. She sat there, supremely innocent.

"Switch on your headlights, indicators, brake lights." They opened the back doors. "This your van then, is it?"

"No, I've just stolen it, I thought that was obvious."

"Got your driver's licence on you?"

"No, I haven't, I've just eaten it."

"Right, that's it! Name and address?" He extracted my details and the van's credentials. "Produce this with your licence, MOT and Insurance Certificate at the police station within the next seven days or you're in trouble!" I was surprised he didn't ask for the size of my left foot.

"Well, thank you very much for your wonderful help. What would we do without the police force?"

They started to walk back to the Panda. "Just a minute, aren't you at least going to take me back to a phone box?"

"No. You can stay with your van until the morning and sort it out from there, can't you?"

You bastards, I nearly said. "So you're just gonna leave me here? What about my parents, they'll be worried sick, at the very least."

"Give me your home telephone number, we'll ring them," the driver replied begrudgingly.

"You will definitely do that?"

"Course we will. Sleep tight," he said with a sarcastic air.

"That's a promise then?" There was no reply.

I stood there, stunned, and watched the Panda disappear from view. So much for our all-embracing police force, I thought. *Z-Cars* had just been crossed off my all-time favourites list. Sorry, Fancy. If I walked back into town, I could miss Dad coming out on a rescue mission if the cops did ring my home. Better stay put for a while and hope.

Back in the van it was past one o'clock. There was no traffic on the road. All was deadly quiet. I sat there, sterile. It was turning a little colder, must try to keep warm. The PA columns were the first pieces stacked behind the bench seat in the back. I removed one of the covers, pulled this over my legs and up to near my shoulders, leaned back in the front passenger seat and drifted off to sleep.

As a heavy lorry passed and rocked the van I awoke from a kind of slumber. It was 6.30 a.m. and daylight. Hell, they couldn't have rung home, Dad would have been here by now. Extricating myself from the PA cover took a while. I closed the door and started the walk back into town again. Thumb-waving and praying resulted in two vehicles passing without response. At the top of Rougham Hill I looked down. A car was coming. As it advanced I realised, *Thank God! It's Dad and the Morris Oxford to the rescue.* With joy and abandon, I crossed the road and he pulled up beside me.

"Where—the—hell—have—you—been?" he said in a raised voice that was totally out of character. "Your mother is worried sick."

I was not surprised hearing him say this. My brother Cliff had died in a road accident while returning after a long weekend at home to his job as a photographer on the *Kettering* and *Corby Leader* newspapers back in 1962. He was only nineteen then, the same age I was now. My father had only ever raised his voice to me once in my entire life, and that wasn't very high even then. He rarely made his emotions known, keeping his thoughts to himself.

"So the police didn't ring you then?" I asked.

"No, were they supposed to?"

I explained the whole story. He was his usual reserved self, making no comment, but I knew he believed me.

"Well, I thought you probably ran out of petrol so I brought a gallon with me."

I was filled up. What would I do without this parental devotion? "No need to replace it," he said.

"How did you know where I might be?"

"Well, it's the obvious route back from Norton, staying on the main roads. I just hoped you didn't come home some other way."

Dad emptied the can into the tank. She started after a struggle and I followed him home; he then went straight off to work. His generosity gave some assurance there should be enough petrol at least to get to Brandon on Saturday, providing I stay at home until then.

The police never rang or made any contact.

Saturday 12th September

Another very important day. Everything was almost in place. I'd collect those strings from Albert Balaam's before picking up the crew in town and then going on to Rick's. Morning came and went. At around 12.15 the phone rang. I answered.

"Hello, Andy, it's Rick here."

"Rick, just thinking about you… may pick you up later than planned as John is having to work on a little later and needs more time to get ready. Probably around quarter-past five. We should still get there by six, gives us an hour to set up."

"Ah, well, that's why I called. I'm not coming tonight. I'm calling it a day. You'll have to get someone else in, sorry."

My heart skipped a beat. "Can't you just do tonight and then we can look for someone else next week?"

"No, I definitely can't make it tonight."

"Why not?"

"Can't tell you why."

I tried to persuade him, using the 'we-can't-possibly-let-the-newlyweds-down' appeal, but it was not to be.

"You can hang on to the drum kit until you get something sorted out."

I tried again, but to no avail. The conversation ended with my parting words, "Thanks Rick, hope everything's ok with you." I did wonder.

Cataclysmic and more, I rang John at the jeweller's straight away.

"Rick's pulled out of tonight. Well, not just tonight."

"Oh, what?… why?"

"He didn't give a reason but it may have been pressure from his girlfriend perhaps, I don't know. He's a good bloke, there's gotta be a genuine reason."

"It's a bit late to do anything now," John replied.

"We could get Clive to stand in but it'll be a bit hairy. You know he'll do it if we ask him, he'll knock out a beat of sorts, but he's not rehearsed enough and only stood in a few times on odd numbers."

"Perhaps the best option is to see if Ray knows a group not working tonight who could stand in," said John.

"Yeah, you're probably right. I'll ring him and call you back," I said, mortified.

Turmoil! This was not good. The couple getting married had already been let down once. I'd ring Dave first before I tried Ray, I decided. Perhaps he'd come up with some miraculous solution. I called but he was not at home. His sister Lynn said he'd be back around three.

"You're using that phone a lot, Andy," said Mum as she passed to go upstairs. "Not cheap those things, you know."

"Yeah, sorry, there's a crisis I need to sort out."

I called Ray with foreboding ringing the alarm. "He's popped out of the shop, he'll be back shortly," said Ron.

"Could you get him to ring as soon as he gets back, it's kind of urgent?"

"Yes, I will, Andy," his genteel response.

I sat waiting, my anxiety increasing as the minutes hurtled by. Half an hour passed, my patience tested almost beyond reason. As I went to call Ray again the phone rang. It was Dave.

"Hello, Andy, can't stop… gotta go out again in a minute. Lynn said you called."

I explained the crisis. "Have you got any instant remedies up your sleeve?"

"No, only to go with Clive. At least we won't let them down completely that way, but I think John's proposal would be the best option. I'll ring back about three, OK?"

I needed a pee. As I was mounting the stairs the phone rang again. Biology would have to wait. I stood at the phone with legs crossed.

"Hello, Andy. Just tried to ring but you were engaged. Ron said you had an emergency, what's up?"

"Er, Ray, yeah, we don't have a drummer for tonight. Do you know of a group that could stand in?"

A pause. "Not at the moment. Leave it with me, I'll get back to you as soon as I can." With that he put the phone down.

I knew he would be busy on a Saturday, which probably explained the short conversation, or maybe Albert was in the office at the time.

The phone rang again. It was John. "Dying for a pee," I told him. "Ring you back."

The anxiety levels were peaking again as I stood at the loo. Thoughts of the debts resurfaced, no money… *Hell,* I decided, *this is a lost cause. I'm going to take all the equipment back on Monday, sell my Strat and the van. Hopefully that will just about clear the debts.* Wishful thinking, without doubt.

Must keep the phone free for Ray's call back.

Another thirty minutes passed; it was approaching 2 p.m.

The bells… this must be Ray! Fingers crossed he'd found a replacement.

"Hello, is that Andy?" Ray's voice had gone soprano.

"Yes."

"I'm glad I've caught you, it's Mrs Bettson. Our neighbour is looking for a window cleaner. Can you and Clive do it for her?"

Thunder and lightning! There was no space in my head for this right now, although we could do with the reward, even if it was only a bacon sandwich.

"Um, can I call you back, Mrs Bettson? In a bit of a rush at the moment?"

Andy in a rush? Impossible!

"Yes, that's fine, there's no hurry."

Immediately I put the receiver down, the phone rang again. Mum walked past. "It's like the telephone exchange in here this afternoon."

"Hello, Ray," I said in hope.

"Found a drummer who'll stand in tonight for you. His name's Jamie," said Ray.

I could hear music playing in the background, he must be in the record department. He'd probably phoned from there to be out of Albert's earshot.

Hesitation mode was in full flow. "Er… ah…well… yeah. I don't know him, do I?"

"He's played in a group before, he'll be fine. And he's got his own car."

I interrupted, "But he hasn't rehearsed with us, has he?"

"Don't worry, you'll manage, Andy. He'll get there around seven. Jamie won't let you down. Can't stop, very busy at the moment. Good luck tonight! Let me know how you get on."

Here we go again! My head was close to exploding. Back on that rollercoaster, so many unknowns and imponderables. Must get a drink and take all this in before speaking to John and Dave. I was in the kitchen, the phone rang yet again!

"Hello, that you, Andy?"

"Oh, hello Uncle Bob.

"Can you bring the ladders back? I must have them today, got something urgent I need to do."

Damn, or something much stronger. I'd got to be ready by 4.30 at the latest. "OK, I'll bring them down straight away," I said with agonizing misgivings.

A call to John then in rapid speak: "Can't stop. Ray's found a drummer so it's still on tonight. Will pick you up as arranged, must rush, 'bye."

I asked Mum to pass the message on to Dave when he called, loaded the ladders and hurtled down Hyde Road to Fornham, dropped them off to Bob who had a problem with his TV aerial, then hurtled back.

"Did Dave ring?"

"Yes, he did. Said he'll be ready."

I jumped in the bath, grabbed a bite to eat and off. "Good luck and do a good job! Make them happy," said Mum as I was leaving.

Must get the strings first! It was twenty to five and I was picking John up at quarter past five.

The fuel gauge had returned from the Arctic Circle though still barely registered. I parked in Risbygate Street car park again, leapt over the low wall and hiked quickly to Albert Balaam's where Ray was busy with a customer. Mick served me with the strings. "Must go, Ray, speak on Monday," I said as I passed him. In my haste to leave the shop, outside I almost fell over a passer-by.

Oh, god, it was the Old Lady in Black! "I am sorry, are you OK?" I said. She turned, looked up at me and paused. The fourth dimension opened before us. I was almost in a trance.

"You're the young man with a kind heart, aren't you?" she said in her frail tone.

"Well, thank you, but not really," I said, feeling bashful.

"Good men always go far, young man," she said with sincerity.

What did that mean? And no mention of my long hair today! I picked up the basket, carefully handing it to her.

"Are you walking down the road?"

"Yes, son."

"Take my arm, I'll walk with you."

We walked slowly, arm in arm. It was much quieter in the early evening. As we walked she spoke only once.

"I dream and sometimes my dreams come true." I had no idea what she meant but I have never forgotten her thoughts.

We reached P.C. Tidy's nearly opposite the car park. "I have to cross the road now, are you going to be alright?" I asked.

Her parting words: "I'll be fine. Be good and be successful. You will do well, I promise, never look back."

That was the last time I saw her.

It was a completely surreal moment, a calm after the storm of all that had happened so far that day. I suddenly felt the anxiety lift completely. I was cool and in control again as I drove to Dave's, Clive's and then on to John's.

I explained all. John's first question, "No fuel, I guess?"

"Enough to get us there – hopefully."

"Dave and I will chip in three shillings each, that should just about get us a gallon."

"OK, I'll add the other thruppence and that'll be exactly a gallon!" I joked. We stopped and spent the six shillings and thruppence; the fuel gauge was off the danger list.

On our arrival at the British Legion in Brandon, the reception was in full swing. Our set up was at the end of the hall. Clive was in his element assembling the drum kit. There was an impressive look to that Laney stuff but I did wonder how things would go with a completely unrehearsed drummer, but for some reason, at that moment, I didn't feel any anxiety or concern.

We waited, in anticipation of Jamie's arrival.

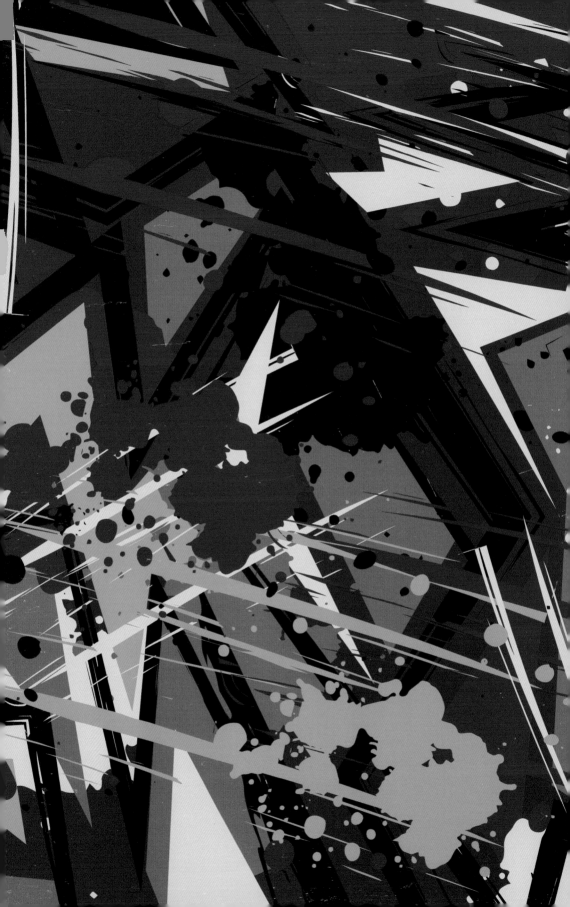

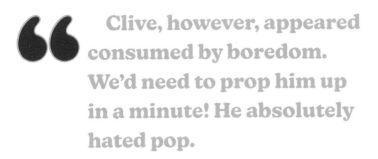

> Clive, however, appeared consumed by boredom. We'd need to prop him up in a minute! He absolutely hated pop.

Chapter 8
Jamie and the Genie

IT WAS FIVE to seven and there was no sign of Jamie. The tension was rising. We all stood there without expression, probably resembling four hairy bridegrooms jilted at the altar.

"Ray said he wouldn't let us down, he'll be here." I was convinced.

"He does know where we are?" Dave checked.

"The clock on the wall is fast, plenty of time yet," replied John, although he knew it was slow.

"All drummers are laid back, and I know what's coming next!" said Clive, anticipating the inevitable.

The real bridegroom appeared on the horizon, another crisis looming.

"OK, lads are you ready? We're all raring to go."

"Er… our drummer is a little on the drag. Hopefully he'll be here in a few minutes, sorry," said Dave.

"Alright, boys, just a few more minutes then."

Those few more minutes passed in three seconds, the audience awaiting our opening with an air of patient expectation.

"Can you get going now, lads?" said the bridegroom. It was nearly ten past seven.

Clive was attracting the centre of attention syndrome.

"How'd I guess that was coming? OK, as long as we start with Black Sabbath's 'Evil Woman'," was his ultimatum.

Heavens! How appropriate for the opening number at a wedding, I thought.

"He's winding us up, isn't he?" said the pale-faced groom.

We sauntered through our first number, slowly of course, the bride and bridegroom dancing with elegance and embrace, the audience locked in the romantic dream. It was all so charming and raised warm emotions at that touching moment. Clive, however, appeared to be consumed by boredom. We'd need to prop him up in a minute! He absolutely hated pop. The next song would have to be 'Evil Woman' or he could be horizontal!

'Love is All Around' followed by 'Evil Woman'! At a wedding! Prepare for an early Exit.

Our next song was about to spring into life when…

…the entrance doors opened. We paused, waiting in suspense. As if the gods granted perfect timing, slowly, a well-dressed, good looking young man with a slight

Mediterranean complexion and dark shoulder length hair emerged. He was holding two drum sticks in his left hand. The drama was near sublime, as though the star of the show had finally arrived. The hall fell virtually silent as he calmly approached us with a gentle smile. What an entrance, I thought, and rapture, *there's that look again!*

"Hello, I'm Andy, you must be Jamie," I said as we shook hands.

"Sorry I'm late."

"Oh, thank you for coming, we're really grateful. It was very last-minute!"

"This is Dave, John… and Clive, our most treasured man for all seasons."

We had no idea who Jamie was until he arrived. I had never met him before, but John was pleasantly surprised to find he knew him from school.

Clive graciously made way for Jamie and headed for the bar.

I was completely oblivious of any expectations and really didn't know how this was going to work out. But Jamie certainly looked the part, the perfect vision of a pop musician.

"Better get cracking, I guess."

After some adjustments and a run round the kit, "Just count me in Andy," was Jamie's prompt.

It was 'Hitchin a Ride', that very first song we rehearsed on the 2nd August. None of us were enamoured by this sugar-coated pop plaything, but it did seem ideal for a wedding reception. Besides, we had given it a savoury flavoured makeover anyway.

So, it was 1–2–6, and we were up and cruising. Jamie, steady, feeling his way, instantly into the right tempo. To my delight nearly the entire audience was up and dancing.

It was a good feeling. Knowing there was a long way to go, and only fourteen numbers to call on, I extended the song by about three minutes, hoping this would give Jamie more time to get familiar with our style and the kit. Dave and John were calm and assured, or at least they appeared so. They kept it together beautifully and released some of the pressure resting on my side of the stage. Let the good times roll! And they did.

The ending provoked sustained applause and a few cheers. Blimey, this set was going to be good. And it was. Jamie opened his shoulders more as the night went on and I realised he must have a decent level of experience. Dave and John were in their element. Me... well, I can't comment. We did eventually play Black Sabbath's 'Evil Woman' but by that time most of the audience were on a different planet. It went well, perhaps very well, and the encore after our final number, which we had already played at least three times, was 'Born to Be Wild'. Clive was zonked, the audience wild.

Relief and calm stimulated the return of those good vibrations. Jamie was the centre of attention after that final set. We invited him to join us, full-time.

"Well, I came here with the intention of this being just a one-night stand, but yeah, I wanna get back out there playing."

That was a special moment. At last, I had inspired hope this was the true beginning of a new journey for me.

"I don't think we'll be rehearsing those numbers again anytime soon, Jamie."

"That's the first time I've done a full 'rehearsal' live at a booking, without rehearsing first," he replied.

We had played our fourteen-song repertoire four times over, some of the songs extended to around eight minutes.

"That was great, lads," said the mother and father of the bride, and paid us the £20 we so desperately needed, John accepting the money without hesitation.

As for Clive... well, what can I say? He stepped up without waver or delay – very special.

As we were winding down with the burden of humping the equipment on the horizon, a young couple wandered up to speak.

"Loved it," they said. "We're getting married next week, can you do our wedding?"

"We certainly can," said Dave. "We'd be delighted."

"The reception is here in this hall, same time."

"OK, we'll be there," said John taking the details.

As we were leaving at midnight, the Monday meeting at Jolly's was arranged for lunchtime, Jamie included. With thanks from everyone, he left in splendour in his green and white Triumph Herald. Rubbed a thousand times, Aladdin's lamp couldn't have conjured up anyone better suited to us.

On the way home Dave and John were in constant conversation on the back seat, Clive fully awake in the front. As I drove through Thetford Forest, that dark, quiet, tree-lined road touched my romantic soul. Everything had fallen into place that night, the whole experience near-perfect. I had to remind myself this had all come together by pure chance. It was just over seven weeks since my meeting with Ray in Albert Balaam's and that timely encounter with Dave. There were times when it had all seemed a hopeless mission, full of false dawns and hazards. As I was drifting, a vision of the frail old lady in black opened before me. How much had she influenced the warm feelings I was experiencing at that moment? I couldn't help but allow my imagination to run free. But there was still a long way to go; this was only the beginning of the beginning.

Monday 14th September

Feeling sanguine, with a free and fresh mind, there was a spirit of determination. Wash the van! She hadn't been clean for ages. Ten to nine, it was much too early. I donned the scruffiest clothes I could find and ventured out to a grey and overcast day. She deserved a bath and I had good reason to smarten her up. She was, after all, the figurehead of this newly-formed group EXIT. Washing the windows reminded me of Mrs Bettson's phone call on Saturday. I'd speak to Clive later and see if he's up for it; the money would be handy however little it was.

A leap into the bath and out, prompted a down the stairs trot with just a towel wrapped around my head. (Just kidding.)

"Where are my jeans, Mum?"

"They're in the wash."

"Where's the other pair?"

"In the wash."

Oh, blast, I'd have to wear those old black corduroy hipsters, bought from Sixteen Plus in 1966. Boy, were they out of fashion.

"What about my tee shirts?"

"They're in the wash as well."

Even worse. Where was that low-collar shirt that I bought with the hipsters? I'd look like something out of the Ark.

"Where's my belt?"

"I threw it out – the buckle was broken if you remember."

Damn! Better keep my hands in my pockets, that should hold them up.

The hipsters were excruciatingly tight. I must have put on weight, the belt was redundant anyway.

"It's Ray on the phone!" A truly pleasant surprise!

"Hello, Ray, where's it at?"

"Digabadcool, wasnit?" he replied.

"Bongtackular."

"How did it go on Saturday?"

"Well, we got rebooked for this coming Saturday, so I guess we must have done something right."

"Ah, good news! How did Jamie get on?"

"Perfect, and he decided to join us. Many thanks for finding him, he's ideal."

"Well, that *is* perfect! In addition I had a call from the father of the bride this morning. He rang to thank me for recommending you lot."

"Oh, really? Nice."

"Also, by some miracle of chance, Phil Beevis from Norwich Artistes rang me a few minutes ago. I mentioned Exit, POP GROUP! to him. He's interested and could see you for an audition at three o'clock this Friday. They'll pay ten pounds for your expenses."

My brain electronics exploded into overdrive. Never done an audition before. What were the expectations? Were we good enough yet, and if we were, what sort of bookings would they offer us? Petrol to Norwich didn't cost £10! Would they want some of their money back? The list of queries was endless.

"That's two packets of pastilles I owe you now and I've only just started saving up for the first one! Truly astounding, Ray, thank you. How many numbers do we need for that, by the way?"

"Oh, you'll manage. Half a dozen or so, I should

imagine," he replied with his usual optimistic delivery.

"OK, we're meeting up at Jolly's lunchtime and I'll call in afterwards. I need to check everyone can make that time."

It was good news after more good news, and wonderfully fitting to take along to Bill Bayliss and the Dodgy Buns.

Gertrude… I forgot to mention. Gertrude was the name of the van, lovingly adopted from Bertha's days. She looked radiant and ready to go as I walked towards her and jumped inside, but the ignition didn't fire the fuel gauge. How far would she take me? Not far enough, I was certain. What were the options? Risk it? Take the number 226 bus? – I could just about afford that. Try to hitch a ride? I loathed doing that. Ask Mum for a loan? That was the only option, the others wouldn't guarantee I'd get there on time.

"Mum, I know it's a pain but can I borrow six shillings? I need to get some petrol before going into town."

"Oh, Andy, you need to get yourself a proper job, you can't carry on like this, you know!"

"I'll pay you back tomorrow after going to see Scrooge."

"You know I can't afford this but here you are." She gave me six shillings from her well-worn purse. "I must have it back tomorrow."

"Promise! I'll repay you then."

"Don't tell me, you're off to New York and then on to Hong Kong?" said Bett as he walked towards the pumps.

"Close. I've got to stop off in Bury on the way first, to see Mary Whitehouse about a naked hippopotamus."

"I'm gonna have to think about how to follow that one," he replied.

That was the six shillings and another fourpence gone and I was a little on the drag.

When I arrived at Jolly's a board meeting was already in progress: Clive, John, Dave and Jamie were all there. I had just enough loose change to buy myself an orange squash. As I walked to the table the pro rock musicians walked in. I nearly left the solar system when they quietly said, "Hello". Completely dumbstruck, I walked past them without a reply. Weird.

As you may imagine, the main topic of conversation was the twenty pounds we'd earned on Saturday. It should have been mounted in a glass cabinet and displayed in the centre of the table. Jamie was very much a spectator, still getting to know us, everyone trying to make him feel welcome and at ease, but the opportunities to chat with him about his background and experience were limited as I opened with the latest news.

There was an air of suspense as my usual long-drawn-out drama heralded the announcement of Friday's afternoon audition.

"It's impossible for me to fit into my extremely busy schedule, but knowing how difficult it is for you all to cope without me, I'll rearrange my sleeping timetable, which means I will have to get up early every day for the next week," said the long-suffering Clive.

Dave was absolutely fine and had an announcement of his own to make: he was starting a full- time job the next Monday, for Beers in Hollow Road. John said it wouldn't be a problem for him as he would be able to get the time off work. Jamie, who'd so gallantly came to the rescue on Saturday without hesitation or falter, was a little less certain. He was in full-time employment, as an apprentice at Boby's, and only here today on his lunch break.

"I should be OK, I'll get the time off somehow or other,

take it without pay if I have to. So count on me to be there," he said finally.

The focus returned to the twenty pounds. "We could always go see Fred Pontin for a day," said Dave, "or the South of France even."

After we'd explained the HP predicament to Jamie, John's more sensible proposal ushered unanimous approval: three pounds ten should be kept in the kitty for petrol and emergencies, and sixteen pounds ten should go to pay off some of the HP. This was heady stuff, a little more weight lifted from my shoulders. John appeared to be taking some responsibility for accounting and there was now a move towards collective decision-making. Rehearsals were arranged with Jamie for the pre-booked Wednesday evening and money for four gallons of petrol given to me, to keep us mobile through to Saturday. Four whole gallons!

John and I went next door together to make our first joint HP repayment. The shop was quiet, it was Monday. Despair! Mr Balaam emerged from the office, alarm bells echoing around the empty shop.

"Yes, Andy?" That booming baritone drowning the alarm.

"Er, is Ray here?"

"He's on the phone at the moment, what can I do for you?"

Hell, this was awkward. "Um, it's OK, we'll wait for Ray."

"Well, if you're not in here to buy anything, don't hang around too long!" He returned to the office.

I looked at John. "Amazing. He didn't mention the arrears."

While we were waiting John was eyeing up a Hammond.

"We'll never get it in the van, John!"

"I'll get Ron to saw it in half! Can't afford one anyway,"

he replied.

"Saw it into quarters, it might just fit, and then buy it a bit at a time." I said seriously.

"*Sacrebleu,*" was Ray's opening line. What the hell did that mean?

"Spiffing," I replied. John was completely bamboozled.

"Come to pay off some of the HP with our hard-earned pennies from Saturday."

While Ray was signing the card we confirmed we were OK for Friday. He gave us directions and said he would phone Phil Beevis and let him know, also mentioning he had updated Albert on what we were doing. We both thanked him for his help, and John and I parted company with the intention of meeting at Wednesday's rehearsal.

Tuesday 15th September

As I was driving to the little white garage shed with its three Esso pumps standing in a row, I was trying to conjure up another bizarre remark I could throw at Bett.

"Don't tell me, it's ten packets of sausages and half a hundredweight of potatoes?" was his opening salvo.

"You've got me with that, I'm stumped. Haven't got anything to match it. Oh, wait. How about this? Four gallons, please, and I need a receipt."

"What! I don't believe it… have you won the pools or something? And a receipt as well!"

"Are you alright, Bett? You look a bit pale. Do you want me to go to The White Horse and get you a drink?"

"No, but I'm going to close and sit down for at least an hour after this shock."

I could fully understand his brain overheating. There was a time when I'd asked him for one and sixpence worth.

"That'll be one pound, five shillings and eightpence. Must be a record for you, Andy."

It was.

On the way back from my weekly Tuesday visit to town, Deep Purple's 'Black Night' was vibrating my passion and electrifying my senses, so much so that I shelled out six shillings and fivepence from the unemployment fund to buy the single from Harper's. I felt flush for once. Oh, and yes, I did repay Mum *and* told her about Friday's audition. She was impressed.

"Was that why you needed the money?" she asked.

"Well, in a roundabout, indirect, about the houses kind of way, yes."

Did I detect a tear in her eye? "Why do you so often take me by surprise, Andy?"

Anyway, let's get back to 'Black Night'. It had charted at Number 50 in early August and taken six weeks to climb to 20; a rock crossover in the charts was good enough to class as popular. The rest of the afternoon and evening was spent learning the guitar riffs and lyrics. It was a perfect fit for the Strat and that bruising fuzz-box.

Wednesday 16th September

Jamie made his own way to the rehearsals that evening. He lived in Barrow, three miles south of Risby. The first hour, including setting up, centred on 'Black Night'. This was a song I felt really comfortable with. As it turned out so did everyone else, and the first number the completed line up added to the set list. It also gave us the first hint of an identity if we wanted to take it. There was something special about how easy it seemed rehearsing, the same sensation I felt when rehearsing that first number with Rick. The rest of the time was spent going over the songs best suited for the audition. The phone box had been restored, glass pristine, no sign of damage as its lights shone brightly as we left.

Over the following weeks we gradually got to know more about Jamie. He was born in May 1952 in Hertfordshire. A year later, with his mother, father and elder brother, he moved to Bury St Edmunds, his father opening the off licence within the modern shopping parade recently built along Lake Avenue. This neighbourhood became a mecca for budding musicians, spawning seven or so groups in the 1960s.

Educated at Tollgate Primary and Silver Jubilee School for Boys, at twelve years old Jamie purchased his first Carlton drum kit for £10 from the Athenaeum manager's son on Angel Hill. Aspiring musicians Michael, Steve and Tony became friends, and Jamie joined their group The Argonauts, rehearsing at The Cricketers in King's Road. They became well-known locally, even featuring in a national newspaper as the youngest rhythm and beat band in East Anglia. At the time Jamie was thirteen years old.

After leaving school at fifteen, he became an apprentice at Boby's Engineering Works in King's Road. By this time his rudimentary drums had evolved into a full premier kit. In 1967 the group changed their name to The Mood and by 1968 were semi-professional and travelling widely, including appearing at Margate Dreamland with The Move in May 1968. Their name changed again in 1969 to Smoke. Their agents by then were Bury Theatrical Agency in Bury St Edmunds.

In June 1969, Jamie and girlfriend Linda's son Roger James was born. Smoke's Michael (Tuffy as he was then known) and Steve were ambitious and decided to turn professional. Jamie, with a young son, felt compelled to complete his apprenticeship and both he and Pete Murrell (the bass player at that time) left the group in early 1970. Jamie turned down the volume and sold his kit to Trevor Warner. At home things were not turning out as he'd hoped and there was an amicable split from his girlfriend. Always attracted to girls, probably as much as girls were attracted to him, he was keen to get out there playing again when the phone rang last Saturday. He was still only eighteen years old. By this time it was already becoming clear Jamie was happy to go along with whatever we were doing. He appeared laid back and easy to get along with – the archetypal personality for a drummer, I thought.

When the power of love overcomes the love of power the world will know peace.
Jimi Hendrix

Chapter 9
Auditioned in Angst

Friday 18th September
THE DAY JIMI Hendrix died.

So this was it, the pinnacle of my one time dream. Well hardly, but it's one small step perhaps. Oh, I forgot, try to pass the audition first.

It was twenty to one, the earliest we could get away. There were five of us in the van with plenty to talk about, and I wondered had I ever been to Norwich. If I had it didn't register; maybe I'd just passed through. An audition, The Melody Rooms, Norwich Artistes, this was all new to me. The conversations were vibrant, no feelings of apprehension or doubt evident. My question, "has anyone been here before?"

"Played there once," replied Jamie.

"Yeah, several times," said Clive. "Saw Floyd, Fleetwood Mac, Jethro Tull… oh, and The Who played there before my time."

Oh, heck, this is more of a venue than I imagined. The expectations must be stratospheric. Are we really up to this?

The journey there was about an hour, weaving our way through the small towns of Thetford, Attleborough and Wymondham and on into Norwich, the avenue of trees warmly greeting us on Newmarket Road. I was already impressed. We passed the Norwich and Norfolk Hospital, The Gala Ballroom, and muddled our way through the city centre, eventually finding Oak Street, still in semi Victorian mercantile mode. The Melody Rooms were set back from the road and looked to be mid-twentieth-century, an unassuming building on one level, perhaps of industrial origin.

The tension was powerful as we walked together through the open entrance and into the main dance hall. There was an air of unbroken stillness, as though Venus the Bringer of Peace had descended to scatter calm before a return of the Tempest. It was surreal. No one was in view, the jukebox to our left silent, lit up and ready for a patron. The stage empty, awaiting its cast to stimulate the masses, strange deserted cages above concealing some mysterious assignment, and the bar at the far end, with its two entrances, to entice the sober. The quiet air was gently broken by our apprehension, some nervous comments taking toll of their sender. We searched for a voice. Just one came, from within the bar. "Be with you in a moment lads."

We awaited, and as we waited, I wandered across to the

Jukebox curious of its selection, mainly up-to-date and current chart material, my thoughts. As I returned, without prompt or command, the piccolo of 'Tears of a Clown' eloquently interrupted the peace, filling the empty hall with melody; it was truly surreal.

The voice emerged from the bar in the form of a modestly tall, well-presented man in his thirties, who strode the length of the hall with an air of confidence to greet us.

"You boys must be EXIT from Bury St Edmunds," his opening line. "I'm John Fisher." We didn't know of him.

"We're here to see Phil Beevis, re the audition," said Dave cautiously.

"Yep, he'll be along shortly. You can set your stuff up over there on the side, away from the stage."

As he left us to it I sensed a modest level of intimidation in his manner, but perhaps I was misled by his vaguely forthright delivery.

An hour passed as the equipment became our stage, our endeavours the only sound to break that eerie silence again. Fisher demanded our attention as he approached with a shorter, more rounded man of a similar age.

"Boys, this is my colleague Phil Beevis."

"Hello, everybody, good to see you all. Looks as though you're just about ready to go," said Beevis.

Pre-performance nerves were at their utmost height as I picked up the Strat and hung her over my shoulder. Jamie caressed the kit with a cautious touch as Dave thumped out a few notes before the call to perform, John's melodic keys replacing the memory of that distinctive piccolo. As I gazed at the two judges awaiting our performance, this was the most nervous moment for me at any time in my modest musical career, even more so than that night back in '68 in front of a thousand plus audience. The weight on my shoulders had returned with a vengeance. I glanced to my right. If only I could adopt the mindset of Clive, sitting sprawled over a chair oblivious of any concerns. Or did I just detect a rare moment of apprehension behind his customary unfazed posture?

It was 'Black Night' as our opener, we'd all agreed, so current and so perfect for us. And we opened. The first few bars before vocals started effortlessly, and then – catastrophe!! – the jack plug sprang from the Strat and fell to the floor. A mortifying halt pursued. It was one of those moments I would never live down. The yawning silence was frightening.

"Sorry about that, just lost my jack," I spluttered. Clive remained apparently unmoved, but there was a look of 'that's torn it' from my group mates. Strangely, it obliterated any sense of nerves I had zinging through my body. Calmly, I picked up the lead and she came alive again.

Those six numbers glided without hesitation or calamity until eventually the hall fell silent once again. I hadn't a clue what reaction we roused within our audience. They looked unmoved.

Across the hall Beevis and Fisher were in deep conversation. The tension was graphic and at least a minute passed before Fisher called, "OK boys, come up to the office, all of you." We followed in procession up a dark narrow staircase to the office above and behind the stage. It was relatively small, pictures of acts strewn around the walls and a singular untidy desk displaying a promotional leaflet headed:

'EAST ANGLIA'S LARGEST ENTERTAINMENT AGENCY'.

Beevis sat at the desk, Fisher standing behind. We all stood to attention.

"OK, lads, we like what we see and hear. You have potential and we'd like to take you on exclusively," said Fisher. Our facial expressions converted to a look of total disbelief and magnified shock.

"An exclusive," said John. "What does that mean?"

"Well, you'll work exclusively through Norwich Artistes and only accept bookings through us," replied Beevis.

"How much should we expect?"

Fisher raised an eyebrow. "How much work have you got at the moment?"

Dave was pressganged for an answer. "Err, one booking, tomorrow actually. We've only just got it together," he replied, with a level of embarrassment.

"That's ideal. We'll keep you busy, don't worry about that. We think you have good marketable potential as a pop group," replied Beevis.

Your turn, Andy! "Sounds good to me," I said, thinking, *I've never worked for a real agency before.*

The others nodded in agreement. We really didn't understand what we were signing up to, but it didn't matter. There was triumph in the face of adversity and that was much more important. Beevis, with his infectious enthusiasm and quickfire, almost unending delivery, ran through the small print. Commissions, expectations, venues, contracts, contact numbers, the importance of… you name it. All of that went over our heads except for John, who was focused to the last. Maybe the only note of caution was struck by Clive who frowned as we all signed a document unaware of its detailed content.

"We'll be in touch next week, add in those chart numbers as much as possible," said Fisher.

"Current chart stuff, dance music for the young and our clubs is what we're looking for at the moment. Try to stick to that and *keep it current.* Do that and there should be plenty of work. Oh, and, Andy – once you've got the jack in, try not to lose it," said Beevis with a grin.

"He's always having problems with his jack," said an amused Dave.

I KNEW I'd never live that down!

Phil Beevis I'd warmed to. I liked his enthusiastic approach and felt he was someone I could relate to. Maybe he went a little over the top at times, but I considered he would go out of his way to promote any act he truly believed in. John Fisher appeared more distant, elusive perhaps, but our John seemed to strike a chord with him and he did hand over the £10 we so badly needed.

Later on, I was to learn a little more about the backgrounds of the partners in Norwich Artistes. Phil Beevis originated from Long Melford in Suffolk, where his interest in the music and entertainment world began. A journey to Norwich in 1967 led to a meeting with John Fisher at the Melody Rooms and together they formed Norwich Artistes. Phil's natural energy and enthusiasm saw a rapid rise in the agency's standing and he was noted for the many top-line acts he secured to appear in the region.

It was often said Phil aspired to become the Brian Epstein of the East, and this was reflected in the enormous effort he made for a number of local groups, lifting their status and taking them from the wilds of Norfolk and Suffolk onto highly regarded London venues and recording contracts. He was, however, still searching for that big breakthrough act that would finally repay his endeavors.

John Fisher was the son of businessman Geoff Fisher, and through his family had connections to several other hospitality and entertainment venues in Norwich, including

Club America and The Prince of Wales, a Free House. He kept a close eye on the management of the clubs in their portfolio.

This was the agency team we'd just secured for ourselves.

On the journey home the euphoria was cosmic, our non-stop talk intoxicating. Jamie was giving us the lowdown on some of the venues mentioned during the meeting.

"So what are the cages over the stage for?" I wondered aloud.

Clive and Jamie answered in harmony. "GO-GO DANCERS."

"Caged go-go dancers? Kinky. What, they're dancing behind bars while a group plays?!" "YES."

"That's one heck of a distraction in the middle of 'Hold On, I'm Coming'."

The euphoria settled as we were approaching Ingham. John, sitting in the front passenger seat, was looking preoccupied and scribbling in a notebook.

"What's that about?" I asked him.

"I thought I should make notes of what we spend and stuff, when we're out and about, in case it gets forgotten."

"Looks like a novel to me," I replied.

"I'm jotting down some of the events of today as well. Might make interesting reading in the future perhaps."

"At this rate it probably will."

For me today had been beyond incredible. Could I possibly have imagined this outcome back in July, things falling into place so perfectly? Not in my most fevered dreams – and I had a pretty wild imagination. Our journey as a four-piece pop group with one far-out roadie officially began on this day. Oh, and I must mention our truly faithful, dependable van, Gertrude.

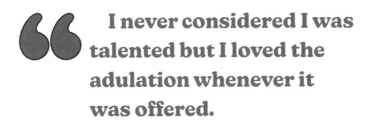

> I never considered I was talented but I loved the adulation whenever it was offered.

Chapter 10
Euphoric Windows

Saturday 19th September

THE JOURNEY INTO town that morning was like a joy ride on the Orient Express. I could afford the luxury of enjoying the moment and Nirvana's 'Rainbow Chaser' was filling the space in my swirling psychedelic head. First, that pleasing visit to Ray, and on the way collect those two packets of pastilles from Herrington's newsagent-cum-sweet and wool shop further down the street. Albert Balaam's was busy that morning, scattered with nattering musicians, so Ray was fully occupied. I had a brief conversation with him, explaining the outcome in Norwich, and presented him with the bag first and then the two packets of pastilles. He was ecstatic as you can imagine – about the pastilles, I mean. I thanked him sincerely for the introduction.

"We may end up on the same bill," he said, offering me a pastille. His own group, Barrie's Magazine, had by then been working via Norwich Artistes for over three years.

For the first time in a long while I owned some true purpose and confidence. Staying in town for the morning and early afternoon, I met up with Dave and Clive before returning home to prepare for our second outing in Brandon. After a short interlude of basking in calm waters, however, there was a subconscious reminder I was not yet out of the woods. Those debts on the Strat and the two personal loans were still to be resolved. The three pound ten a week hand out was barely enough to keep me going with the basics, the odd gallon of fuel for the van for my own use; the occasional drink out here and there at bookings perhaps. It didn't go far. As far as the group was concerned, the promise to 'keep you busy' from Phil Beevis was still only a vague statement. We really didn't know how much work they would put our way. There was £20 to come from the booking this evening and the £10 from the audition to throw in, but beyond that was still the unknown. I decided at the first opportunity to go meet the three people I owed money and explain the current position with the group, in the hope they would allow me more time. Not that they hadn't been extraordinarily understanding already.

Arriving home, I was greeted with "Mrs Bettson rang – can you call her back?" Completely forgot about that! I telephoned her straight away.

"Hello, Mrs Bettson. Sorry I didn't get back to you."

"Oh, that's OK. Vicky, our next-door neighbour, would like to get her windows cleaned. Are you interested?"

Could I afford to refuse? Probably yes if it was still only two shillings each. "Would you tell her I'll be round to have a look on Monday?"

"I'll give you her telephone number. She should be at home, I've just spoken to her."

So I telephoned Vicky and arranged to call on Monday afternoon.

Late afternoon we all assembled to revisit Brandon, collecting John outside the shop at 5.30. Gertrude came to a lethargic halt at the traffic lights before taking a left turn down St Andrew's Street.

As we waited for the lights to turn green, Dave enquired, "Have you heard anything from the cops about that phone box, Andy?"

"No, it's all gone quiet. Perhaps they discovered the truth."

"Probably waiting for a delivery of charge sheets. Takes a long time to stitch those together," said Clive.

"A bird in the bush is worth a stitch-up in time," someone said, wisely.

"WHAT?" said a voice from the rear.

The lights turned green. I was struggling with the column change again.

"Come on, Andy, you know they don't like it up 'em," said Dave.

The sound of crashing and grinding gears was echoing around the street, passers-by looking round in disgust.

"Well, if history repeats itself we'll be here till midnight," was Clive's cryptic warning.

"While I'm working on this, can you pop back to the

shop, John, and ring to tell them we should arrive at twenty-past nine? We're reversing all the way there." Horns were sounding from the queue behind. "I refuse to PANIC!"

"Everybody out and push!" said Clive.

"I sense a change is coming," Jamie announced, mystic-style. The lights turned red again!

First gear suddenly crashed in. "Anchors aweigh, Cap'n Pugwash," said Dave.

'A Life on the Ocean Waves' was the chorus as we juddered off when the lights turned green, again. That was the first time Gertrude had embarrassed herself in front of a capacity audience.

"What's this about a phone box?" said Jamie. We explained all on the way.

This was Jamie's first outing in the van and I did wonder what he was making of it all, but he was just as light-hearted as the rest of us.

The wedding reception went well and we travelled home full of animated cheer. Our regular Sunday rehearsal in the hall was to be held the next day. I had prepared three more current chart numbers over the past few days. Bobby Bloom's 'Montego Bay' had climbed to Number 15 after three weeks and I vowed never to whistle again, not even in private, after this had left the charts. 'Band of Gold' had just reached Number 1. I developed female tendencies whilst singing this Freda Payne classic – oh well. Then, desperate to stay true to my roots, I added Sabbath's 'Paranoid', totally not pop, but it was in the charts after all, having reached 28 after two weeks.

We had a good rehearsal that Sunday, lasting nearly three hours. Clive looked devastated after the first two numbers, really quite ill, but incredibly well and full of colour after 'Paranoid'. Add in 'Black Night' and those post-chart numbers from earlier in the year, Status Quo's 'Down the Dustpipe' included – oh, what a mix! – and God willing such variation should cater for the differing venues Beevis had mentioned. I was hopeful.

Returning the keys, we paid that day's hall fee and all the backdated amounts.

"Whottayew rubberedur bank or sumtun, Andie?" said the caretaker.

"Yep, the Midland, Abbeygate Street actually. Should be in the *Bury Free Press* on Friday."

"Asa useul yew heven alarf, arrntyew?" *Hopefully that story's not circulated around the entire village before Friday,* I thought, belatedly.

"Have you had any complaints about the noise recently?" I asked.

"Noww, Andie, noht laytly. Oicud ear utthouw wen oiwus inur garrdun," she replied with an 'oim ownley pullun yer leg' expression. She lived about half a mile from the village hall and was a lovely old lady, bless her. In a conversation sometime before she'd commented, "Yew noht wunna dem Smook's arryew? Thay scrats moy vynuls." Let me know how you get on with translating this one.

Monday 21st September

I had barely had chance to come round the next morning when Mum crashed into the bedroom. "It's that Mr Beevis you were talking about on the phone, Andy, quick!"

This was unexpected. Had he forgotten to explain part of the contract or something? I picked up the heavy Bakelite receiver.

"Hello, Mr Beevis."

"It's Phil to everyone who knows me, Andy," he replied.

"Oh, OK, Phil."

"We've decided to put you in at The Melody Rooms this Saturday." Bombshell! I'd not expected that!

"What! Who are we supporting?"

"No, you're on your own, main attraction if you like."

I hesitated. "Er… do you think we're ready for this, Phil?"

"Based on Friday's audition you'll be absolutely fine. Two one-hour spots."

My mind was spinning. We still hadn't enough material for two hours as a support, let alone as a 'main attraction'. We should have told him at the audition we were not the finished article… should I tell him now? Firstly, I was flustered – then hesitant – then resolute. Hell, we could do with the work and I didn't want us to get off on the wrong foot. Two hours… we'd just have to repeat some of the more popular numbers.

"What can I say Phil, but thank you for your faith? Is there anything else we should know?"

"How much you're getting paid perhaps?" he replied with a satirical slant.

"Oh, yes, didn't think about that!"

"Twenty-five pounds on the night."

I had no idea whether this was the going agency rate. At that time it sounded like a fortune.

"Thanks, Phil, look forward to it."

"I may call you later with some more work," was his parting line.

This was a lot to take in, another eureka moment. What joys would the rest of the day bring? Although I was meeting up with John, Jamie and Clive in Jolly's at lunchtime, I couldn't resist the temptation to express my delight to John, so I rang him.

"I'm blown sideways," he replied. "We're not really ready

though, are we? I didn't think we were going to see any work for at least two weeks. That's astounding."

"Me neither. Still, hopefully we can live up to their belief in us. See you at lunch."

Our call lasted about five minutes. No sooner had I murdered my breakfast than the telephone rang again.

"Phil here. The Carlton Hotel, Yarmouth this Friday – can you put that in your diary? And pencil in Sunday as well."

Wha…? "Yeah, OK. What… er… times and stuff?"

"I'll fill you in later. Call you this afternoon."

"I'm off out shortly, back mid-afternoon. Can I call you around then?"

"Yep, that's OK, Andy, speak later."

Mum walked past. "So what's happening then?"

"You wouldn't believe it! Must get ready to go out… let you know at dinner."

The one thing that hadn't occurred to me: are Jamie and Dave OK for these dates? Dave probably would be, his natural enthusiasm would carry him there. He was at his new job so I decided to ring him that evening since he wasn't going to be at Jolly's this lunchtime. I was not quite so sure about Jamie. He wouldn't have been expecting work at this level so soon and may have made other arrangements.

Our Monday lunchtime rendezvous at Jolly's was fast becoming a religion. We were all on first- name terms with Bill Bayliss and he with us. The tea was awful, the sandwiches average, but the atmosphere hit the heights when we got together. The news I opened with was a heady surprise to all, John included, when I explained The Melody Rooms booking and quite possibly two others that weekend.

"Bloody hell!" amplified Clive. "In demand, you're not

charging enough."

That one went over our heads. We weren't at all concerned. For us, this was another defining moment. Why and how Beevis made this work so readily available didn't even register, it was just great to feel wanted. We had arranged that contracts and all paperwork for bookings should be sent to John, who was evolving into our volunteer group accountant and keeper of the books. More money from the last booking fees should be used to pay off the overdue HP. John agreed to deal with this and I could at last relax, knowing he would oversee the repayments in future provided there was money available.

Jamie was fine for the weekend, easy-going and laid back about it all, true to first impressions of him. There was a spring in our step as we left Bill to clear up behind us.

"See you all Wednesday at rehearsal," I said.

Clive had arranged to meet Keith that afternoon, so I made my way to Vicky's on my own to see about the windows.

I pulled up outside the house. *It's even bigger and has more glass than Mrs Bettson's*, was my immediate thought. *How much should I ask for doing all these? Clive's gonna kill me for taking on such a big job.* I knocked on the door. An attractive woman, probably in her early thirties, answered. The low-cut dress was an immediate distraction.

She opened with, "You must be Andy?"

"Yes, come about the windows."

She gave me a guided tour. *Hell's bells*, I thought, *how long will this lot take?* I hadn't a clue what to charge. We arrived back at the front door. Thoroughly distracted by that plunging neckline, I couldn't concentrate. "Er…" Just as I was about to blurt out a figure plucked from infinity, she interrupted, "Come inside. Would you like a drink?"

She opened the door, I followed her in. As the door closed, she asked seductively, "Would you like to have some fun?"

Well, I thought I knew what she meant but I couldn't be sure. *I'll just agree.*

"Yeah?" I said nervously.

She closed in, pressed her wonderful breasts against my chest, kissed my lips and began to slide her hand down inside my blue jea...

(Sorry to interrupt, but I'd better fill you in at this point. You're probably thinking: 'He's played in two groups, in his late teens, must be fairly experienced, at the least.' Well, sorry to disappoint, but not really. I'd had a few girlfriends, and if asked (not that anyone did ask) I could have replied openly that I was experienced. But those very limited times, two actually, were with girls of about the same level of experience as me. Very little. I had a feeling this was going to be something completely different.

Anyway, where did we get to? Oh, yes.)

...ns. She had reached my vital senses; you lead I'll follow, my instincts were screaming.

"Let's go to bed," she breathed. The temptation was irresistible.

My God, I was thinking, *could this day really get any better?*

Bing-bong!

The adrenaline rush
subsided. Oh, well,
anti-climax. In that at least
I was very experienced.

Chapter 11
A Brutal Ten Bob

THE DOORBELL RANG.

"Better answer that," she said, walking to the door while straightening her dress. Me… I was trying to make sure my jeans were not giving anything away.

"Hello, sis," said Vicky. "What a surprise – come in."

Oh, Christ, better leave.

"This is Andy, he's here about the windows."

Sis was older, more mature, with a less liberal outlook perhaps. "Really?" she said, eyebrows raised.

"I'd better be going," I said in haste.

"Will you call and let me know the price?" said Vicky, almost suggestively.

Sis was radiating 'Price for what?' with her suspicious expression.

"Call tomorrow, let you know then," I replied.

As I walked through the door the devastation effect kicked in. My sex life in the main was full of missed opportunities or roads leading nowhere. But my true love affair at that moment was with the group and what Phil might offer when I called him later. Although I have to say there was a passing thought, *window cleaning, it could have some attractive merit.*

It was gone four o'clock when I eventually arrived home. "Mr Beevis called about half an hour ago. Said could you ring him back as soon as you get in?" was the greeting. "Oh, and someone from Haverhill called just after you left this morning. His number is by the telephone."

Phil was his enthusiastic self when I called him, opening with, "Sunday's booking is RAF Lakenheath, the American base, at the Airmen's Club. Three fifty-minute spots and a one-hour final spot, ten-minute intervals every hour for the first three."

Total bombshell!!!

"Oh, and incidentally – the intervals are strictly ten minutes, absolutely no more. The club reserves the right to deduct from the fee if more than the permitted time is taken."

Seismic shock!!!

I was speechless! Another mega challenge. We did manage at Brandon with an excruciatingly limited set list and there were a few more added since then, but would the Americans notice us playing the same songs in every set? Then, there was always the possibility I would be chasing the others around, gathering them up every hour on the hour.

"The Friday booking at Yarmouth, need some details," was my businesslike request.

Phil reeled them off, then added, "And we've put you in at Club America, Norwich next week, Thursday the first of October," in what I was beginning to recognise as his customary thunderbolt delivery.

I couldn't keep up with this. "What are the expectations there, Phil?"

"A more mature audience, current stuff, some slow numbers for the smoochers, and keep a low profile in the intervals. Be professional at all times and KEEP THE VOLUME DOWN!"

He signed off with, "Must rush. I'll send John the contracts. May call you tomorrow."

That was four bookings over seven days. It was hard for me to take it all in. From nothing to busy in less than a week! I had never experienced this, it was always a struggle to find work without an agent or manager in groups I'd played with before. This was a whole new experience. It was odd and almost unreal to have such faith shown in us after just one short audition. The true test perhaps would be when we performed in front of Norwich Artistes' own clientele and then the post-booking reaction.

I telephoned the Haverhill number. The answer was instant.

"Hello, it's Andy. You called earlier and left a message with my mum."

"Are you the chap with the group?" a man's voice replied.

"Er, yes." Strange. Who would be ringing me from

Haverhill about the group? Or was it someone chasing money I didn't know I owed?

"Ray Broome at the Music Centre gave me your number. I'm looking to book a group on Friday the ninth of October for Haverhill Youth Club."

Hell, this was a dilemma. We'd only just signed an exclusive deal with Norwich Artistes, so should I accept or decline? Ask him to book through our agents with their commission to pay on top. Why would he? We hadn't a booking for that night so should I take a risk? It was eighteen days away.

"Er, yeah, umm… that's, er, OK," gurgle, "I think. Can you give me some more details, please?" My mouth was operating involuntarily, words coming out with no prompt from my brain. I just couldn't turn it down. That made five bookings already and we still only had a repertoire of sixteen or seventeen numbers. I thanked him and the repercussions theory opened as soon as I put the phone down.

Just before our evening meal the phone rang again. *I'm getting familiar with dazed and confused*, I thought. What now?

"It's Dave, wass happening?"

"Oh, you wouldn't believe me if I told you… couldn't make it up."

"Are you going out later?" he enquired.

"Hadn't planned, why?"

"Just wondered if you fancied a drink at The Joiner's Arms? My treat."

"I'll definitely take you up on that one! Why don't I ring round the others, see if they fancy meeting up? Eight o'clock?"

"Yeah, sounds good. Eight o'clock, righteo, see you then."

There had been no real chance to explain in any depth to my parents all that had happened over the past four days.

When we sat down to dinner that evening with my six-year-old sister, there was surprise and delight that perhaps at last, some five years after that first group practice in the front room at number 4 (our old house, in the same road), something worthwhile and even exciting was emerging. As you would expect from parents, as parents do, they would always come up with some level-headed down-to-earth practical stuff and '*do I really need to do that*' reminders.

"If you're going to travel a lot, you'll need to get that van fixed, Andy. The gear linkages and door locks for certain. And it needs an oil change, plugs and that."

Practically-minded dad was often to be found in the shed-type garage working the mechanical on his Morris Oxford, mending the speedo with parts from the clock on the mantelpiece in the living room, creating Frankenstein bikes from mangle parts; nothing was insurmountable. Mind-boggling.

"I'll do the oil and filters. See if you can find some replacement gear linkages somewhere, maybe from a scrap yard."

"If you play with anyone famous, can you get their autographs?" Mandy's gentle request.

"Especially if it's Des O'Connor," Mum added.

"Are you going to play 'In the Summertime' and 'House of the Rising Sun'?" Dad wondered.

"And if you play with The Singing Postman, can you get his autograph for Nan?" added Mum.

Later that night all five of us bundled into Pete Murrell's parents' pub, The Joiner's Arms in Garland Street. As you can probably imagine, having missed the lunchtime revelations Dave was in peculiar mode and in danger of needing resuscitation therapy when I broke the news about four bookings in seven days plus two rehearsals. "Just one night off then," said Clive. We arranged on weekdays to pick up Dave from Chedburgh where he was currently working on site. John and Jamie were fine, Jamie suggesting that on weekdays he might make his own way by car on occasion, to give him more time after work to get ready.

John was already aware of the mountain of paperwork he'd receive if work came in at this rate in the future, he took it all in his stride. The friendship between us all was growing stronger by the day, and there was a clear message of union and a total lack of disharmony. Of course it was early days, but so far this was turning out to be a joyful experience. We unanimously agreed that if Phil offered us work for the ninth that clashed with the Haverhill YC booking, we would explain the van was on loan to Pink Floyd that night. What really stuck in my mind that evening was the definitive image of pop musicians gathered around a table socialising in a quintessential old English pub. Maybe you didn't have to be aloof and self-important to succeed in the music world. My high regard for those pro rock musicians was beginning to fade.

The next day was all about practicalities: that dreaded weekly visit to the miser's lair and on to find some linkage leverage for the van at the scrapyard. I *absolutely hated* these places, but needs must. As I drove in it was to the expected raucous greeting from the guard dogs – and boy, did I fear aggressive dogs! They were up to the van door before I could open it. The brutal-looking yard owner, I assumed, sauntered up in a string vest with hair sprouting out of every orifice.

"Wassa matter? Dogs putuh sh**s up yer?" he blasted, laughing.

"As a matter of fact, they do," I whimpered out of the

small sliding window.

"Goo-on, git back daren nere!" he roared at the dogs. "Whatta you want 'en?"

I explained all. Through the window.

"Air's un old CA long-wheelbase down 'er bottom uv ur yard. Gorn av a look at ut!"

"What, just have a look to see if the bits I need are there?"

"Well, if you want 'um, you'll 'ave tuh f*****g well take um off yerself, won't yer? Leave 'er van 'ere!" he commanded, with the same tone he'd used on the dogs.

Dad did warn me I might have to do this and had supplied the tools for the job, saying: "Don't leave any there, you'll never get them back!" So I fell out of Gertrude, nervously, fearing at any minute a loud, hostile, warlike dog would appear, charging towards me with foaming mouth ready to devour my vital parts.

I walked down the yard. He hadn't told me exactly where it was, I had to find it. Boy, did I have a job finding it. And when I did, God, what a mess: mud, oil, you name it. The inside was full of other old stuff and the only way to get at the parts I needed was to crawl underneath, so I did. *Must be mad*, I thought. The smell, the filth, everything I most hated, was all there in abundance. Even a chicken turned up to see what was going on. There was very little light under there either, but I did get what I needed and managed to extricate myself from the swamp, mud in my hair, over my clothes, hands filthy, and feeling completely demoralised.

"Ha! Are yer same bloke as come in earlier?" the brutal-looking yard owner scoffed. Both of the dogs were chained up by his office-cum-shed-cum-hut and I could see a twelve-bore standing by the open door.

You bastard, I thought.

"How much then?" my blunt request.

"Ten bob," he demanded.

"Here y'are."

I'd be damned if I would thank him and certain he wouldn't show any gratitude to me.

"Cheers, mate," was his parting gesture. I looked on, dumfounded, as he disappeared into his shed-cum-hut. Completely traumatised, I ambled home.

Submerged in the bath I was daydreaming, charmed by the melody of my tiny transistor radio I'd had since 1965, Radio Caroline and Radio London filling its circuits back then. So many iconic sounds had passed through the speaker and she was still working fine. Matthews' Southern Comfort's 'Woodstock' beautified my fantasy with its melodic tones. Tony Blackburn had been giving this regular airplay on his Radio 1 breakfast show. Ideal, I thought, a kind of Phil smoochy he had recommended for Club America. Well, my idea of a smoochy anyway. I leaped out of the bath, donned my black tee shirt, blue jeans and St Christopher, and headed straight for Harper's.

That evening was spent fixing Gertude in the shed, Dad doing most of the work. I know you won't believe me, I was trying to help. Replacing the gear linkages was top priority, servicing the engine with parts he got at trade price from his works, fixing the driver's side door lock, though the passenger one was beyond saving.

"What about this piece of steel wire I just cut off the washing line?" I suggested.

We secured one end to the body and made a loop to drop over the internal handle. How could we have survived without bonk it, bend it, shoe-horn-and-shove-it technology, back then? But the back door lock was beyond redemption, the only answer, a bodge job, sticking on a latch with a lock across the two doors, as you do. There was just about every commodity conceivable in that shed for anything requiring a botch job. So what didn't quite fit was forced to fit, even an old lock. A rummage through a box of orphaned keys presented a total misfit, but a whopping great file soon cured that! Confounding. It was past midnight before we finished. The old girl was ready for action. I was ready for bed.

Wednesday 23rd September

The day before I had completely overlooked contacting Vicky and that unfinished conquest. How could I forget about such a potentially fulfilling moment in my life? I telephoned her but there was no answer. By thrift, famine and fair means, I had scraped together £5 over the past two weeks and decided to pay some more off the Strat. In Ron's Café I met Ralph. He was fine and didn't mention anything about a timetable to pay off the £30 balance. I was lucky, *what a good bloke*, I thought.

Vicky's house was my next port of call. I had time on my hands and felt a real adrenaline rush as I walked up to the door. There was no answer when I rang the bell. It all looked very quiet, with no car on the drive. I wandered around the back. No one at home. *Mrs Bettson*, I thought, *I'll go ask her*.

"They've gone to Vicky's sister's in Warwickshire for a few days, back next week, I think. Do you want me to give her a message when they're back?"

"No, that's OK," I said politely.

The adrenaline rush subsided. Oh, well, anti-climax. In that at least I was very experienced. I'd telephone her again, maybe next week.

With time on my hands, I spent the rest of the day with 'Woodstock' and Chicken Shack's 'I'd Rather Go Blind' from a sabbatical in 1969, not current but another I'd hoped would satisfy the audience at Club America. Both of these were rehearsed that evening, plus 'Are You Ready?' from Grand Funk Live, a set number from Bertha days, massively heavy and in your face, totally not pop, but I wondered if this would find favour with the American airmen at Lakenheath. So all, finally, was set for the weekend. How would we get on?

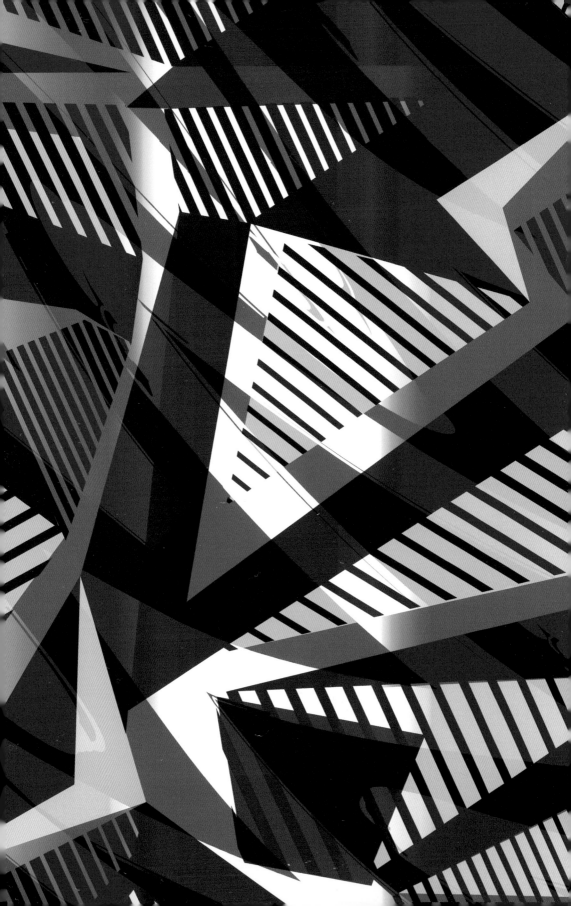

It's rather difficult to think of anybody being interested in me.
Syd Barrett.

Chapter 12
The Syda Sophon Incident

Thursday 24th September

I didn't sleep as well as usual, couldn't keep my mind from straying to that brief encounter with Vicky, even though I was sure it wouldn't be a distraction. Ray G, bass player in our former group Sung Dynasty back in the mid-sixties, unexpectedly came into view as Clive and I were passing The Crown and Castle in South Street, Risby. I hadn't seen Ray since he stood in for Bertha's bass player Brian when he was ill one time. He waxed lyrical about his time at college in Cambridge and musical free-for-alls at the Red Cow. Syd Barrett was a regular acquaintance, visiting Ray's home on the village green from time to time – probably why he had an hallucinogenic air encircling his complexion, or was that over-fanciful invention on my part? Anyway, we agreed to come together sometime for a session to see if we could rediscover some inspiration, write some material perhaps. Of course, like so many good intentions, they failed to materialise. I had largely turned my back on my old song-writing ambitions since I'd been with EXIT, but maybe not completely.

Money concerns surrounding the group were beginning to fade, but there were still the debts of £102 and 10 shillings of my own to resolve. I called in to see Dick that morning about the outstanding loan with him. I was certainly more optimistic than when I'd bumped into him last in Risbygate Street but still had no money to pay. He was as understanding as ever and not in any way voicing expectations. I gave him an assurance I would try to clear the debt by Christmas, a promise I had no real prospect of honouring but perhaps that would drive me to find some way of clearing this and the other amounts I owed. I still needed to see my former workmate Bob and address the £41 overdue to him.

After returning home, Beevis rang. I hadn't heard from Phil for two whole days. Should I be worrying? I thought.

"Have you got your diary, Handy Andy?" was his opening line. Handy Andy! Another tag I'd be lashed to in perpetuity.

He came with a swathe of bookings, including: 10th October The Metro, Colchester; 15th October RAF Oakington; 23rd October The Regal, Wymondham; 24th October The Tyneside Club, Sheringham; 31st October The Town Hall, Eye; and then a few pencilled-in dates for

November. By good fortune there was no mention of 9 October. He signed off by stating he would see us all on Saturday at The Melody Rooms.

Once again, exhilarating stuff – and we still hadn't performed a single booking proper for Norwich Artistes. I was at a loss to understand why so much work was being offered so quickly. I only hoped this was not some kind of false dawn.

Friday 25th September

Thoughts of Vicky and that unexpected interruption were riveted to my conscience. Hoping she hadn't forgotten, I telephoned. She answered.

"It's Andy, how are you?" I said nervously.

"I'm glad you called," she replied softly.

"Err, I was wondering if you would like—"

She interrupted. "I can't talk right now. Can you call me on Tuesday morning?"

I paused. "OK. About eleven then."

"Look forward to it." She ended the call.

God, that felt good. I was up on another high that would probably last the rest of the day.

It was just past four o'clock in the afternoon and we were on our way to the first agency booking – another important milestone. Clive and I drove to Chedburgh to collect Dave. He'd managed to get away early. Jamie and John made their way to Yarmouth after work in Jamie's Triumph.

Dave's first remark on climbing into the van, "Can you call at the off licence in Lake Avenue?"

Great, Dave, I thought, *running a bit late as it is.* He rushed in and rushed out with a bottle of wine in hand. "Important night tonight, I need a stimulant," he said jokingly.

"Try Phyllosan."

"Or a Double Diamond – works wonders."

I was totally calm, no sign of panic. There was no gear-change car crash this time at the traffic lights.

"Blimey," commented Dave, "have you looked up the manual on how to change gear at last?"

"No, I saw a hairy monster and a pair of Rottweilers. I feel much better now."

Our journey of around two hours across country, along the A143 scenic route, took us through numerous villages and old rural centres like Harleston, Bungay and Beccles, these wonderful old places still largely unspoiled and full of Suffolk charm. The mood was happy and exuberant, the main topic of conversation our burgeoning bookings list. Oh, and of course the two EXIT signs, proudly displayed in the back windows for the benefit of those following who probably hadn't a clue what they represented.

The Carlton Hotel Great Yarmouth

We gathered outside this impressive hotel building, John with our first pink agency contract in hand. Greeted by our hosts we were ushered to a basement room with a small alcove stage. Then came the arduous task of humping the equipment downward and setting it up. Drinks, a vital ingredient, were courteously donated and we awaited the curtain call. When it came, the audience were principally girls, well-dressed, much in the image of well-to-do teenagers. For two one-hour sets we stayed with the current and earlier chart material, including the Purple and Sabbath numbers. The audience was close up and I couldn't help but notice some keen and focused attention from the young ladies. Was that image already having some success? Dave was in his element, playing up to this blatant female interest. Jamie was behind me – I couldn't see what he was focused on though I had no doubt where – and John was almost sideways on to the audience, kind of in a world of his own, in Bill-Wyman-behind-a-keyboard mode. It was a good night. Our audience dancing with happy go lucky sparkle came to mind. So, any anguish I had about our performance and how we would be received was perhaps unfounded. We left on a high.

A walking tour along the seafront ensued, a fitting way to burn off our post-performance high. On our return to the van, parked in a side street, everyone was in good spirits, but this was about to be rudely interrupted. *Not again,* I thought, *it's Panda and its two keepers.* They made an arresting approach.

"Hey, come off it," I heard Clive and Dave harmonise, quietly.

"Your van then, is it?" one bobby probed.

'No, it belongs to the Queen Mother,' I was tempted to say, but decided I must bite my lip after that last A45 encounter.

"Yes, we've been playing at The Carlton."

"Really?" he replied. Where had I heard that one before! "Wass in the back then?"

Silent thoughts. *It's obvious – sausages!* "It's full of our equipment."

"Oh, yeah? Let's have a look."

I unlocked the latch across the back doors. He insisted on opening them himself.

"What's them Syda Sophons doing in the back there?!" he blurted.

I was having difficulty in holding my humour. Syda Sophons? They're something to do with Ancient Egypt. Aren't they?

"We take them around with us for a drink on-stage and spray the audience occasionally." What a load of rubbish that was, but Clive's quick wit held up the criminal investigation for a split second or two.

Just as our interrogator was about to reply, a large cymbal on top of the equipment, in true patriotic style, fell downward. I stood frozen, unable to stop its slow-motion descent, the sharp edge grazing his shin as it careered loyally onward, crashing directly onto his right foot. The sound was wondrous. It was a magical moment that aroused a distinct look of pleasure on all of our faces. "Painful," someone verbalised, quietly.

"Hope that hasn't damaged it!" Jamie grumbled.

"On your way then," was the PC's quick but muted reply, supported by a red-faced frown.

The cymbal was fine and we were, kind of, jubilant.

In earlier collective negotiations which resulted in an ultimatum, Clive and I were allocated overnight sleeping quarters in Great Yarmouth, entirely in the interest of monastic thrift. Well, to put it simply, gasoline frugality. The sleeping quarters were in the van! John, Jamie and Dave headed home, to the tune, "See you at the Melody Rooms, six-thirty sharp."

So we made the best of it, messing about along Yarmouth seafront in the early hours, crashing out on the beach until dawn. The morning was much the same, lazing our way to Norwich in the afternoon, wandering around the city and its music shops to pass the time. Sublime, isn't it, the life of a penniless pop musician? Carefree and careworn at the same time – but I was loving it.

Saturday 26th September

"Sleep well, did you?" was the six-thirty greeting outside The Melody Rooms.

"Yeah, like Jack's giant – completely shattered," Clive quipped.

He was in good spirits, as were John, Jamie and Dave. Me, I felt a little tentative walking into this place for the second time. "Big night" as Dave suggested on our way in. He was right, and it would probably set the tone for our future relationship with Norwich Artistes.

I stopped on the way and peered at the promotional posters. There was our name – the first time I had seen it in lights, so to speak.

Following their Successful Norwich Debut – We Proudly Present EXIT

I was startled by that. Never before had I been granted such a grand introduction in either of the two groups I'd played with previously. It kind of put me up on the must-do-well shelf again. Agent's licence was another thought; after all, our 'debut' (last week) was only an audition, with just two non-paying onlookers.

We ascended the same narrow stairs we had climbed on our way to the office the week before, this time turning right on the landing into the modest dressing room where we prepared for our opening. I think all of us were nervous, Jamie less so perhaps. Dave had already murdered half of his bottle of wine; Clive was standing with his pint in hand. "Good crowd out there tonight," he said with an enthusiasm that wound me up a little tighter.

Thirty minutes or so passed before the door opened and Fisher walked in.

"OK, lads, you're on."

We descended the stairs in a line, dressed for the occasion, Dave and I with guitars strapped over our shoulders, Jamie with drumsticks in hand and John with nothing but himself to carry. Out into the main dance hall filled with the sound of Freda Payne, the whole place vibrant, energetic, lively – so different from the week before. Onto the stage, the jack plug was securely taped in and the nerves were jangling. I looked around. *This is where we are right now*, my perception. I was very much in the moment. There was a sense of calm as we prepared ourselves for our opening. The cue came from the DJ, the count in… and we exploded into our aggressive version of 'Down the Dustpipe'. It felt good, but I was too preoccupied to notice early on, hardly focusing on the audience, more on our performance. Still with only fifteen numbers, our choice for the first set included a few of the best that would be repeated in the second. As we played on, some of the audience were dancing and others standing watching. They were close, and almost on our level. There were moments when I seemed to lose all sense of my own presence, my eyes wandering across the stage and gazing at these three performers with me who had rapidly become my friends. It was like watching them through tunnel vision or a camera lens, an almost out-of-body experience.

After that first set the retreat to the dressing room sanctioned a breather, and then down to the dance hall for drinks. There was a general sense of satisfaction, optimism, and on my part relief. Girls were already curious; one young lady around my age asked if we could meet up after our last set. As we sat around a table, Fisher walked by on his way to the bar.

"Great, lads," he said. "Keep it up."

We glanced at each other, mystified. "Well, it can't be going too badly then, can it?"

The second set was much the same as the first for me, like being in a bubble at times, unable to see beyond the four of us on-stage. I did get to wet my whistle before 'Montego Bay' and managed to overcome fairy-like qualities, singing 'Band of Gold' with a level of meaning. Dave had polished off his bottle of wine by the end the night and Jamie and John were off on a girl hunt, I think. Clive was more laid back than a Chaise Longue. I did walk that attractive young lady home; we embraced at length against a Victorian wall behind some Victorian terraces. She was nice. By that time I had no idea where the others were or what they were up to. Phil didn't appear that night but we were humbled when John Fisher came by to congratulate us on a great night.

Somehow we had navigated our way through a performance at a premier night spot in Norwich without failure or fiasco. I drove home on another high, John writing the genesis of our story and that night's events, Clive nudging frequently to keep me awake as I started to drift off at the wheel on the long straight road to Thetford. He was interrogated on four occasions about some [fictitious] gorgeous ladies of Great Yarmouth, flatly refusing to admit or deny guilt. Well, you know what the truth is, but if you bump into Dave sometime in the future, don't let him know what really happened. Promise!

Sunday 27th September
The Airman's Club, USAF Lakenheath.

Odd, up until then the closest I had come to the USA was my brief encounter with Dave2 the American happy hippy. Never had I before experienced the USAF airbase phenomenon. This was the nearest to home we had appeared so far under Norwich Artistes' semi management, although as we drove through security, which was pretty lax, I could have been 4,000 miles away in my mind. First impressions were of the Stars and Stripes fluttering in the wind, cars, hell they were big, lorries an odd shape. For some reason walking styles appeared laid back. Surely not on a military base? Strange. The confidence I felt in knowing the lingo came from the Dave2 encounter; little did I know.

From the outside the club appeared as a typical military, utilitarian, single-storey building. As we walked through the entrance, nothing seemed spectacular other than the modest poster announcing: 'Appearing tonight EXIT Pop Group'. We asked a burly regimental-looking gentleman with an MA label on his jacket lapel where to set up. The room was unassuming, a modest stage, about two feet high, and the bar was in a separate area off to one side. Directly in front of us was a parquet dance floor with tables and seating each side. There were a few figures scattered around already, sitting or standing. I really didn't know what to expect. We lumbered in the equipment and set up. As I was giving the Strat the full fuzz-box treatment, a red-faced, heavy-duty airman approached wearing a mean expression.

"TURN THAT GOD DANG THING DOWN FOURTEEN NOTCHES!" echoed from his deep Yankee voice-box.

Wha…? What a greeting. This, my first-ever encounter with an American GI and member of the audience we were about to entertain, and we hadn't even started yet! I was at a loss for words for a few seconds, but then, without further hesitation, I blurted out, "Carnt, there's only ten!" The rest of the group looked on in amusement. He stormed off without response.

As he disappeared through the bar entrance, I calmly

bent the E string as far as possible, high on the fretboard and with full-on fuzz. The Strat screamed with delight. A high-pitched "Wh-ow!" was the reaction from someone in the tiny audience. Was this a precursor to the night ahead? Dread was beginning to flood the onward advance.

With just five minutes before our scheduled curtain call, was there time to get a drink? Beevis had warned about the need for punctuality. But we had no dollar currency, so what to do? Time ran out before I had a chance to find out.

That first set, and half way through the second, was like playing to a non-existent audience, not many there, and no reaction from those who were, everything carrying on as though we were part of the decor. We did manage to get some drinks, paid for in sterling and change in dollars, without a clue what the change represented. We didn't really care. There was little room for manoeuvre in the excruciatingly short first set break, barely time for a pee. But the room started to fill by the end of the second set as drinks began to flow, and we did, surprisingly, muster a ripple of applause, once! As I looked out through the glare of spotlights I could see the audience had assembled in two halves. To my left, seated and standing, were all black faces, to my right all white. *Odd*, I thought. *Why?*

When John, Jamie and I returned for the third set, Dave was missing. We waited in vain for him to appear. The Master at Arms was there in a flash. "Hey, you guys, get started, you're overtime!" came the demand.

"Our bass player's gone missing. Give us a couple of minutes, we'll find him," said John, and he did, outside with Clive and Keith, who were having a smoke of the mind-enhancing kind with a couple of GI's. Just to keep your thought processor on the right track, Dave loved his wine but never looked for any other form of stimulant other than the opposite sex.

That third set was something special. I do believe, in this one session, we discovered more about our respective abilities on-stage than we had collectively so far. In my desire to please the audience before us, I perhaps went further than anticipated. We played a couple of soul numbers from that early rehearsal, which did go down well with the black audience, but not, it appeared, with the white. So, without telling the rest of the group, I decided to rectify this imbalance, and with the next introduction aimed to please both sides. "Here's The Temptations and a Grand Funk Live! Are you ready... 'cause here I come!" No one else on-stage had a clue what I was about to spring on them.

There was a holler of "GET DOWN" from the left, and a loud hailed "FAR OUT" from the right. After two verses and chorus of The Temptations' 'Get Ready', I slammed to an abrupt halt, screamed "ARE YOU READY" and launched into our Grand Funk Live.

The once-silent white side erupted as we thundered through this heavy-loaded animal of white stadium anarchy: a six-minute lead break, screaming guitar from just about everywhere on the frets. I couldn't help but notice Jamie let loose, as though all of the discipline instilled in him had broken free. John's storming keyboard playing ripping across the keys; Dave, with that fantastic hair swirling around like willows in a gale, was thumping out riffs I wasn't aware he was capable of. And you can imagine the reaction this provoked in Clive and Keith, who were already on a major high. For me it was brilliant, and I realised how far we had come in such a short space of time. After the long, long, long outro the audience on both sides erupted. To my amazement, the "Get Downs" were applauding and the "Far Outs", standing, beer bottles held high, screaming: "FAR OUT HEAVY MAN THAT'S COOL." Or something similar. I was humbled. Thank god for Woodstock.

But!! To my dismay that heavy-duty airman returned at speed and with meaning, towards me, with a bottle in his hand. How many notches will it be this time, I thought – or was he going to use that bottle for something other than drinking from? I was astonished and relieved when he held out his hand in a gesture of friendship. "GOD DANNG, DUDE, THAT WAS COOOOL!" he exhaled and handed me the bottle of Budweiser. It was very small and cold. Odd?

I learned a lot that night. Little did I know what further education would come my way while revisiting our new American friends sometime later in this story.

The only way you can get good, unless you're a genius, is to copy. That's the best thing. Just Copy.
Ritchie Blackmore.

Chapter 13
A Summons for Numbar 26

Monday 29th September

SO IN JUST sixteen days we'd gone from a group that was still on the assembly table, with no drummer, one booking, a set list that in normal circumstances lasted at best forty-five minutes and no true direction, to one that had completed a successful audition, landed a contract with a leading regional talent agency, had a rapidly filling diary, made a debut appearance as the main attraction at one of Norwich's premier nightspots, and completed five bookings in ten days. My most fertile imagination could not have evoked this whirlwind outcome in view of what had gone before.

I couldn't that morning recall feeling so good about life since leaving school four years before. It was special to wake up the day after the night before with that enormous sense of achievement. Well, it was for me anyway, but I had no glorious illusions; this was after all comparatively modest in the grand scheme of things. Mum was eager to know how it all turned out, as so often I barely uttered a full sentence in reply, "yeah pretty good I think!"

It was 11 a.m. when the phone rang. I was already expectant of Phil's contact in the morning, and yes, it was him.

"And good morning to you, Andy, you're awake then," was his jaunty opening line.

"Still in my pyjamas."

"So, how did it all go?"

I hesitated, not sure how to respond to that. "Well, OK, I think."

"What about Lakenheath?"

"Not sure. Seemed to get an audience reaction, finally. So OK, I think."

"I'm going to ring them shortly. I'll let you know later how things went from their perspective. I have more dates, I'll give you a call this afternoon. Will you be there?"

"Should be. After two-thirty, say."

The call ended. Quite formal that, no mention of Yarmouth or The Melody Rooms?

The 'have more dates' thing was becoming familiar, not prompting the surprise reaction I had experienced up until then. But I did realise we should never take anything for granted. If our journey was to continue we must always endeavour to prove ourselves.

"Andy, there's a letter for you in the hall, came in the post this morning, it's official," Mum stated.

I picked it up with optimism. Maybe I had at last won something on that Premium Bond. When I saw what 'official' meant on the front of the envelope, my heart sank. As the paper emerged from within, the euphoria drained completely. It was a summons to appear at 10.30 a.m. on Wednesday 4 November, before Thingoe Magistrates Court, Shire Hall, to answer charges of wilful damage to the telephone box, Risby, on Sunday 6th September 1970. Completely downcast by now, I immediately felt a huge level of anger toward the police. No warning, no contact, not even the courtesy to consult us. It was totally out of the blue. By then mum was standing by giving her support.

'Don't Bring Me Down' echoed in my head as I walked into Jolly's that lunchtime. Keith was there with Clive, an air of gloom and disbelief resonating around the table. All, except Jamie of course, had received the same summons. After debating all the negatives, police, the girl, you name it, the conversation surged into defensive overdrive. Not guilty was our verdict and we should all defend ourselves stoically. We agreed unanimously – that was decided! The sense of achievement that should have followed that weekend was muted but not buried. We were still completely immersed in this fast-track journey and wondered where it would lead to next. There were just too many positives for a setback like a court appearance to be a major distraction. Or so we thought.

I returned home that afternoon, having almost cleared

my head, only to be confronted by a written message from Mum. 'The police called this morning, want to arrange for all of you to go to the station together on Wednesday. You can telephone them if that's easier.'

Oh, no! Now what? Well, they could wait. I wouldn't see everybody again until rehearsal on Wednesday and was certainly not going to chase around for the benefit of the police. And I didn't.

The awaited call from Beevis was a welcomed interlude. An oasis in an ocean of doubt you could say. It was late in the afternoon, gone five, when he rang. My opening greeting was perhaps unintentionally reserved, not surprisingly perhaps.

"Andy, glad I've caught you. Everything OK?" his opening line.

"Yeah, I guess. Just some bad news today, that's all, nothing to be concerned about really."

"Well, let me cheer you up if I can. Spoke to Lakenheath, they were pleased with your performance on Sunday. So much so they want you back."

"Oh, right."

"But I don't want to make EXIT too easy to get so I've told them the earliest you're available is early December, is that OK?"

"I'm sure we'll go with whatever you suggest."

"Just means that if you're in demand and elusive, if you like, you can also be more expensive. I offered December the ninth, over two months away, for thirty pounds and they accepted."

"That's fine, Phil."

"Don't get overexcited!" My tone was probably much more muted than in our previous conversations.

"Yeah, sorry, a little preoccupied at the moment."

"Well, here's some more good news! Tower Ballroom, Great Yarmouth on the eighth of November. You should be supporting a chart act, not sure who yet."

"Many thanks, Phil, it's great to be wanted."

He gave me three further dates to pencil in. "If I don't speak to you before, have a good night at Club America. John Fisher will be interested in how you get on there."

"We'll do our best, Phil," I confirmed and the call ended.

Sorry to harp on about this, but we must also have made an impression at The Carlton and The Melody Rooms. If we hadn't Phil wouldn't have been so enthusiastic today, would he? But at least we had yet more dates to fill the weekends over the next six weeks.

That next morning was not going to reflect the joy I had been granted more recently. Before I had chance to eat my first cornflake the bobbie was at the door.

"Andy! I left a message for you yesterday. Just to make it absolutely clear, all of you at the police station, Wednesday, without fail. Understand?!"

"What time? Don't forget, three of us have to go to work."

"After work then, six o'clock."

"I'll need to speak to everyone first, make sure they're available."

"Well, don't waste any time. And come back to me at the station to confirm you've made the arrangements – today!"

I could almost have told him to get lost, and when I reflect on it now I wish I had, particularly when we discovered later why he was calling us in.

I did contact Dave, Clive, John and Keith, suggesting we should get there at 6.30 not 6.00; this would be more convenient as we normally arrived at the village hall around

7.00 to set up for rehearsal. They all agreed, and this at least gave me some satisfaction, that we didn't totally submit to the dictatorial demands of the police. Although, to my utter surprise, when I contacted the station the bobby was completely accepting of that time and almost polite. Strange.

So we all congregated outside the station house at 6.30 p.m. that Wednesday and trundled in with trepidation. No one looked at all at ease. Our neighbourhood bobby was standing behind the reception counter, immaculately dressed in his sergeant's uniform and peaked cap.

His opening line, "Well, boys, I'm glad you all managed to come along." His tone was almost inviting, even stranger, not a trace of command or menace. There was no response. "Now, we don't want to have a long-drawn-out court case, do we? Much easier for you all to plead guilty and get this over and done with," he said in a *would you all like a drink and is there anything else I can do for you* manner.

We were all knocked sternward. Why should we plead guilty to smashing up a phone box that was already smashed up?

Although by that point we hadn't uttered a word, he could see clearly our expressions were radiating 'no chance'.

"Look, boys, you must understand that you don't have a leg to stand on. We have two witnesses."

There was still no answer, just cold silence.

"Now you wouldn't want to drag the poor girl and that old gentleman through the court process to testify, would you? After all, you've no chance of winning this case."

I was completely at a loss. Who was this old gentleman with eyes like binoculars, and why the soft-soap approach to persuade the guilty plea?

"So what will it be?" he probed.

Clive opened the counter-attack with, "Who *is* the

other witness?"

"I've told you before, I'm not at liberty to disclose that, I'm afraid. Go away and think about it for a few days, boys. You know it'll be better to get it over and out the way without any fuss."

We left. Boy, were we naive even to 'think about it', but we did. Not once had we been interrogated, asked to give our version of events, individually or collectively. A classic example of Guilty before Proven Guilty.

That evening's rehearsal was shorter than usual, not so harmonious. Jamie could see we were all subdued, but despite the official arm-twisting we were still all in agreement there should be no guilty plea.

Our next booking was just a day away, Club America. We needed to pick ourselves up and perform.

Thursday 1st October

Not a word was uttered about the events of yesterday on our way to Norwich that evening; it was almost as though it didn't happen. The happy band had re-emerged, Clive's obsession about Midnight Mints baffled everyone except me. Dave's wine was the main attraction. I just drove, completely oblivious of where our venue was. We found it eventually, down a narrow, cobbled, sparsely lit street called Lobster Lane, in the heart of Norwich. The unassuming entrance was arched, enclosing tall double doors probably as old as the building itself. As we entered the only way was up. Up a steep narrow flight of stairs flanked by a wall to one side and an open banister on the other. I peered upward but couldn't see the top. Maybe my eyes were failing in the dim light. We were greeted by a burly Pacific Ocean gentleman dressed in a gaily decorated Hawaiian shirt. He escorted us into the club beyond the landing. The room as we entered opened to a small low stage, compact dance floor and gaming table off to the left. A selection of tables surrounded by chairs were discreetly positioned around the room, very intimate and truly clublike. You could say it was upmarket. I asked our 'Hawaiian' chaperone if there was a lift. No, was the polite answer, it's all up the stairs I'm afraid. We looked down in horror at the thought of humping all our equipment up, step by step. But we did, without comment or contempt.

A reminder of Phil's directive was ringing between my ears when Vic, the club manager, confirmed that volume was a major charge. "Keep it down, lads, particularly early on." Well, we did, but it wasn't low enough apparently. It had to go lower until we could hardly hear ourselves and almost mimed our way through numbers without any real conviction. I could see this was all quite comical to my mates, but in the interval Vic appeared happy enough. Nothing much happened in the club until later, when the audience loosened up and we increased the volume to barely audible. I didn't know if our performance was what they'd expected or not, but anyway Vic seemed pleased and our Hawaiian friend, who we discovered was actually Polynesian and known as Pineapple, in a very friendly and accommodating manner, offered his help to haul the equipment down those rock-face stairs. We accepted without any hesitation and watched in amazement and awe as he carried two 4 x 12 speaker cabinets, one under each arm, without toil or delay, down the stairs and out into Lobster Lane.

That night was quite an experience for me, a completely different take on the entertainment world, a mature, refined audience, cocktails and all. I actually enjoyed it and John, Dave and Jamie all appeared pretty happy we'd got through without incident or misadventure. Our repertoire appeared to strike a chord with the audience. After all, it included four of the current Top Ten chart singles: 'Band of Gold', 'Montego Bay', 'Black Night', 'Paranoid', and Southern Comfort's 'Woodstock', rapidly finding recognition, was up to Number 34. But the most popular song with our audience that night was 'Black Pearl', a reggae gem that had reached Number 20 that week; the dance floor was packed as we played this and Pineapple was visibly ecstatic. Had he become our biggest fan. Most significant for me was John's keyboard input in this song. It made the whole thing and we had only completed rehearsing this the night before at Risby. Our version was longer than the original recording, the intro deleted and replaced by a reggae drum-roll introduction before launching straight into the vocal. We did refrain from performing 'Paranoid' and 'Black Night' until the volume was raised and most of the audience were under the influence of alcoholic enhancement, including to some degree Vic and Pineapple.

Our journey home down the A11 was uneventful until Jamie suggested a visit to Red Lodge.

So, what about Red Lodge? Well, it was past Mildenhall and on the way to Newmarket, a mixture of fair-and poor-quality transport cafés dotted around on both sides of the carriageway, some of them open 24 hours a day. When Jamie made the suggestion I agreed but didn't let on I had never been there before so had no idea what to expect. Parked up between a Foden and a Kelloggs Corn Flake, as we walked in I realised this wasn't going to be the exquisite cuisine of Mayfair, but I suspected Jamie knew this place was better than the rest. There didn't appear to be a female in sight, not even behind the serving counter. Maybe it wasn't a good place for them to be at 1am in the morning. Looking around, there were some dodgy-looking characters, tattoos, scruffy, or was I being paranoid? We lined up to order.

Dave: Sausage, Beans and Chips.
Clive: Sausage, Beans and Chips.
John: Sausage, Beans and Chips.
Jamie: Sausage, Beans and Chips.
Me: Err. Beans, Chips and a Sausage.

Quite an interesting choice from us all; what are your thoughts?

We were given a double-digit number for the whole order and found a table with just about enough space to seat us all on the bench seats, three on one side, two on the other. The wall-hung lighting was toned-down red. I did wonder if this was to mask the not-so-palatable food. As we sat down the low rumble of male chat around the café was muted by the jukebox gently pumping out the sound of 'Black Night', a reminder of the warm reception when we'd played this earlier. For me this night café was all very atmospheric and totally unfamiliar.

Dave decided to spend a few bob and select some tunes of his own, standing by the jukebox scanning the list for some time. In his absence, a tall, tattooed, late twenties man, posing as a waiter, emerged from behind an end wall with five plates, some in his hands and others balanced on his arms. He stopped and bawled out: "TWENNY SICK!" There was no reply. "NUMBAR TWENNY SICKSA!" There was still no answer. "FOR F**K'S SAKE… TWENNY BLOODY SICK!" We were all locked in conversation and not really paying attention. Jamie had our ticket. When he heard 'TWENNY BLOODY SICK' and realised it was microscopically comparable to our number he hailed our servant. "Over here."

The tattooed waiter headed straight for us. Rounding the last table in our row, his left foot caught the leg of the bench seat, he lost his balance and the whole 'twenny bloody sick' landed on the floor, one plate upside down. Gathering himself, the quasi-waiter picked up the plates, one by one, including the upside down mutineer. Only a few chips and a sausage had spilled onto the floor, the rest still firmly glued to the plates. He picked up the loose chips and one sausage in his fingers, one by one, chucked them all onto one plate, reloaded his burly arms and hands and walked over to present them to us! By then we all knew which was the duff and unpalatable plate. This appeared to be a normal occurrence here as no one else in the café took a blind bit of notice. Of course, there was only one plate left by the time Dave returned from his musical mission.

The next time I saw Dave after that night he didn't look at all well.

Phil's call that next morning was full of enthusiasm. "Club America went well, didn't it?"

I couldn't answer that with full on optimism since I didn't know. "Yeah, seemed alright, no problems."

"Well, you're back there again on Sunday the eighteenth, this month."

"Really?"

"Yeah, it went well, very pleased."

After a brief chat he signed off with, "You're doing great!"

Even now all this it was hard to take in. We had no grand illusions that we were 'great' and had no real ambitions. The journey had been so rapid, like being carried along on a tidal wave, there'd been no time to plan or to be creative. But for now we were riding high on the adrenaline and joy of being wanted.

This week's events had been so all-consuming, I had completely forgotten that tentative liaison with Vicky. Strangely, I had no real desire to chase it down now. After all, she was a cracking-looking woman and clearly experienced. Why wouldn't I want her? Cleaning windows had completely lost its appeal, perhaps. I did eventually call her several weeks later but there was no answer, and there it was left. Pity.

THE CLUB AMERICA

DANCING - CASINO
CABARET

LOBSTER LANE
NORWICH

Telephone
NORWICH 29060

Only Personal
Application for
Membership will be
entertained

OPEN
EVERY EVENING

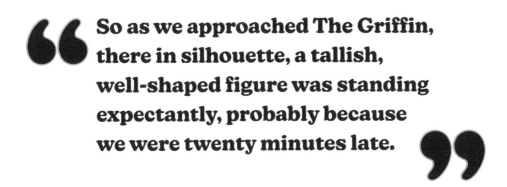

> **So as we approached The Griffin, there in silhouette, a tallish, well-shaped figure was standing expectantly, probably because we were twenty minutes late.**

Chapter 14
The Naked Snake

TIME AND BOOKINGS flashed past over the next nine days or so, Beevis continuing to add dates and the learning curve was near-vertical. For me, the phone-box incident was an enigma hanging over my persona, village gossip never far from the door and speculation ever-more distant from the truth. As a result I felt a little detached from the place where I was born and had lived all my life, but thank the heavens my parents were ever-supportive.

Monday 12th October

The boardroom meeting in Jolly's was the centre of attention for the phone box incident that lunchtime; no contact from the police, but a dark, sinister phenomenon had come to light that our parents may have been coerced by the police to persuade, or even insist, we plead guilty. We still refused to compromise.

Dave and John had recently visited The Centa in Out Risbygate and were on about using this as our rehearsal venue. Built within the grounds of the old Gibraltar Barracks, this new single-storey complex had been designed as a social centre for teenagers. The main building housed a coffee bar, function hall and three further meeting rooms, each with one wall fully glazed and overlooking a central courtyard. Modern and inviting, it was both popular and busy. John's suggestion we should move from Risby Village Hall to The Centa for rehearsals was a guaranteed winner, and we decided to reward him with a half a bottle of Coke, especially as there was no charge to use one of the function rooms and it would definitely help us to avoid getting icicles on our noses in the winter. I didn't hold much sentiment for my home village at that time, although I would miss those weekly visits to the lovely old caretaker.

But the most surprising item of interest, written on the back of a Jolly's menu, was changing the name of the group. An earlier suggestion that we should lose EXIT for something more appealing, more distinctive, had been given air-time, and a number of proposals were still on the table including mine, Emily. In fact, I'd been thinking about inviting her along to support my nomination. I'd had total confidence that Dave, John and Jamie would vote for her as soon as they saw those stunning looks. A name change now, I was not so sure about. EXIT had been the vehicle for our arrival on the circuit. There was a high level of luck and good vibrations connected to it; for me it would be sad to jettison a name we had established successfully. But I kept that opinion locked inside, not wanting to rock the boat at a time when everything was going so well. With a court case on the horizon, which would almost certainly feature the name of the group EXIT, bad publicity would not be helpful, particularly in any newspaper, so perhaps it was wise.

Julius Pam

John had recently been trawling through G. F. Herbert Smith's book entitled *Gemstones*, a bible for those in the jewellery trade, when he came across the name Julius Pam.

Julius Pam #1 was a diamond recovered from the Jagersfontein Mine, South Africa in 1889, and reported to weigh 248 carats. The rough stone was cut to produce a stunning 123-carat gem. It all seemed very impressive when John articulated this over drinks and Bill's ham sandwiches. Unanimously, we adopted the name without hesitation. It was unusual, and had an air of mystery. For me, there was a romantic ring about our name honouring a stunning gemstone. John's imaginative genes had emerged with an air burst of sparkling colour. (Oh, he'll love that). So we decided to gift him the other half of that bottle of Coke. Beevis was to be informed that day; as it turned out we would appear for the first time under the new name on 18th October at Club America.

So we said hello to Julius Pam, goodbye to EXIT and Risby, and moved on to the next chapter of our journey. The group was maturing rapidly, decisions made more individually but with collective agreement. I was perhaps becoming less influential, the mantle of group founder feeling less important than it used to. Essentially the group was founded on our need to make money to meet a burgeoning debt crisis. But I was fully aware that having a business model was not a sure-fire platform for success within the pop world. Sourcing new material, musical arrangement and organising rehearsals to create the finished product were my most significant contributions these days. Fundamentally, creativity is the key ingredient in any career in music, whether from within the performer or introduced to their act from outside. So far we were successful at producing covers but not at finding our own unique musical identity and material. With everything happening around us at lightning speed, would there ever be time to stamp our own creative mark, or did we perhaps need proper management to take control of this element for us?

So we had stepped onto the circuit and were busy, but there was no money in return, as yet, and I was still broke. Effort was needed to find full time employment, and in truth I had no motivation whatsoever; no job that had gone before gave the slightest incentive to make a go of it. So I just kept managing with what I had and reminded myself this is great compared with what went before.

Engagements at the Metro Club Colchester and RAF

Oakington flew past. Beevis had, as promised 'kept us busy', but not surprisingly there were bound to be a few unfilled dates early on. It would have been extraordinary if he had been able to fill every weekend date from a standing start within the first month of our introduction. As it was, he was plainly performing miracles without the assistance of a magic wand. So RAF Oakington on the Thursday that week was followed by a vacant Friday.

Dave and Clive decided to visit the London club scene that Friday and stay there overnight, returning Saturday morning. They set off with endeavour and optimism to hitch a ride, walking from Bury to Newmarket without a single response to their raised thumbs. Completely demoralised by then, they ground to a halt around midnight, halfway down Newmarket High Street. Abandoning all pretence of venturing any further on this crusade, they curled up in the entrance to Laying's Family Grocers and Wine Merchants shop and fell asleep. But nothing escapes the notice of the police, or at least it didn't in those days. They were accosted by Midnight Plod around 1 a.m.

"What are you two up to then?" he asked in his broad copper accent.

"Er, well, we're on our way to London, thought we'd stop off here for a drink at midnight but they were closed, so we're waiting till morning when they open."

"NAAMES!"

"Clive ****"

"David ****"

"David ****? Not the famous trainer from Bury Road?"

"Well, no, but I am a distant relative. He's my great-grandmother."

"Reeeealy? Come on, on yerr bikes!"

But without bikes the fourteen-mile walk home was

pedestrian, until, half a mile from Clive's front door, they were offered a lift by a Wartbug two-stroke. It travelled a further 200 yards and broke down.

Sunday 18th October

I was actually looking forward to our return visit to Club America, but the daunting prospect of humping all the equipment up that sheer cliff again was not exciting any of us. Jamie suggested recruiting an unsuspecting new member of our backroom staff to lend a hand. His name,

'Richard'.

He lived in Ingham, the village on the A143 we had passed through already at times on our way to the wilds of Norfolk. Jamie arranged for us to meet him outside The Griffin (now The Cadogan Arms). On the way there he gave us some background on the new recruit. Tallish, well-built, strong, if you like, he worked alongside our drummer as an apprentice at Boby's. Cripes, would we get him in the van? There were already five of us plus a ton of equipment, he'd have to sit on someone's lap! There was also a reminder that all of us were brought up in Suffolk, yet throughout our conversation there was hardly a whisper of Suffolk dialect in our vocal repertoire. For some reason I was absolutely convinced Richard would have a 'Cord Blast' Suffolk drool, particularly as he had lived all his life in Ingham.

So as we approached The Griffin, there in silhouette, a tallish, well-shaped figure was standing expectantly, probably because we were twenty minutes late. He was smartly dressed, with near shoulder-length, groomed, thick black hair, and wearing a smile. As he rounded the van, *girls will love him!* I thought. Having said that, the lingo might just be a distraction. But none of it! To my utter surprise, when Dave slid back the door, "I was wondering if I had got the wrong day," he said with an air of confident optimism and upbeat delivery, completely void of any 'Blarss me ut hooly snew lars noight'. Exhilarating, and yet another handsome addition to this journey as we meandered our way to Norwich, not early but not drastically late.

Club America was little different from our last visit; Jamie barely tickling his kit, me with the volume turned down to minus 3. I could hear John's keys rattle as he caressed the keyboard and Dave hardly moving for fear of making too much noise. This was all-consuming and comical on stage as we endeavoured to uphold Phil's mandate for a successful evening. Richard, well, he appeared taken with it all and clearly viewing the attractive sights dotted around the club.

After a totally exhausting first set, not because we were working very hard but because we were expending so much energy trying to keep awake, we sat around a table during the 'interlude'. In the centre lay a copy of the *Norwich Evening News*, Saturday edition. John inquisitively thumbed the pages to the entertainment section. Within the listings was an ad promoting our appearance at Club America that evening. It read, 'Tomorrow – Sunday – Long-awaited Return of Favourites Julius Pam'. *Well, agent's licence again,* I thought. The last and only time we'd appeared here we were EXIT, and now we were Julius Pam 'Favourites' even though no one here would have heard of us! Phil's or Vic's creative imagination was certainly widespread, but it didn't matter. I loved the publicity and it confirmed that all had indeed gone well the last time we appeared here.

The expectation of another mind-numbing set before the club sprang into life later continued, until Vic approached us between numbers with an explicit, completely unannounced directive. "Play some music suitable for a stripper. Ursa will come on and perform." That was all he said. What the hell?!! Totally dumbfounded, I hesitated and looked across to the others for inspiration. They shrugged their shoulders in unison. "Oh, let's just improvise," I said, so we did.

Ursa serenely entered the arena, radiating glitter and boldly embracing a very large snake.

A SNAKE!!!!

Dave was mortified. He had a chasmic dread of snakes, so much so he looked totally unrecognisable, nervously laid down his guitar and headed for the nearest exit. We carried on regardless as Ursa, calm and composed, peeled off her clothing with incredibly suggestive movements and eye-popping evocative use of that highly tensile snake. During all of this thought-provoking scene Dave boldly returned, looking completely transformed, took up his guitar and carried on from where he'd left off. What had transformed him?

As I gazed beyond Ursa's wonderful rear-view, Richard and Clive stood at the back of the room watching all of this unfold with expressions of faux-shock and utmost joy. I wondered what Richard in particular was making of all of this. His expression was totally naked of any bashful inhibition; I did think he must be delighted Jamie persuaded him to come. Ursa by this time was totally naked, except for the snake! Clive swiftly reverted to his usual unshaken-not-stirred demeanour, as though nothing out of the ordinary was happening. Perhaps he had seen it all before? For me it was yet another totally virgin experience and the first time I had witnessed the entire group smiling in unison on-stage.

The following interlude opened yet another thought-provoking moment as Ursa, by now fully clothed and minus her flexible friend, came to sit with us, occupying a station directly next to John. She appeared fascinated by him – and this was a girl who didn't blink an eyelid while face to face with a python! John looked flattered within the bounds of his usual polite, conservative manner. How rapidly things were evolving for us, I thought, whatever next?

The rest of the night came alive, just as it had the last time, including the introduction of 'Elizabethan Reggae' by Boris Gardiner, which we'd had fun with during our first rehearsal at The Centa earlier that week. John was in his element with this keyboard number and I loved it. I didn't have to sing! Followed by 'Black Pearl', the Caribbean sound was all so perfect, stimulating an audience already set free from the grind of everyday life. Ursa dancing expressively in front of John, so distracted, he missed the odd note or two. A delighted Vic stated, "Great night, lads," as we were exiting the club, but the most radiant expression of delight came from Richard as he watched the Pineapple phenomenon, fully loaded with Laney under his arms, rapidly descending those stairs.

It was quite a night, and on the way home the van was quiet, some asleep, others in thought. It gave me time to reflect again; there was so much to take in and we had barely been a month on the road. I did ask Dave what had happened to his bottle of wine. "I finished it off during Ursa's snake trip, powered my Dutch courage," he replied. We dropped Richard off at The Griffin and arranged to see him again at the board meeting the next day. "Thanks for a great night," he said, walking away from the van. With the exception of Clive and me, it was back to work for everyone that morning and the humdrum reality of everyday life.

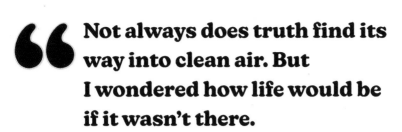

> **Not always does truth find its way into clean air. But I wondered how life would be if it wasn't there.**

Chapter 15
Court, Plums, Bosoms and Deutschland

SITTING WRITING THIS chapter I find myself thinking, as bookings and events began to follow all that had gone before, how do I stimulate you all with what's ahead as you read on without repetition or fear of losing your interest?

The next week was uneventful. Well, come to think about it, there was a significant moment at The Centa, our new rehearsal venue. John's introduction of his restored Farfisa Compact Duo twin keyboard, which he had originally purchased from a guy in Cambridge, lit up the surroundings. So let's speculate to the near-extreme… Pink Floyd's masterpiece 'The Piper at the Gates of Dawn' and single sensation 'See Emily Play' were loaded with Richard Wright's Compact Duo. A guy in Cambridge flogged it to John and the band had a black Bedford van, who knows? What's for certain is this Farfisa fashioned a new and distinctive sound dimension and created many varied tonal options for John to conjure with, plus it was much larger than the Vox Continental and far more visually impressive. I liked that.

That night we played around with the new single from T. Rex, 'Ride a White Swan', making its debut in the charts at Number 47 along with mega radio exposure. But the most pleasing feature throughout the night was the interest our rehearsal attracted from a group of very pretty girls who would frequently accumulate in another function room, able to watch us curiously through the glazed walls.

Performances and bookings were becoming, for me at least, less of a major event as they came and went; familiarity and more confidence added to this I guess. Harmony within us all also blended differing personalities, it was good, and there seemed no possibility this could fracture. The fun, the casual, unregimented, happy-go-lucky, take it as it comes, mindset crafted a joy to be part of the whole thing.

Our first visit to The Regal, Wymondham that week very much reflected where we were in this journey. We were received enthusiastically by a mainly teenage audience within this intimate disco club that was part of the Regal Cinema complex, owned and managed by the larger-than- life former boxer Les King. Youngsters from around Wymondham and its satellite towns and villages congregated weekly to enjoy this very well-run venue. I felt a rush of euphoria as we left that night, so well were we received. Seven songs in our repertoire occupied a place in the Top Fifty, six of those in the Top Twenty, including the Number 1 and 2 spots. This reflected the work we had put in to create this collection following Beevis's remit only a few weeks earlier. Our playlist was unoccupied by old classics or self-indulgence, and we worked hard on material tailored to appeal to the audience before us.

A local newspaper five months later recorded: 'One of the most popular groups to visit the disco has been Suffolk-based Julius Pam. They'll be returning for the fourth time tonight. Many disco-goers will remember their successful debut back in October. The four-strong group have made quite a name for themselves.'

The Tyneside Club, Sheringham the next day was another happy night before an embracing audience. Richard accompanied us on the journey beyond Norwich to the heights of the North Norfolk Coast. In one memorable moment, Dave was accosted by an extremely enthusiastic member of the audience who expressed in a broad local accent his vast pleasure in our rendition of 'Paranoid': "Nevur urd soo meny noots in 'Parinoyd', borr." Bless him. The whole occasion was a joy and we decided to celebrate, Jamie suggesting an excursion to the centre of Norwich on our way home to enjoy the exquisite cuisine served up from King Beefy, the burger stall. After the Red Lodge fiasco and the displeasure of devouring unpalatable concoctions from other fast food vans, I had my doubts. This was another first for me as we rounded Castle Hill at 12.30a.m., and it turned out Jamie was right, the food was terrific. The odd group van arriving, leaving or parked, hadn't escaped my notice either. It was the long-wheelbase transits in particular that caught my envious eye. Our faithful transport, Gertrude, looked humble and forlorn beside those ultimate macho road machines.

It was always the atmosphere I soaked up on these journeys, the venues, the characters, the lonely roads, the cities, towns, villages, and even the inclement weather, as we passed on the way and then back in the dead of night. It was all magical, and at that time a journey I didn't want to end.

Wednesday 28th October

Our Monday Jolly's meeting was overlooked that week. Perhaps it was a good thing, the intensity of it all needed some space. But it was soon to be resurrected as we each were told of visits the fuzz had paid to our parents in turn, in an attempt to seal their ambition to nail a guilty plea from us all. The pressure was all-consuming, and that evening at rehearsals, under overwhelming duress, we agreed to accept our parents advice and plead guilty without mitigation. We hadn't a leg to stand on apparently, or so our parents were told by the hardly disinterested plod who no doubt wanted to boost their zero conviction figures for phone box vandalism. Jamie was of course a bystander in all of this but still supportive. To be so unconditionally subservient in court, and accept punishment for charges that ought by rights never to have been brought, did not sit easily with any of us. But there it was, our visit to Honey Hill Magistrates Court was now a week away and our fate sealed. We took a deep collective breath, got back up and brushed ourselves down.

I shouldn't forget here to mention Keith, who had been

with us during the phone box débâcle and occasionally came along with us to bookings, donning his long RAF greatcoat that looked perfectly at odds with his mane of bushy red hair. He was tall and slim, had an avid sense of non-humour, and lived off Hollow Road near the sugar beet factory. We would pick him up from his home after work on the way to bookings, so as you can imagine the van was crowded at times, but it didn't matter. Doing what we did felt like a total detachment from the routine of everyday life. Keith's greatcoat was a match with Clive's and cast an upmarket appearance missing from the average trench coat. Perhaps it was just as well their rhetoric didn't match that of the RAF jet set elite. You can imagine the heady mix of 'chocs away', 'tally ho' and 'I say old boy', regularly interspersed by graphic renditions of expressive swearing.

That said, our visit to Eye Town Hall on Saturday 31st October with a disco in support was without either Clive or Keith; they had gone to London to absorb the music scene. Richard and his friend – yes, another – Clive squeezed into the van with us that night instead. Clive B was an apprentice at Boby's alongside Jamie and Richard and lived in Great Saxham. We quickly realised he had the cryptically bizarre sense of humour that seemed to be fashionable for roadies: for instance, "I've come prepared with my wellingtons and a jam roly-poly." What the expletive did that mean?

This old Victorian Town Hall in the centre of Eye appeared unchanged in the one hundred years of its existence. The audience however, particularly the girls, were definitely modern in appearance and up-to-date in every way. The reception we received in those ornamented Victorian surrounds with its high-set stage was exhilarating

– so much so I almost felt important, a proper pop star perhaps, or was it living in the wilds of Suffolk that nurtured such enthusiasm for any new sensation among the young folk? As we were packing the equipment away to leave, Richard was nowhere to be seen. "Where the hell is he?" one voice echoed another.

After what seemed like several days of waiting and searching, we discovered he had been snatched by an extremely buxom blonde and whisked off to her father's allotment shed – and it wasn't to share the delights of his home-grown fruit and vegetables! After a healthy romp amongst the plums and bosoms he looked completely knockered on his return, two hours after our final number.

Monday 2nd November

Consumed by the group by this time, I couldn't function outside or beyond what happened daily: the rehearsals, bookings, the social side, the mundane tasks and all the other elements surrounding everyday happenings totally absorbed my attention. Days started and ended with Julius Pam. A summons to Norwich, for a meeting with Beevis and Fisher at the Prince of Wales on Tuesday evening, came as a surprise that morning. So, when asked around the table at Jolly's "what's on this week", the reply was Tuesday 7.30 p.m., The Prince of Wales pub (we had no idea why we had been summoned); Wednesday, our first performance of the week, 10.30 a.m., the Magistrates Court Honey Hill – "can we cancel that one? I've got a hair appointment" said Dave, – rehearsals in the evening at The Centa; Friday, The Labour Club, Bethel Street, Norwich; Saturday, RAF Brampton; Sunday, The Tower Ballroom Great Yarmouth.

Beevis by now was in racing mode as he filled dates at Mach 4. In December alone, bookings already near-equalled the number Bertha struggled to complete in just under a year of existence. Trying to be cool, I could barely hide my inner warmth when reflecting this near vertical transformation. All of us were soaring on this mystery tour, but none of it nurtured a sense of superiority or grandeur within our ranks. We were all very grounded, respectful of our place, and unconditionally unpretentious of our talents.

Tuesday 3rd November

The call to meet Beevis and Fisher that evening was filled with intrigue. All four of us travelled there together in Gertrude, with much speculation about the reason for their call. Our arrival was on time as we walked like a crowd with uneasy meaning into The Prince of Wales. Our two hosts were sitting at a corner table surrounded by plush sofa-style, upholstered seats. Very comfortable, I thought.

The greeting: "Ah, good to see you all. What would you like to drink?" requested Fisher.

We accepted the warm welcome and sat down, shaded by caution.

Fisher continued, "Well, you may be wondering why we called this meeting. It is good news, you're doing a great job, without doubt. Getting good reviews and being asked back everywhere. Keep on as you are and the work will flood in."

Beevis interrupted, "The run up to Christmas provides an uplift. At Scampton you're headlining with a support group, then it's your first visit to The Links, Cromer on the twenty-first – you'll love that, it's a top venue – plus, a couple more dates to add to your diary: Kettering on the nineteenth of December, The Links again on Boxing Night, their biggest night of the year, with Raymond Froggatt, not forgetting The Melody Rooms on Christmas Eve at the top of the bill!

"I also have your first pay cheque here, up to the end of September, covering bookings paid to us direct. But that's not the main reason we asked to see you!"

This must be the downside, I thought. But then came another one of Beevis's barnstorming deliveries. "How would you like to go to Hamburg?"

"Hamburg!" exclaimed John.

Fisher added, "Yes, there are so many opportunities there – it's a great place to go and build a reputation for yourselves. The first possible slot would be early in the New Year. If not then, certainly not long afterwards. The initial contract would be for a month or so."

"Are we good enough to go do something like that?" I questioned.

"On what we've seen so far, yes," replied Fisher.

We were all taken aback – well, speechless again. This was totally unexpected. I was intoxicated by the prospect of playing in Germany. I couldn't believe that after barely two months all this could possibly be on offer. But it was!

Beevis summed up by saying, "Back here afterwards all billing will mention your return from Hamburg, which will add to the prestige and up your fees. What do you all think?"

Germany… so many questions, so many possible scenarios. Well, for me it was a fantastic opportunity; the scenarios could go whistle. What a prodigious thing to do. Dave was in grand agreement, despite his new job, but the euphoria didn't appear universal. Jamie was a little reserved, or just unmoved as always. For John there were many queries to make, and perhaps, rightly so.

"Well, do you want some time to think about it?" said Fisher.

After an extended conversation it was decided, disappointingly, "Yeah we need to do that."

"Don't leave it too long, let us know some time next week," replied Beevis.

I found it difficult to understand why we needed time to think about it. How many more windows of opportunity like this would open before us? I would absolutely go to Germany, in the nude if requested. Dave was already preparing.

The meeting was finalised with a call from Phil for promotional photographs, an essential for any entertainments agency and one we hadn't given a shred of thought to. Not that we'd had the time.

On the way home the mood was a little disjointed for the first time since coming together on that unforgettable night at Brandon. It felt unfamiliar. Dave and I were keen beyond keen to go to Germany, Jamie perhaps not sure, John concerned. The roadies, we couldn't take them, space was at a premium.

"It would have to be just the four of us," said John.

"Yeah, more room for us to sleep," said Dave.

What about the costs, petrol, passports, where would we stay, would Gertrude survive, how much would we be paid? But for me none of this even touched reality. We must take this opportunity, we might never get another. Caution of any kind was totally out of character for us. So far we'd just leapt at everything thrown our way without a care or concern. Was this a new vault forward that for the first time could fracture our unity?

We agreed to sleep on it.

I arrived home early that night, around 10.30. Mum and Dad were in the living room. I couldn't help but open with Germany. Dad was elated and I knew he would be mentioning this to his workmates the next day. Mum replied, "Oh, I am pleased for you, Andy. The Beatles went to Germany, didn't they?" But did I detect a tinge of sadness in her tone, or was she just tired?

"No, I think that was The Singing Postman, Mum,"

She giggled. What a moment for me. Perhaps at last I would give them something to be proud of. But! The next day it was back down to earth and stark reality.

Wednesday 4th November.

Judgement day had arrived. I *had* to be up early. Our engagement was at 10.30 sharp. Strong parental advice came in the form of: must dress smartly, no jeans or tee shirt, brush your hair, brush your teeth, and without fail wear a tie. Mum gave me Cliff's jacket and tie that she couldn't let go of and had kept all these years. I felt totally out of character, soft, acquiescent, and tempted to take my guitar along to counter that submissive appearance with a rendition of 'Jailhouse Rock'. We congregated outside Thingoe, Thedwastre and Blackbourne Magistrates Court, Shire Hall. Strange. I should have been accustomed to giving stand-up performances, but today's was altogether alien and I was more nervous than on that visit to Mr Lee the dentist when I was nine years old. So, in regimented fashion, well, no, not really, more like, we sauntered aimlessly into the Court House.

All was so vividly evident in that courtroom waiting area. There was a morbid presence, a scene of downcast oppression, a production line for the establishment coffers, a place where people go to have money extracted to maintain the quota of fines for the week, which is then totted up with glee by the court accountant. The young, and not so young, summoned to court for the first time, many here for misdemeanours as little as having a defunct light bulb on their nearside rear. The anxious worried faces of ordinary people who have been accosted for the most trivial transgression, like the teenager who faced charges for riding his bicycle too fast in 30m.p.h. zone on his way home from school. You just couldn't make it up, could you?

So when the hail for case number 808 came – thank god it wasn't that bloody 'twenny sick' again – with horror, to the chamber of doom we toiled. It was almost as though the main attraction had arrived as we entered the arena. The press box apparently occupied with more reporters than normal, those within gazing upon us with zealous curiosity. As we stood, smartly dressed for persecution, my eyes wandered around a courtroom filled with glum faces, some expressing distaste, others trying to look officially authoritarian. Oh what a different world this was from the joyous, exhilarating bubble we were encompassed by.

"You are hereby charged that on the 6th of September 1970 at Risby, being concerned together, did commit wilful damage to a telephone box thereby doing damage to the amount of one pound and eight pence." One pound and eight pence!! Is this slapstick or something?!!

As we stood perfectly in line across the dock the customary request was raised: "How dost thou plea?" (Well, that's what it sounded like to me.)

John replied with his eternal calm, "Guilty."

Dave, in an uncharacteristically quiet voice, "Guilty."

Clive – did I hear him mutter (bloody) under his breath? – "Guilty."

Keith, graciously defiant, "Guilty."

Me: "Guilty." Looking our persecutors straight in the eye.

None of which had an ounce of sincerity but we were submissive to the last. Our unanimous pleas brought a look of radiant joy and relief to the bobby's face, so much so that when he thundered through his statement that look of utter delight never subsided, and he just couldn't resist satirically mentioning the name of our group, EXIT. Downtrodden and dejected we were, as the case blundered its way to the predetermined verdict, GUILTY on all counts, without remission, and may that be a lesson to you all. *Poppycock* flashed through my eyeballs. Well, actually it was a much stronger word than that but as I'm sure you will understand I couldn't possibly include it here.

'Each Defendant shall be fined £10.0.0d and 5/- each compensation.' After some negotiation with the clerk of the court a payment schedule was demanded.

John "pay £2.0.0d on account balance in 7 days".
Dave "pay total in 7 days".
Keith "pay total in 7 days".
Clive "at £2.0.0d per week".
Me "at £2.0.0d per week".

"NEXT!"

We were herded to the 'Exit' like a disposable commodity, and out into the glorious sunshine, clean and true, every tie loosened. As a group, never were we seen wearing ties in unison again.

"What a farce!" Clive's outcry. 'Absurd masquerade' went through my mind.

"This is bound to be in the papers, a real coup for the Police," John lamented.

"That's more than a week's wages after deductions," said Dave, still recovering from those weeks on the dole.

So, how did this outcome impact on our unity? Well,

without doubt we were supportive of each other throughout. There was no fracture, blame game, or innuendos. Some would have had good reason to defend their minor or zero involvement in this affair, but no one did. However, our time in the dock completely obliterated my faith in law and order, and I don't think I ever fully recovered to trust in that again.

But already we were away, drifting from this débâcle and thinking of that night's rehearsal and the busy weekend.

As Gertrude and I ambled homeward I was lost in thought. We passed old Fred Smith labouring along on his ancient high-handlebar bicycle, closing in on the final leg of his journey home from Bury. *The perfect simplicity of it,* I thought. And then, *Fred Smith, what a great name for a group! A real homage to the old boy.*

Some weeks later, as Gertrude and I passed the phone box in the village on the way to visit Bett at the White Horse filling station, at least half of the new glass panels had been broken. Not a policeman in sight. Irony of ironies.

My nerves before a gig got worse. I had terrible bad nerves all the time. Once we started I was fine.
John Bonham

Chapter 16
Press for Pilloried

Thursday 5th November
A QUARTER TO two, much to do, I desperately needed to find a job!

That blasted fine had bulldozed my precariously balanced finances to the very edge. I just had to find work, whatever it was. By some strange coincidence there was word from Fred Babbage that Thedwastre Council – the irony of it! – were looking for a general labourer to work at their rubbish pulverising plant in Great Welnetham. God knows what it would entail, nothing pleasant that was for sure, but I applied and was granted an interview on the coming Monday.

But before I describe what happened, here's an interesting piece of headline news. Richard, of Ingham and Austin Healy Sprite fame, had just dropped off Clive B at Saxham. Richard was not yet fully recovered from the vegetable and plums incident within the notorious Eye potting shed. Totally distracted, on his way home, approaching Westley crossroads, for some mysterious reason yet to be determined, the little Sprite took to the air upside down, gliding gracefully in free fall then making an unconventional landing on its soft top. Richard was trapped, petrol and oil cascading from every available nook. He didn't possess the same delicate lines as his sports car. Getting in was difficult enough upright; this was a challenge of monumental proportions upside down, the doors were jammed! But, by some miracle of good fortune, an old farmer with muscles of sizeable dimensions, on a Fordson Major tractor, chanced upon his plight, and with one almighty yank he had the door open and extracted Richard from the potential inferno. Unmoved by his escape to freedom, he hitched a lift when, by the marvel of mechanical splendour, an Eastern Counties bus of the Albion type made an unscheduled stop in deliverance mode, offering him a ride back to Clive's. Furthermore, the petite and delicate Sprite proved to be tougher than an old boot. Once standing upright, she showed little evidence of her flight of fancy. Richard was back at the wheel within two weeks. You could say he was a lucky young man in many ways.

Anyway, where was I? Other than that, nothing much happened during the day, and for once I had almost switched off any thoughts of the group. Early evening was Bonfire Night and the traditional family get together around that weird garden bonfire made up of just about everything and anything Dad had thrown on it over the past four or five months. I could go on about all the different scenarios that emerged from trying to light it but I won't, I would be here for several months. Let's just say we enjoyed that box of tiny Standard Fireworks that go *phut*, jacket potatoes, sausages and fizzy pop. My little sister Mandy was still a little nervous of fireworks and stood watching, enchanted, from the window. I disappeared around eight to meet up with Clive at The Chequers in Risbygate Street, home of young John Stannard who went on to become a hugely fêted Country guitarist. After a glass of water and a long surreal conversation about Coconut Nice mingled with 'TURN THAT GOD DANG THING DOWN FOURTEEN NOTCHES', I returned home closing on midnight feeling totally normal. The house was quiet as I walked in through the kitchen, but unusually for that time there was a light on downstairs. Entering the living room, I found Mum standing facing the fireplace. As she turned to greet me I saw she was holding in both hands the framed photograph of Cliff which had been such an important presence on the mantelpiece since 1962. There was a look of melancholy.

"Hello, Mum, where's Dad?

"He's gone to bed. Tired."

 "Are you alright?"

She came to me and stood close.

"You will be careful when you're out there, won't you?" There was sadness in her voice. "It's a dangerous world. You know we love you and don't want to lose you."

I knew the heartache of losing her first son was a memory that never left her, and a powerful reminder of how a happy, secure life can change so dramatically.

"I will, Mum, don't worry. There are four of us, we'll all look out for each other."

We embraced. It was a rare moment, and one I will never forget.

"I've got a job interview next Monday, Mum."

"Oh, good – where?"

I explained. The sadness was lifting and I could sense a level of quiet contentment that there may be a regular job on the horizon at last.

"See you in the morning. I'll be up early as usual to do the papers," were her parting words.

Friday 6th November

A copy of the *Bury Free Press* lay on the dining table that morning. Mum had already completed the paper round and been to visit Nan and Granddad in Alexander Way. As I sat eating my breakfast, contemplating the weekend ahead and that night's Labour Club booking in Norwich, she walked into the room with a copy of the *East Anglian* in her hand.

"Have you read the *Free Press*?" she asked.

"No."

"There's a column inside about the court case!"

She opened the paper to the headline, which read:

'Five pop group members fined £10'

I was mortified. There in black and white, before the whole town and surrounding villages, was every detail of the guilty verdict and each of our names in full, mine heading the list. And all of our addresses! They, the journalists, couldn't possibly overlook the name EXIT, ideal drama fodder for the creative press, and they didn't.

"Nan found this in yesterday's *East Anglian*." My mother pointed to another report containing much the same detail.

So most of Suffolk were informed of our apparent dastardly

deed, and the passing line from the East Anglian read:- 'The youths—none of whom had anything to say about the incident in court—were each fined £10 and ordered to pay restitution.'

I had visions of grannies, uncles, milkmen, postmen, farmers, road sweepers, from Lowestoft to Haverhill, Woodbridge to Newmarket, at that very moment reading with vast interest and commenting, "Ruddy hooligans! And hooray for the cops." John was right, it makes good fodder for the local press and a storming headline heralding the success of the Police.

Mum was annoyed. "I'm furious with that policeman. Best for everyone indeed! This could quite easily have been resolved if you had been allowed to see the girl and her parents and explain."

"Sorry."

"Don't be. Put it behind you and go out and enjoy the weekend. You deserve it."

There was a knock at the door. "I'll get it."

I opened the door to see Bob, my former workmate, who had generously loaned me that fifty quid for the deposit on the Laney equipment, back in November 1969. It never thunders without lightning.

"Hello, Andy, come about the money," he said, almost nervously.

"You'd better come in," I said with a multitude of dread. When things are low there's always something to send you lower. I totally deserved this visit. I had been far too hopeful in thinking Bob would allow this debt to continue unpaid indefinitely. Why should he? Better sound positive though, I thought.

"Things are far better than when we last spoke. I have a job interview on Monday, and if I get it I will try and repay you regularly."

"Well, with interest it's up to forty-four pounds now and I'm keen to get this settled sooner rather than later."

I had £1 10s 7d to last me for the rest of the week. I couldn't immediately offer any amount that would reassure him.

"Next Tuesday I should be able to pay you three pounds from my dole money and let you know then if I got the job. If so, I will make a concerted effort to pay off the balance by the end of the year."

"OK," Bob said mildly.

I was surprised; perhaps it was the sight of Mum standing by me with reassuring support that influenced him. He was a decent man and had just been trying to help me back then. I had stretched that generosity to the limit.

Of course, I had forgotten the first payment of the fine was due next week. That only impacted when Mum reminded me and hammered home the dire importance of getting some regular work, whatever it was.

The journey to Norwich that Friday evening was without John and Jamie; they followed in the Triumph Herald. Conversation between Dave, Clive, Keith and me was dominated by the newspaper exposure, and overshadowed the much more important and uplifting debate surrounding Germany, and whether we should go or not.

Sunday 8th November

The Labour Club and the westward RAF Brampton flew past like a sonic bang and we were on our way to The Tower Ballroom, Great Yarmouth. I was super-apprehensive when we ground to a halt at the tradesman's entrance in Apsley Road. I'd never been inside or seen the back of this modern structure, its brutal lines such a stark contrast to many of the quaint old inviting buildings we were frequenting. The descriptive rhetoric on our journey there outlined this place, and as we mounted the steps I felt a wave of nervous tension I had never experienced, ever. It consumed me. Why was there such an aura in my mind about this place? The stage appeared vast and high; the ballroom imposing, almost grand. Or were my senses amplifying my vision? I didn't detect any outward signs of anxiety among my companions. Or was it all part of a splendid deception?

As it turned out, great it was. We shared the stage with a chart-topping act – quite possibly Edison Lighthouse of 'Love Grows (Where My Rosemary Goes)' renown. Clive remembers there being a 'chart group with us' that night. But, because of his anti-pop affliction and loathing of anything sung in harmony, he has completely blanked out any recollection of their name. We almost certainly appeared with Edison Lighthouse *somewhere* and I think it was at The Tower. Perhaps someone could enlighten me.

Taking all of that into account, you may be surprised I wasn't charmed by our reception; perhaps I was setting the bar to high. But my downbeat view was unfounded. We were invited back on four more dates, on one occasion as the main act and with a brief mention in the Stage.

During our breaks, girls were interested and interesting. In the bar area a young lady of about seventeen approached our table. Lesley was fascinated by the group and wanted to know more, offering to create a fan club, but disappointed when I said we had no photographs or promo material. Flattered by all of this, I was happy to stay chatting with her when all the others had disappeared to watch the main attraction. When Dave thundered back across the floor, calling, "They're on, Andy, are you coming to watch?" I couldn't tear myself away. She was nice, I liked her personality, and despite my pessimism about our reception her interest didn't fade, asking for my address.

I would have walked Lesley home, however far, but the compulsion to make our way was overwhelming after a busy week. It was early Monday as I dropped everyone off one by one, Jamie the last, in Barrow. My interview with Mr Casson at the Council Offices was at ten o'clock.

Monday 9th November

I could hear the angel gently calling again, beyond the swirling mist.

"It's quarter-past nine, thought you had an appointment this morning?"

"Chrrrist!"

Instant panic. No chance to wake up, tripped over my pants on the way to the bathroom, a frightening image in the mirror, started to clean my teeth with the soap, stood in the bath to have a pee, thundered down the stairs like a bonking hippopotamus.

Mum looked on. "Your jumper's inside out and you've got odd socks on."

The van. Petrol! Gauge! Empty!!

Wing! Prayer! Horror!!

Calm.

I drove to town without a care in the world. Didn't want the job anyway!

Made it! To the council office car park. "Gertrude, you're a miracle."

Terror!! Ten minutes late.

"I'm here to see Mr Casson."

"You're late!"

She announced my arrival. "He'll be a while."

Tick tick tick tick, the clock, and that silence in between.

Hair raising.

Thirty-five minutes passed. The door opened. "Come in," a voice said invitingly. "Take a seat."

"So you're interested in the job at Welnetham?"

Well, not really. "Yes."

"Your employment record's not great, is it?"

"Yes."

"Can you start on Monday?"

"What!"

"Ok, the wages are £12 a week."

"No."

"Demands good timekeeping and keeping the plant clean and tidy!"

"How much?"

"See the plant manager at 8.00 a.m. Monday."

BLANK.

"Be prepared to get dirty," he said as I was shown the door.

Crikey, I sensed a sizable modicum of desperation. How bad *is* this job?!

Gertrude struggled the fifty yards around the corner to the nearest garage, Hawkes in Mustow Street. I had precisely three shillings left from the weekend and blew the lot on petrol, then stayed in town till lunchtime for that all-important board meeting at Jolly's.

Germany, *Wir werden es lieben...* or would we? Dave and I were desperate to go. "We must, too good to miss." "Chances, like Coconut Ices, don't come along everyday." Clive and Keith were in agreement, but no decision was made. Fisher and Beevis were not pressing for a response. It was left on the shelf.

On Tuesday morning came the beyond-the-real-world hike to Triton House and home again on the gallon I'd fed Gertrude. "There's a letter for you on the table, looks personal," Mum said as I walked in. Odd, I'd never had a letter addressed informally via Royal Mail. It was from Lesley, dated 9th November. I was more than flattered; she, so sweetly, had written extending our conversation on Sunday. There was an enthusiastic air in her neatly typed text mentioning the fan club.

"I could look after the newsletters and membership cards." "I have joined a few fan clubs in the past." "I know if I didn't get a photo of the group I would be very disappointed." She signed off, "Anyway thank you for our little chat."

Well, what can I say? Loved that. *Must reply soon,* I thought.

I visited Bob that evening as promised, paid him the £3, and confirmed I had been conscripted as a general labour in a rubbish pulverising plant. He was impressed, as you can imagine!

But, drastically, I had nearly zero funds again and the dreaded £2 fine instalment was due tomorrow. Painful though it was, I had to consider using my final get-out-of-jail-free card and try to sell part of my cherished 1960s singles collection. A collection of around two hundred I had amassed since that first purchase when I was eleven years old, Bobby Vee's 'Take Good Care of My Baby' in 1961, and the last, 'All Along the Watchtower', Hendrix in 1968. But it was heart- wrenching to part with any of them: Stones, Who, Kinks, Beatles, Yardbirds, Animals, Dylan, and eleven of The Small Faces' charts singles, made up over fifty of those.

Perhaps the most influential was 'Shapes of Things', every spine-tingling note of Beck's breathtaking solo etched in my memory. The searing guitar through the whole of a wonderfully produced masterpiece, so ahead of its time and such a major influence on my musical direction during Bertha's days, was a guarantee I would never part with this.

I set about selecting those I felt less connected to, ending up with eighteen. I phoned Robert from Great Barton and called to see him that evening. The best I could achieve was £2, precisely the amount I needed for that diabolical first instalment.

The next morning, completely traumatised, I handed over the extortion money to a clerk who had a dramatically more elevated dour expression and demeanour even than the Charles Dickens character in the dole office. I felt like some kind of heinous convict put asunder and shamed by the boot of the Judiciary. He gave me a receipt! How wonderfully generous and considerate.

Wednesday 11th November

So back to excruciating, on the brink, temporary, financial parity. Rehearsals at The Centa were a return to the wonders of normality.

By this time we were all making our own way to rehearsals. As I arrived at the back entrance the doors were flung open to the greeting, "Wassup, doc?" There was an air of quiet enthusiasm among us as we unloaded the equipment for a rehearsal that turned out to be a PHOTO SHOOT! I was completely unaware and unprepared, walking in wearing my normal stuff and eating a bag of crisps. All had been arranged, John and Dave recruiting Trevor, a friend of Dave's. If only my brother had still been alive he would have loved to have taken these for us.

Wall curtains and lighting perfectly placed, Wendy the pretty hairdresser who was often present at rehearsals marshalled us all into styling mode – and what a blessing that was. When I'd arrived my hair was totally gnarled; it was windy outside. All so well presented for the occasion apart from me, Jamie suggested the pose, sitting and standing, a PA column laid on its side as not-so-comfortable seating. After many adjustments and a remit not to smile but not to look serious – harder than it sounds – Trevor snapped away. There was hardly time to blink. "Great, should come out well, let's see if we can get a standing pose." We all stood shoulder to shoulder, me with my arms folded. "Look tough," Trevor instructed. Hell, how do you do that? A few other stances followed. The grand reveal of our youthful features would be early next week.

There was minimal rehearsal that night and our production line of new and fresh content was slipping. We were off to The Melody Rooms again the next night ahead of another busy weekend.

 **Fairy-tales are nice.**
Syd Barrett

Chapter 17
Beyond Reason

THE MELODY ROOMS on Thursday night wasn't at all the occasion we had expected; the main attraction was completely alien to our virile male rationale. I stood aghast as I read the poster headline: "A Club America Night Spectacular with All Star Cabaret Female Impersonators THE DOLLY SISTERS, Doors open at 8pm licenced bar till 1.00am everyone welcome." So we were supporting a drag act! Yet another first-ever and this time for all of us. Heavens! *What will be expected of us tonight*, I thought. But the real test of our nerve was playing high up on the balcony above the main stage, performing between those thought provoking empty cages. Getting the equipment up there was a challenge in itself, but we had no comprehension of how we sounded, lost in the clouds. Clive and Keith were downcast. "It sounds f****g awful." But that didn't seem to deter Fisher, who once again sang our praises as he passed by.

Late into the evening we were all pretty relaxed, almost detached from the audience below as they danced the night away. No wonder! By now the cages were adorned with very scantily dressed young ladies. Twisting, turning, evocative, sensual motion… the distraction was overwhelming, so much so Jamie probably missed a beat or two and I'm pretty sure I was playing a totally different tune to the one we were supposed to be playing. John was trying desperately to carry on regardless, and Dave *absolutely* in his element. But it was great, and the atmosphere on our level alive and distinctly more attractive than the floor show. It was near 4 a.m. when we arrived back in our home town that night, the fatigue evident on that journey, magnified by the thought of returning to work in just a few hours' time. There was barely a sound from anyone until the departure announcement, as they all left me and Gertrude to wander home alone. I knew I was fortunate, but that blessing was to come to an end the following week.

That morning was the last for some time that Beevis and I spoke via the telephone during work hours. I explained I was starting work on Monday next. There was a note of disappointment in his voice as he acknowledged my statement. John became our communication hub with Norwich Artistes at that point as he was the only one of us with a telephone at hand that Phil could contact during working hours. John, however, working in a busy shop, couldn't extend the time to Phil that I had been blessed with. I knew I would miss those invigorating near one way conversations and blockbuster deliveries. He did ask if we had made a decision about Germany but I couldn't answer positively.

Time would be at a premium in the future, my input probably curtailed, and I was not at all aware how demanding this job would be. I was also mindful our collection of chart material was becoming dated, some of those tumbling down the charts. Woodstock had arrived at number one, T. Rex were slowly climbing, but there was nothing on the horizon to beautify our stage act. Scouring for potential new material, 'I Hear You Knocking' by Dave Edmunds and McGuinness Flint's 'When I'm Dead and Gone' were getting airplay but not yet hit the charts. With no money to buy the records, I had to listen out on the radio and recorded both on an old reel-to-reel recorder, which sabotaged the sound quality until it was absolutely rubbish. But perseverance was key; both were ready for rehearsals the next week and I hoped they would have a crossover appeal to our younger and more mature club audiences.

Saturday 14th November

Our journey that day wasn't into the urban jungle of a big city, but away to the Lincolnshire wilds and all that goes with truly rural places. Our first long-distance haul. Until then the furthest I had ever travelled was Hastings, seriously! I had been to London three or four times, and North Kent once, but other than that Lowestoft, Clacton and Walton-on-the-Naze occupied most of those summer breezes when I was young.

We set off at 3 p.m. that afternoon from our assembly point, the faithful car park in Risbygate Street. The van was laden with equipment and personnel, the fuel tank filled to capacity – the first time ever during my time with her. Gertrude never once complained, plodding away through Brandon, on into the Norfolk countryside to Kings Lynn and beyond, over Lincolnshire fenland, Boston to Sleaford then onto the A15 where the panoramic Lincolnshire landscape and expansive skies were fading from view before the glorious setting sun. Remote, and beautiful. She rattled her way to the city of Lincoln in the dark and onto the seemingly endless strait beyond to RAF Scampton set on a high. Conversation on the journey surrounded not much more than something and nothing, comedy, tales, why and when, and there was almost a driven path avoiding the Germany subject.

As that endless straight guided us to the airbase enclosure, Dave's grasp of world war two history enlightened us, "Scampton – home of the Dambusters."

I had no idea. "Really?" I said. Weird, Germany had only been in my mind just a few minutes before our arrival…

We made our introduction at the guardroom and were ushered in the direction of the Flying Bowman. My imagination was going wild with nostalgia – the buildings, the daring do, the glorious history – as we gently came to a peaceful halt in front of our destination.

We were early and had time to prepare, time to wander and discover the poster heralding our forthcoming appearance.

EAST ANGLIA'S TOP POP GROUP JULIUS PAM

Not again! I thought. What has Beevis been articulating to

our hosts this time? Headlining, a magnified proclamation, and presented again with an exaggerated reputation to defend. It raised my nervous tension to jeopardy.

Our support was stationed at the far end of the hall. The main stage we occupied was quite high with a view down the long narrow interior. As the vacant space began to fill, the sound of rock and roll echoed from the far wall as our support sprinted through their set.

In the dressing room we awaited our call.

"Two minutes boys," came from the face peering around the door.

As our support raced to the end of their final song, the audience gathered before us in curious wonder, gazing at this apparent new phenomenon as we took our places.

The Tannoy came alive.

**AND-ER NOW... EAST ANGLIA'S TOP POP BAND
THE NEXT BEATLES...
JUUULIUS PAAAM!**

OH----------MY---------GOD! *Live up to that one if you can,* I thought. Phil's gargantuan over the top sales rhetoric was sensationalized again!! If I was ever tense this was 'Beyond Reason'.

"Yeah! One – Two – Three – Four." Our raunchy personalized version of 'Down the Dustpipe' erupted and our performance as East Anglia's Top Pop Group blasted off.

But not for long!!

A fuse had blown it. Two bars in.

You could hear a gnat sneeze.

Bloody hell, surely Guy Gibson never had this problem.

"Hang on a sec!" Frantic, I disappeared. Behind our set.

Our moment of glorious fame lasted just ten seconds. As I scoured for the source of our car crash, Dave launched into a stoic Tommy Cooper roll and stumbled through some jokes that had been aired on our journey there. They went down like a lead balloon. But he was unmoved, determined to get to the punchline aided by Jamie's occasional drum roll. I had no doubt John was impassive, as ever. After just ninety seconds I re-emerged, unscathed and victorious.

"Thank you everyone. It's good to be here in this famous place. Let's take you 'Down the Dustpipe.' Again." 1-2-6…"

Our content was popular, and current. Teenage girls were instantly up and dancing, young men and women quick to join them. The dance floor before us was crowded. And the most popular number on our playlist? Believe it or not, my impersonation of a female song with a male voice makeover, 'Band of Gold'.

So through endeavour and guile, by the end of the set near credible normality had been restored. We returned to the dressing room spent and unresponsive.

Although an hour, it seemed just five minutes before we were called to perform again. As that final set advanced, intrigue was heightened and our most vociferous supporters in the audience were all female. Loaded with our best material and all that personified our appearance, the crescendo finale and our jewel, 'Black Night', we thundered to an extended end.

Suddenly, a rush of enthusiasm washed up a sea of sexually aware teenage girls and young women onto the stage as we were pursued to the dressing room. The chaos of normality did eventually return, but not before an extended non-musical performance.

Magnified a thousand times I could not comprehend how we arrived at this place in our journey. It was all there that night, and yet somehow I was still not captivated by our abilities. That didn't seem to matter to my colleagues; the fun and attention was all-consuming to them, and a carefree joy ride into the unknown.

It was close on 2 a.m. when we found ourselves outside with Gertrude, contemplating the journey home. A darker than dark night, all was quiet, within and outside, as I navigated our way towards what I thought was the right direction to the Guardroom.

Mysteriously, a wider than wide road opened up before us, lined with small white lights on each side trailing into the distance. "Don't remember this on our way in!" my anxious declaration.

Out of the shadows and darkness the sound of 'The Dambusters' theme rose from the depths of the back seat, in painful harmony.

"CHRIST we're on the runway!"

The romance! Is this the very same runway 'The Guy Gibson' lifted into the air from on that momentous day. My fanciful genes were soaring; what a story to tell the grandchildren. Well, not quite so romantic perhaps. Gertrude looked nothing like a Lancaster.

It must have been the first and only frenzied U-turn performed on a RAF runway by a 1962 Bedford Van, and at Scampton of all places. The way out did eventually appear before us, but without one single encounter, alien or otherwise. I was renamed Bader of the East after that, and Gertrude, The Bouncing Bucket.

John had taken to the pages of his chronicle again. There was so much to record from that night, he hardly stirred from thought for the first hour. The journey home seemed endless as we floundered our way under dark deep clouded skies, over barren fenland and back into the Norfolk landscape. Closing on home it was cool, and those massing clouds opened in downpour. The tiny wipers were barely able to function under an all-out assault from the headwind of rain as the dim lights of old Gertrude struggled to illuminate the way ahead. Her top speed on the level was 55 m.p.h. and the journey was becoming tedious as we trundled through Brandon in the dead of night and on into Thetford Forest, darker than dark, like something out of a fairy tale. I could barely find my way whilst all were asleep around me, Dave lounging on the front passenger seat.

As the road dipped downhill her speed quickened. *Get her up to 65 and hasten our journey home,* my thoughts. I could see only a few yards ahead; the momentum was awesome as she hurtled down the hill to the bottom and straight into a torrent washing across the road. Gertrude ploughed in, and through the gaping hole in the floor gushed a fountain of rainwater up into the nearside cab, showering a wondrous cascade over the dozing Dave. The reaction was like a sleeping giant suddenly awoken in tempestuous rage.

"Sorry, didn't see that coming, Dave," and I didn't. Gertrude was unmoved, carrying on regardless; we didn't stop.

I know what you're thinking, that hugely dramatic over the top lead up to the heart stopping moment ended in a damp squib. Well, that's the best I could do I'm afraid. I could have said the van rolled over 20 times and on its final roll landed upright carrying on as nothing had happened.

But I knew you wouldn't believe me.

And then we were back where we'd started, in the car park. Sunday, 5.30 a.m. Little was said as we parted and there was no booking for that evening. A blessing perhaps. On Monday morning I was joining the wonderful world of Regular Work.

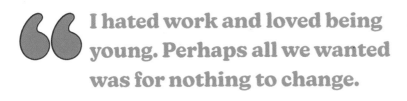

I hated work and loved being young. Perhaps all we wanted was for nothing to change.

Chapter 18
In the Manglings of my Mind

Sunday 15th November

WITH TIME ON my hands that afternoon I just had to keep my promise and return to Mr Matheson with the story of our journey so far.

My perspective had changed radically since my last visit. Uplifted and positive, I was looking forward to meeting him again and felt sure he would be fascinated by all I had to tell. I was eager to let him know this almost certainly would not have happened without his generosity on that day back in late July. Entering the driveway the weather was much the same as when I last visited, wet and overcast, but this time not raining. The house opened up before me. Its appearance was different, somehow, a little downcast perhaps, uncared for compared with before, the ivy untrimmed and mildly overgrown and beginning to invade the window panes. The lion's head was still in place and I rapped it against the doorplate with two short knocks. There was a delay. I wondered if anyone was at home. Should I knock again? As I reached for the lion a second time, the door gently opened.

"Oh, hello." It was Emily. As I'd hoped it would be.

"Sorry to come unannounced."

"Oh that's OK. Good to see you, do come in," she said with that wonderful mellow voice. "Come through to the Drawing Room."

Gracefully she led me to a door off the entrance hall. A fire was burning in the grate as we entered. It was wonderfully calm, timeless even, just the old large glass-domed skeleton clock on the marble mantelpiece above the fire, ticking towards 3 o'clock. This elegant old room was filled with character: high ceiling, an oak floor adorned with rugs, walls hung with gilt-framed paintings, dark, cared for antique furniture. A place filled with peace and privacy. To my instant surprise, standing on an ancient chest was my father's old tin plate car, clean and restored, the missing wheel no longer missing, looking perfectly at home within this glorious interior.

"I imagine you have come to see Mr Matheson."

"Yes, I promised I would return. I'm looking forward to meeting him again."

There was a pause. Her charm turned to sorrow as she announced, "I'm afraid I have sad news; Mr Matheson died just ten days ago."

I could hardly respond; the shock was debilitating. "My god, how?"

"He died of a heart attack. It was very sudden – and unforeseen."

There were no words I could convey. My thoughts were silenced.

"Do sit down. Would you like a drink?" she offered.

"Please, a glass of water would be fine."

As I awaited her return in those quite surroundings the gentle ring of the clock's bell struck three.

We sat in conversation for at approaching an hour. Emily was Mr Matheson's niece; she was to inherit his estate. There was a true sense of sadness in this disclosure and I was humbled she chose to share it with me.

"He was quite fascinated by your story and wondered if you may return," she expressed warmly.

I found it difficult to find a way to explain all that had happened since we last met without losing sight of the emotion surrounding Mr Matheson's death, but she was sincerely interested and encouraging as I revealed our tale.

"So what will you do now Emily?"

"The funeral is this Thursday at three in the local church. Would you like to come to pay your respects?"

I was more than surprised by her invitation and at a loss for a positive response.

"I am starting work, a new job, tomorrow. I would like to, but I'm not sure if I could get time off in this first week. I will try." I couldn't possibly explain I was to become a rubbish pulverizing plant conscript. "Can I say, I'll come if it's at all possible?"

"Please do come, if you can."

As we walked together to the door, I turned to shake her hand. Instead she embraced me in a gentle, warm hug.

"Good luck in everything you do," she whispered.

I couldn't find the words. "Thank you," was the best I could do.

Emily stood at the open door as I started Gertrude. She waved goodbye. I felt empty when I left the beautiful old house and its equally beautiful owner, subdued and sorrowful that I couldn't express my thanks in person to the old gentleman who had shared my love for a collection of old battered toys.

Monday 16th November

It was devastating having to even think about getting up at quarter to seven in the morning. I had settled into the self-possessed habit of oversleeping since July and it was going to be a habit that was hard to break.

Groggy and irritable, I staggered to the van, sandwiches and Vimto under one arm. On my way all the imponderables invaded my head, not least the irony of going to work for Thedwastre to earn money to pay Thedwastre. No work wear was supplied so I'd dressed in old clothes. It was damp and overcast again, not the most inviting day, as Gertrude mounted Station Hill. Truly apprehensive by now, I introduced myself to the manager, immediately realising he was an amiable character and not so old as I had anticipated. He suggested we tour the plant to explain its varied functions.

My opening line: "I have a funeral to go to on Thursday afternoon. Is it possible to get that time off?"

"What? You haven't even started yet!"

"Well, I didn't know about this until yesterday."

"Blimey, this is going to go down well with Mr Casson. I'll ask him for you but I doubt it… plus he's bound to ask me whose funeral?"

"Well, not a relative, but someone to whom I owe a debt

of gratitude."

I guess you're wondering, Great Welnetham Rubbish Pulverising Plant, what the hell has that got to do with a pop group without a manager? Nothing whatsoever really, but it was where I was at that moment in my life. Strangely strange – but oddly normal.

The plant was set in the grounds of the former Welnetham Railway Station, on the Bury St Edmunds to Long Melford line, which had closed around five years before. A new building had been erected on the track bed east of the station building to house the pulverising plant. The machinery was roof covered, the south side of the building and the operating plant open to view. A sunken ground-level hopper was the feed for the conveyor belt that ran the length of the covered area, and hanging above this were mega magnets. What for? As the rubbish shuffled along the conveyor the magnets extracted metal objects, a kind of crude recycling-sorting mechanism if you like. It was a surreal visual spectacle as cans, bicycle parts, wheels, metal- capped boots, a tin toilet, you name it, flew up into mid-air at breakneck speed, instantly locking onto the magnets with crashing precision. Simple, but effective. What was left, which was most of it, ended up in a tall hopper like drum. The pulveriser, which gurgled and ground at high speed, then spat out a heaving mess of crushed and mangled rubbish into an awaiting trailer with a little grey Ferguson tractor attached. All of this was carted off to a deep cutting further up the track bed as infill. Fascinated? No, me neither. My job, to keep the machinery clean of all the bits of stinking rubbish that constantly fell off it.

Arrrrrgh.

I definitely didn't need this job!!

My first assignment was to clean out the long rectangular pit below the conveyor. As I descended to the depths I could see why I'd been urgently conscripted. There was no doubt in my mind, right there, why I got the job, without accepting it. The pit was full to overflowing. The dust, dirt, grime, filth, was almost overwhelming, the stench overpowering, but I struggled on until that longed-for thirty-minute lunch break. Seeing nowhere to wash my hands, I was directed to the station waiting room. It was cold, damp and dreary. As I sat there my gloomy recesses hauled out a trailer load of negatives. *This must be a sentence of penal servitude for all of my misdemeanours throughout my life, however small,* I thought. Please, someone, come and rescue me! The British Railways poster on the wall showing a family on a beach in Clacton-on-Sea was the only ray of sunshine. Oh, to be beside the seaside. But I did see out the day, got that horrendous job done, and what a blessing – the knocking off time was 4.30 not 5. I drove home and sank into the bath for an hour. Boy, did I need that. I didn't think I'd last the week.

The next morning was less taxing, more manageable, and out in the open air. But I knew I would have to return to that pit sooner or later. Throughout the day the Council dustcarts rumbled in, emptying their grotty, tangled mess. I had in some ways settled to the task. At lunchtime, curiosity caught hold as I wandered across to an old wooden building on the far side of the station. I opened the door and peered inside. Antiquated crude machinery, wood piles here and there, and a heap of what looked like handmade rakes? Intrigued, I asked.

"What do you do here?"

"We make rakes und stuff, bin doin' it fur yonks.

Und 'andles uz well."

Old crafts and skills handed down from generation to generation. "So a rake factory?"

"Thas it."

I was captivated and, seeing this, the bloke gave me a guided tour: overhead belt-driven shafts, crude cutting tools and all. Perhaps something you'd have expected to see a hundred years earlier. That occupied me nicely for twenty minutes or so, but sadly, back to the rubbish pile I had to go.

The afternoon came and went. The plant manager was, it turned out, the only other person employed there. As I was leaving he called me over to explain, "I've spoken to Mr Casson. He said it's OK to take Thursday after lunch off if you really need to, without pay. But don't make a habit of it!"

Well, I didn't really need to take the time off, but I accepted with open arms. The £1/4 shillings lost by not being at the plant was a blessing in disguise.

You're probably wondering why I haven't mentioned the weekly fine due that day. I was broke, completely. I'd decided to risk being hauled before the justices and run the gauntlet of taking it in after getting paid on Friday.

So Wednesday came, another day, another shilling, and there was an exhilarating moment at lunch from a day-old *Sun* newspaper the plant manager thought might be of interest. Page 3, a new introduction featuring the wonders of the female form. I'd never before seen anything so uplifting in the pages of a newspaper.

That evening after a mammoth bath I prepared for rehearsal. And what a revelation that turned out to be.

I hadn't seen or spoken to any of the group since Saturday; our next three bookings were Thursday, Friday and Saturday this week. I couldn't afford the luxury of a social life so I stayed at home.

When I arrived at The Centa that evening I felt a little detached from the others. I never saw the inside of Jolly's again before Christmas, so any decisions going forward were relayed to me during bookings and rehearsals. I didn't know what had been going on, what if anything had been discussed, and was not sure what was on the agenda for this evening other than the two new songs I'd come prepared with.

Dave came with the proofs from the photoshoot, and these occupied our enthusiasm for some time. Six differing images, but one stood out as perfect: the first take of us sitting on or standing by the PA column. It portrayed a serious but significant presence. We were unanimous, and Jamie proposing the creation of some postcard-sized images with Julius Pam in print included that we could offer to our extremely limited number of fans. Paul & Matthews, general printers in St Johns Street, were definitely the best option to get this shot reproduced as Ray G (I mentioned him earlier coming out of Crown and Castle if you remember) worked there and we were bound to get them done on the cheap, and we did! He probably worked on them in his spare time. What a good bloke.

So the image was set. Beevis would receive copies as soon as possible.

There was still no mention of Deutschland. The need for rehearsal time was critical if we were to bring those new songs to the stage. At 10 p.m. all was done and it was time to vacate. John asked if I could drop him home off Westley Road. His opening line as we sat in the van outside the house was, "Germany. We've decided not to go."

"We?!!"

"Well, Jamie and I. He has his apprenticeship to complete and I can't be away from the shop for that length of time. Besides, our earnings would barely support our costs."

"What about Dave?"

"Well, he wants to go."

"And no one's asked how I feel, have they? I'm desperate to go! Books balanced or not, it would be a great experience and something really good to look back on."

"We're doing OK as we are. Do we really need to go so soon? There could be other opportunities to go when the time is right."

"Maybe so, but maybe not. I really think we should reconsider when everyone's together… perhaps take a vote."

"Well, like I said, I can't go and Jamie doesn't want to jeopardise his apprenticeship."

I had no answer to that. The disappointment was etched on my face. "What about Beevis and Fisher?"

"I talked this through with Fisher this morning."

"Oh, really?"

The conversation was sliding into tense territory. We agreed to leave it there for now as RAF Coltishall beckoned in less than twenty-four hours.

This decision came as a huge disappointment to me, a let-down on a monumental scale and one I never fully recovered from. My whole perspective changed from that moment. I couldn't get over the way the decision had been taken and communicated without even consulting me, and I did wonder how this would impact on our relationship with Fisher and Beevis. They had implied that they'd be more inclined to push us harder once we'd done the German tour, to brush up our skills and prove our commitment. Now we'd knocked them back, just how much effort would they be prepared to put in on our behalf?

True adventure rarely comes from uncompromising caution and we'd been offered just that: an adventure. I could see nothing but negatives all around me at the moment. I'd been serious about a musical career, prepared to shoulder debt, endless chauffeuring, song research, living like a pauper while always putting the group first. I sensed a lack of ambition. Perhaps this was more of a fun thing without an added desire for success.

Mum and Dad were about to retire when I arrived home. "Have you paid this week's fine, Andy?" Mum asked.

I explained.

"I think it will be too late to pay after work on Friday. I have to go to town tomorrow, Dad and I will pay it then and you can repay us when you get paid."

When, oh, when, would I be able to stop relying on their love and support?

I wasn't sent to the pit that next morning and departed at 12.30. I travelled home to bathe, and onwards to the little village church and its rural surrounds. The congregation was small but select, men in conventional suits, ladies in black wearing hats and high heels. I stood back, a little detached from the other mourners. Emily was there in all her glory, even on this solemn occasion, and 'All Things Bright and Beautiful' raised her profile even higher in my eyes. From the tribute I learned of Mr Matheson's contribution to industry and high regard for his rise from a poor background to the heights of directorship and beyond.

At the end of the service the congregation filed out of the church behind Emily, supported by a young man who had taken her arm. As I waited to be the last to leave, a thought filled moment emerged when Mr Casson came into view. Outside he stood with a group of other well-to-do mourners; he nodded, but didn't encourage conversation. My mind raced into overdrive. Did Mr Casson know I was acquainted with Mr Matheson, or was this pure coincidence? It seemed most likely he knew Mr Matheson too, and if so, had he worked out whose funeral I was to attend from the date and time? But I hadn't mentioned the time to the plant manager. And there was another conundrum. Mr Casson knew my full name, but I couldn't recall mentioning my surname at my meeting with the old gentleman and Emily back in July. Or did I?

Emily made a warm gesture as I was leaving, coming over to speak.

"Andy, you came. Thank you so much. So you managed to get time off then."

"Yes, I have a considerate boss to thank."

"This is my husband-to-be, Daniel. We're to marry in the spring."

Daniel was tall, mid-twenties perhaps, handsome and eloquently spoken as he greeted me. "Hello, very pleased to meet you. Emily has spoken a lot about your recent visit."

"I hope it wasn't too boring. My rambling can be very extended at times."

"Not at all, it was very interesting."

"May I ask, Mr Casson over there… what relationship did he have with Mr Matheson?"

"He was a friend who sometimes visited my uncle. Why do you ask?"

"Oh, nothing really. Sorry, I must rush, we're off to RAF Coltishall tonight to entertain the masses."

"Once again, thank you for coming today. And do keep me updated with all you are doing. I know my uncle enjoyed talking to you," Emily replied.

"Yes, I will. Something to look forward to."

She gazed at Daniel, who nodded. "Oh, before you go, Andy, would you mind giving me your telephone number?"

With time on my hands I was ready early for RAF Coltishall, a journey time of around an hour and a half with all six of us and the obligatory bottle of wine. The immediate topic of conversation once we were on the open road was Germany. Clive and Keith weren't aware of the rejection until then.

The tone of conversation plunged from eloquent and considered, in the afternoon, to raw and blunt, in the evening.

"You absolute prats!!!" was their reaction.

"What the f**k are you thinking?! Are you off your heads?!!!"

"You're in danger of losing the momentum with Beevis. And what about success? You'll get nowhere if you don't take a bloody chance or two!!"

The response was muted, any explanation was shot down with a verbal barrage. I sat in silent agreement with our two roadies, on another of those 'don't rock the boat' moments, with Dave in vocal support. You would have thought this kind of event may lead to outright fracture, but it didn't. We got over it. Or rather shelved it. The busy highway to Christmas didn't allow for any fundamental disagreement. In my mind, we must continue to perform as well as possible, but at the same time there was a hint of apprehension within me. Where would this B-road we had taken lead us?

It was our first appearance at this British airfield. Our playlist was popular and those two additions from the previous night's rehearsal were fresh, current, and near-ideal for an audience not dissimilar to Scampton's, other than the young women who were more reserved and didn't stampede. It was work for all of us tomorrow except for Clive, so we packed up without delay. I crawled into bed at gone 2 a.m. to prepare for another full day among the refuse of perdition.

Friday 20th November

It was PAYDAY!! The first I'd had since July. I was elated, despite nearly all of it being accounted for already. Work was down the pit again but nowhere near as polluting. The garbage was at about half the height compared to that first visit.

That night at Beccles Public Hall was the first truly after work booking for me with Julius Pam. Critically, the leaving off time of 4.30 had to be precise. It was vitally important we arrive before seven. Journey time of around an hour and a half included collecting Dave and Clive on the way and the mandatory call into an off licence for Dave's liquid of uplifting sustenance. I drove home from work, leaped into the bath and out, applied fragrances and dress, had something to eat, and thought, we're going to be late! I think we arrived about ten past seven; not bad considering! John and Jamie came in the Herald again along with Richard and Clive B, arriving a few minutes earlier. Unfortunately, it was one of those nights where I have no recall of how it all went, other than the poster promoting EXIT, clearly Beevis had forgotten to tell our hosts of that new adopted name. Oh, and yes, I do remember loading the van outside in the pouring rain and getting soaked.

Those excruciatingly tight timings reflected the plight of many semi-pro groups who struggled to make their way to bookings after work in those days. Hard work and very long hours were commonplace. But the joy of doing what we were doing was ample substitute for the morning fatigue...

> Although I had never visited this seaside town in the past, we found our way, but the darkness spoiled the view. Looking for guidance it had to be a mini-skirted young woman, and we found one.

Chapter 19
A Coastal Electric Ladyland

Saturday 21st November

I WOKE FROM a deep sleep and a dream about being pulverized in Germany. It played on my mind for weeks... Germany, I mean. I never mentioned the depth of my feelings to anyone within the group. Concern for how Beevis and Fisher reacted was never aired, and I didn't have any contact with Beevis again until after Christmas. Our engagement diary was as full as we could accommodate for the next six weeks, and there were already a number of filled dates in January.

That lunchtime I sat at the table trying to compose a reply to Lesley:

Dear Lesley,

Thanks for your letter, and thanks for the compliments. Photos are coming next week, it would be great to form a Fan Cub and pleased if you could do this for us, we will help in any way we can. We're back at The Tower Ballroom on the 24th January. Be nice to see you again there, I will bring some photos along for you. There's a lot of work coming up for us before Christmas, we are headlining at The Melody Rooms on Christmas Eve. It would be great to see you there if you can come along.

Happy Christmas,
Love,
Andy.

The Royal Links Pavilion, Cromer

This was one of those uplift venues Phil had mentioned. Dave, John, Richard, Clive B and I had never been there or had any idea what to expect. Jamie thought he had played there but wasn't sure, so this was a journey into the unknown. We set off early, in the dark, six of us in Gertrude, Richard and Clive B standing in for Keith and Clive. Although I had never visited this seaside town in the past, we found our way, but the darkness spoiled the view. Looking for guidance it had to be a mini-skirted young woman, and we found one.

"The Royal Links Pavilion, Overstrand Road, could you direct us?" Dave asked, fluttering his eyelashes.

She walked past without a sidelong glance or a reply. That was probably the worst rebuff he'd ever experienced.

"Let's try a bloke next time!"

"Hello," we asked an old codger.

"Ar ya reet, borr?"

"Had one last week," someone replied from the back.

"Wass ar want?"

"Err, can you help us… we're looking for the Royal Links Pavilion."

"OW! Usuh orkud un, uts owut ut way," pointing.

"How do we get to that?"

"Royt, usuh bout haher myle."

John, with contract in hand: "It's in Overstrand Road."

"Arr, yurl hutta tun roun un goo back unnen tun lef."

"Right."

"Noow, lef!"

"Left."

"Zackly."

Confusion!! That's completely the opposite direction to where he pointed.

"Are you sure?"

"Were wuz ut agin?"

"Royal Links Pavilion."

"Unt got noo iydea!" Like a ghost in the night he suddenly vanished.

"Less goo up uh rood und troy agin."

A bloke wearing wellingtons on a pushbike was overtaking the van. "Do you know where Overstrand Road is?" I shouted through the open door while he was pedalling like mad.

"Arr, yus, yur gorna rong weigh. Tun rowund un goo baak up ut weigh." He was wobbling, a lot.

"How far?"

"Us uh nurly ouwta towun, goo dowen thar un arsk someun," he said frantically.

There was a hedge on a left-hand bend. He carried on,

straight – disappearing – in the hedge.

"Locals around here have a habit of disappearing into thin air!"

We tund rowund.

After intense debate we parked on the side of the road for an analysis of the situation. A very well-dressed gent with a beard and a closed brolly in hand walked straight up to the van. "Are youw losst!?"

Dave tried: "Scuze me, could you tell us where Overstrand Road is?"

"Oooh, hello, you boys, lovely to see you. Where did you say?"

"Ooverstrund Rood."

"Ooo, are you a pop group?"

"Well, yes, we're playing tonight at the Royal Links Pavilion."

"How lovely! That's in West Runton. Would you like me to hop in and show you the way?"

Everyone said in unison. "No! No! That's OK!"

Dave persisted, "It is in Cromer."

"Oh, I'm dreadfully sorry, I can't help you, I'm afraid. GOOD LUCK." He disappeared.

"Anyone got any other bright ideas?" Richard protested.

"A little further, maybe?"

A very scruffy-looking bloke appeared from a side street.

"Overstrand Road, any ideas?" I asked.

"'Ello, boyo, where'd youw say?"

"Overstrand Road."

"Sorry, can youw speak up?"

"OVERSTRAND ROAD."

"Oh, eye norr where tha is! Where exackly are you gowinng?"

"OVERSTRAND ROAD!"

"Norr, norr, I mean – where are youw gowing in Orverstrrand Rrroad?"

"Oh, THE ROYAL LINKS PAVILION."

"Playing golf, are youw?"

"NO, MUSIC!"

"Oh, well, your gorwing the wrrong way. Turn rrround and gorup there a fairway until youw come to Crromwell Rrroad. See."

"WHAT, ON THE LEFT, RIGHT OR STRAIGHT AHEAD?"

"Carn't hear you, can you speak up?"

"LEFT OR RIGHT!!" "Norr, well, yes, isn't it?"

"SO LEFT OR RIGHT INTO CROMWELL ROAD?"

"Thas it, boyo."

"BUT HOW FAR IS THAT UP THE ROAD?"

"Oh, a fairway."

"WELL, THANKS, TREMENDOUSLY HELPFUL."

"Yes indeed."

"Are you sure this is Cromer, Andy?"

So we turned round, again, drove on a 'fairway' and tossed a coin for right or left. "Turn right, boyo."

"Now what?"

"Just keep going, it must lead somewhere."

"Probably into the sea!" We were going uphill and Gertrude was huffing. Slowly up and up.

"Keep a look out."

"What's that place we just passed behind those trees?"

I reversed back.

"Doesn't look anything special. There's a sign over the door, can't read it..."

"Well, the lights are on, let's go look."

As we pulled up outside, the sign read 'Royal Links Pavilion'.

I was underwhelmed, it didn't exactly look spectacular from the outside, yet Beevis had put this venue up on a pedestal. All the same, the tapered steps up to the front entrance were old, worn, and trying to look grand.

We mounted them in concert, pushing through multiple double doors and into the main entrance. Up more steps, another set of doors and into the former ballroom, where the interior opened in charming maturity before us. There was such an inviting feeling in that place, a warmth. It was old, quaint almost, but with so much to delight the eye as I turned around 360 degrees. The stage was over to my right, set high, the flanking walls decorated with murals of Venetian scenes and Arabian visions. Steps led up from the wooden dance floor to balconies on three sides, with wooden handrails and balusters strung between heavy timber vertical roof supports. It was unlike any other venue I had visited and I was convinced the acoustics would be great.

John tracked down our contact, a lady for once. "Where do we unload our equipment?"

"Through the front entrance."

Up those steps, and we did.

The main attraction, St Cecilia, from Corby, had already arrived and set up. We didn't know of them. You may have dim, long-suppressed memories of their one-hit wonder 'Leap Up and Down (Wave Your Knickers in the Air)', a chart success in July 1971. With a view looking out into the hall we occupied the left side of the stage, St Cecilia the right; there was room. My position was in the men's toilet… no, not really, but far left on the stage, close to the balcony on that side. Two forty-five-minute performances seemed minor in comparison to some of the grinding nights on those USAF bases. Totally unaware of expectation, that nervous tension was rising fast.

The call for our services came, and from the little backstage room we stepped out onto the stage. Lights illuminating our arrival – and we were only the support. The space was full and the atmosphere electric within this grand old lady. I felt privileged and strangely overwhelmed. Looking up and to my left as we performed, the balcony was overflowing, the faces of our young audience filled with enthusiasm, intrigue and joy. Many were leaning over the banisters, peering curiously down on the stage, some smiling and others in conversation with their friends. It was an Electric Ladyland, a place of power and fulfilment. Special it was, and Dave, John and Jamie performed without stutter or flaw; this sublime venue had found a passion within all of us.

We watched St Cecilia with interest, then returned with our most cherished content for our finale. After ninety minutes of pure adrenaline, we were ready to come down, relax and find our feet amongst this genial crowd.

Dave, John and Jamie were busy in the bar during our sabbatical, girls never far off their radar. I was otherwise preoccupied, captivated by all that surrounded me, hoping that perhaps one day we would appear here as the main attraction. St Cecilia brought their show to an end.

So the night was not as feared after encountering those strange characters on the way, along with that uninspiring view from outside. We'd played to an intelligent, modern crowd, loving life, full of being there and living the moment. Phil was right, it was special, and for me a unique, memorable experience.

But the slog of reloading Gertrude felt less onerous after our performance as the audience drifted away, some lingering inside and out to enjoy the last of their evening, midnight coaches whisking away those they delivered in darkness with such enthusiasm earlier.

Our lady host paid John as we were about to depart. "Well done. We'll see you again on our big night – Boxing Night," she said.

"Look forward to it," John replied, as he signed for receipt of the cash.

We travelled home full of heart, around Norwich and beyond, to our homeland and content, peaceful, slumber.

Sunday 22nd November

The pressure of having penniless pockets didn't even register as I woke at eleven that morning. At home the joy of articulating our adventures to my family was exhilarating, and my little sister at times sat spellbound. But, there was concern. My dark day work just didn't fit or endure. I had to find something more rewarding.

The working days passed relentlessly until Wednesday, where at rehearsal those photographic images in print were revealed. Postcard-sized, titled and ready, John had arranged with Beevis to deliver a large glossy print and a number of cards to Norwich on Friday, before our Pinebanks appearance. Fisher was John's contact at The Melody Rooms that evening and he in turn gave us a number of the promo leaflets they had produced.

Here's the text in full:

The ideal 'pop group' for just about any venue! Four good-looking young boys in the 'teeny bopper' image, playing almost anything from the charts in their own 'poppy' style. Julius Pam are only interested in making the audience enjoy themselves and have found that the best way to make this happen, is to get everyone dancing. Strongly recommended by this company, you will have no volume problems with this act, and no hesitation in taking them back for a second time. Julius Pam are working four and five nights each week, so book them now.

I was mortified, dumbstruck, completely demoralised when John passed a copy to me at Pinebanks. To be portrayed as teeny bopper style completely destroyed my will to live. So much of my guitar work was centred on Bertha's days, aggressive lead solos and all that went with heavy. Yes, Julius Pam were playing some chart songs, but not with any boppy make-up add on. I was regularly ribbed about my habit of breaking into massive searing full-fuzz ad-lib fretwork in the middle of 'Montego Bay' or 'Band of Gold' or even 'Woodstock', during rehearsals, and had been known to do this on occasions at USAF bases in front of a non-existent audience. But it was fun! Anyway, what will be will be. We were on the roller coaster and Christmas was coming fast with no time to ponder.

Gertrude carried just three of us home that night, Jamie and John travelled homeward in the Herald. I was tired after a physically demanding working week and not in the best of spirits. Dave's work commanded a similar physical ultimatum, shuttering silos out at Chedburgh. The long A11 strait towards Thetford was tiring in its own right in the dead of night and a challenge to maintain concentration without conversation to keep me alert. Dave was flat out asleep on the back bench seat, Clive drifting off in the front. Me, I had no vision ahead and needed matchsticks as Gertrude started to wander. Clive suddenly came round in panic, startled to see a roundabout rushing headlong towards us.

"F——!" bellowed with horror from his lungs. Brakes slammed, PA columns tumbling to the rear, we shuddered to a halt against the central island. Deadly silent. Nothing stirred from behind. We nervously looked back. Dave was invisible, PA columns and drums covering the back seat like an avalanche.

I probably forfeited three years of my life in that heart-stopping moment. There was no movement, no sound. Gently, we lifted the equipment, fearful of what we'd find beneath. Dave lay rigid. Clive blurted, "He's not breathing. He's dead!" Suddenly, and frighteningly, he sat bolt upright. We both rocked back.

"What the hell are you trying to do, kill me?!!" There was absolutely nothing wrong with him, but there could have been. He smirked. "Had you going there, didn't I?"

It was a lesson and one not forgotten. Future journeys were loaded with ingenious ways to keep me awake on those long hauls home. I'll tell you about one or two of them a little later.

So it was onward to the next night. Raining again and out in the sticks to the first of only two village hall engagements. No remit from Beevis, so we were not prepared. On arrival all seemed perfect: a young audience, lots of girls, idyllic for us. But as the night progressed the landscape changed radically, darkened by the mighty force of heavy boots and the sudden abundance of leather jackets. Pop was not in the newcomers' vocabulary, and any attention paid by girls to us or by us to them was like committing hara-kiri. We carried on, intimidated, and the tension was steaming.

Midway through our second set, Keith wandered across the stage behind our equipment, oblivious to the unfolding drama, and tripped on the main feed to our entire speaker system.   Jamie was left solo and carried on regardless; perhaps he didn't realise. I was still strumming, Dave was still thumping, John was still plonking, all silently. Keith gathered himself with astonishing speed and plugged us back in, the speakers blasted into action. Seriously, no one noticed. Were we that bad?!

But it didn't shatter the forming ice, so much so that

Clive B's concern for our safety intervened. He had a naturally commanding presence as he stood front and side stage, arms folded. What may have pursued was dampened by his bravery aided by Richard in support. We saw the night out without a brawl. Spoiled of what was a night for the young and free, it was part of an acceptance of all that came with a group out in the wilds of Suffolk. But, there was a little sting in the tail.

We all loaded the equipment for the journey home. John, Jamie and Dave were taking the Herald, the luxury option, and Clive B with Richard in his Sprite. Just Clive, Keith and I were left to find our own way home in Gertrude. What we hadn't yet realised was that the back offside tyre wall had been slashed. Someone who didn't like us, either for the music we played or our fascination with the local girls, had taken their resentment out on Gertrude. So in pouring rain and mud we unloaded the van to lighten the load, jacked her up and said our prayers as we bolted on the totally bald threadbare spare.

That was the last night Clive and Keith came with us, their decision undoubtedly influenced by disappointment that we had not taken the Hamburg option. Our lack, in their eyes, of the ambition to keep driving forward and seize every opportunity that presented itself. Clive voiced in his familiar uncompromising tone, "You'll end up as one of the journeymen of the music world if you're not adventurous, bold and inventive." He was right, of course, and I knew that. Clive was always straight-talking, said what he said, meant it, and stuck to his beliefs. He could be cutting at times, but honest and loyal too. Not once did we argue – disagree, yes, but we never lost respect for each other.

As it was, just a week or so later Clive at last found work again, with Plessey, or 'fiddling around with wires' as he would explain. The job came with the proviso to work in London. Not that it was any hardship. He grabbed this opportunity with both hands. Keith, who was already working for Post Office Telecommunications, moved with him and they both forged careers in the rapidly evolving communications industry. On the doorstep of all that glistened music, London was near heaven for Clive. He was in his element.

Their departure echoed the end of a chapter for me. They retained the connection back to Bertha Dorn and all I had learned within that group. We agreed to stay in touch.

So a new chapter opened. Richard and just 'Clive', as the former Clive B from now will be known, evolved into our type two roadies. Of course, the usual pay and conditions applied. No pay, hump the equipment about, pay for the drinks, keep me awake on the way home, make sure the jokes are as risqué as possible, and push Gertrude if she breaks down. I think that covers it all. They were pleasantly surprised by how lenient we were. But in truth they were there for the fun of it all, the adventure, a night out at many venues they would never otherwise have had the opportunity to go to, free entry, an abundance of willing girls to choose from, and the pièce de résistance: travelling with an up-and-coming pop group. What more could they ask?

December was upon us and the last rehearsal until the New Year. We were too busy to find space for any more. Our repertoire was still current and enduring and the euphoria of Christmas we hoped should sustain that. Dave Edmunds was at Number 1, 'When I'm Dead and Gone' and T. Rex's 'Ride a White Swan' both in the Top 10. 'Woodstock', 'In My Chair', 'Band of Gold', 'Black Night', and 'Paranoid' still hanging on to the top fifty. I had nothing new to offer so we had to invent something.

"Christmas is coming, how about a Christmas carol?"

"'Silent Night'?"

"No."

"'O Come All Ye Faithful'?"

"No!"

"'Holly and the Ivy'?"

"No!!"

"'Away in a Manger'?"

"No!!!"

"'We Three Kings'?"

"No!!!!!"

"'First Noel'?"

"No!!!!!!!"

"'Jingle Bells'?"

"No!!!!!!!!"

"Paranoid!!!"

"Change the words?"

"Possibly."

"'Ding Dong Merrily on High'?"

"No!"

"'God Rest Ye Merry Gentlemen'?"

"NO!!!"

"'When a Man Loves a Woman'?"

"Wait a minute."

"What about 'Good King Wencesluslusalasus'?"

"Why didn't I think of that?!"

"Better still, let's try a reggae version."

"Brilliant idea."

So a crude version of this Christmas carol was crafted, up tempo reggae. We only knew the first verse, that'd do. Repeat 'deep and crisp and even' again at the end of each verse, repeat, organ solo, repeat first verse three more times, end. Completed in twenty minutes, we had an early night.

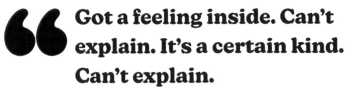 **Got a feeling inside. Can't explain. It's a certain kind. Can't explain.**
The Who

Chapter 20
Mr Balaam:
An Act of Salvation

THAT NEXT NIGHT we returned to RAF Coltishall for the second time. It was a charm to perform at this venue. The audience, made up of RAF personnel and civilian young from surrounding villages and towns, were always there to enjoy their night, and made such an impact on the pleasure of being there. And what a godsend, no aggro, no slashed tyres.

I wondered how long we could sustain this sparkling ride; other than Germany little had laid itself across our tracks as we travelled blissfully on. So far any obstacles we encountered out there had been negotiated without blunder or rebound.

10th to 18th December

Coming off the back of USAF bases we started our assent to Christmas, with seven bookings in ten days, followed over Christmas by seven in nine. With all of us working, John off on Thursday afternoons but in on Saturdays, at all other times it was group first – anything else, forget it. Our success was breeding adrenaline and there was plenty hidden in our diamond.

A non-stop run to the 13th found me still in bed at midday on Saturday. Sixteen tons, another five weeks older, I was starting to ache. The debt pressure was lifting, just a little. The phone-box fine was cleared, the debt to Bob reduced, but Ralph and Dick were still playing a cheerless tune to my inner senses. Thoughts of Ralph re-claiming the Strat I was welded to unloaded dread into my veins, so I decided to visit both of them that day.

But I had nothing to fear, Ralph was cool. "No hurry, good to know how things are going." Dick was just about as laid back. "As soon as I've got some money together, I'll try to settle it outright." But he was more interested in our progress and told me, "Hope I see you on the tele."

I was lucky. Lesser men might have reacted differently. But the real heartache was my demeaning, mind-pulverising employment, which was taking its toll on my sanity.

That night was our third visit to Club America in the heart of Norwich. You may ask why there's been little mention recently of Dave and his exploits as a magnetic stud. Perhaps he wasn't the out and out lady killer I'd first envisaged. There can be no doubt girls were mesmerically drawn to him, but most of the time I didn't know what he was getting up to anyway.

Club America was allegedly an exclusive 'Members Only' venue, but that didn't deter them from encouraging young ladies who were non-members to enjoy the entertainment on display, in whatever form. Two young females made a point of attracting our attention that night, and we were having difficulty prising Dave away from one of them, Angie. So much so that Gertrude chaperoned her to Unthank Road while she sat on Dave's knee. Outside her home we waited; they were gone for an eternity, so we all went for a King Beefy and came back later. Was this to become a love match and a turning point in our evolution? Time would tell.

Southwold

Another one of those wonderful East Anglian coastal towns left to mature gracefully, Southwold and its pier epitomised all that was tranquil seaside in Suffolk. We found ourselves performing in the Neptune Bar within the lower part of the pier building.

Clive came into his own on that night, just as you would expect from a young virile male immensely attracted to young fertile females. The throbbing sound of our performance echoed along the sea front, interrupting the still night and the sound of waves gently lapping the shore. Under the boardwalk the throws of heightened passion were coming to a climax to the enchanting melody of 'I Hear You Knocking'. Whilst we were slaving away in a steamy enclosure, Clive was enjoying the fruits of seaside hospitality deserved only of esteemed gentlemen visiting this lovely old coastal resort. He was very quiet, actually, very, very quiet, on the way home.

A return to The Regal, Wymondham came the next night as the Christmas spirit was starting to rise. 'Good King Wenceslas' rose to this occasion along with all the new material we had to offer. Could we do no wrong? I was never so complacent. Every night was a fresh challenge as we journeyed through a sea of pleasure. More and more my faith was re-building, no distractions, no failures, no time to reflect.

Onward then, to Saturday 19th and another journey away from the safety of our heartland, this time to Kettering. But before that, a visit to Albert Balaam's and Ray, who I had seen so little of recently. Those Ultra Light Picato strings were vital, I had none to spare.

"*Morceau morue*," was my opening salvo.

"*Briser le vent*," was his reply. I hadn't a clue what he was on about and I don't think he did either. I hadn't a clue what I was on about come to that, but it didn't matter. The absurdity of it brightened my day.

So much to tell, so little time. Whilst being served I explained my new employment and expressed my downtrodden mindset and need to find brighter horizons. Ray, with his instant mind, as always, would look for ways to help, if he could.

Completely out of the clouds Ray produced this thought-provoking statement,

"Linda is leaving after Christmas, there'll be a job available in the record department. I can have a word with Albert if you're interested?"

I was lifted by the thought. A music shop, where else could I possibly find a better fit for my persona?

"Would you? I'd be grateful."

"Can't guarantee anything but I'll let you know."

"Could you leave a message at home if I'm out?"

The shop was busy and my need to make haste pressing.

There so often seemed to be something good on the horizon whenever I met Ray. Or was it the Old Lady in Black still guiding me to better things? Risbygate Street was, after all, the stage for our first and last encounter.

Kettering was around a two-hour journey, perhaps a little longer. A drive through central Newmarket and Cambridge, upward to Godmanchester, Huntingdon, the A604 past Thrapston and onward to our destination. This was the same route my brother travelled that fateful day on 20th June 1962. As we approached the Lolworth turn, north-west of Cambridge, memories flooded back to that rainy day when my mother and father stood on the verge at the precise spot Cliff had died. The tears were there. I mentioned nothing to my friends with me at that poignant moment. It was a reminder of the fragility of life locked into my memory ever since that day. I was only eleven years old at the time.

Just the four of us travelled that night, no roadies. There was space, elbow room for some to sleep on the way home. Wellington Street, with buildings tightly squeezing the narrow cobbled road, guided us to the Working Men's Club, another of those Victorian buildings, but this time with the poster reading: **The Swinging Blue Jeans supported by Julius Pam.** I was almost slightly disappointed. Not that I should ever show disrespect to those we supported, but I hoped Beevis had overlooked telling us we would be in support to a high profile current group. Nevertheless we had a mission, and that was to perform as well as we could. Our equipment kind of dwarfed the set-up of these early-sixties idols who'd had a number of early pop hits, 'Hippy Hippy Shake' and all of that. But that counts for nothing in terms of talent; they were polished, their stage presence undeniable, and the audience appreciation reflected that. As for us, well, it wasn't outstandingly memorable. The second set was vibrant and cheerful, the audience up close, but the reaction wasn't quite what we were becoming accustomed to.

Jamie, always genial and friendly with all those he was acquainted with, said as we walked across the dance floor before our performance, "God, they're a stuck-up lot! Anyone would think they were royalty," reflecting on his attempt at conversation with two members of The Swinging Blues Jeans. Maybe he'd caught them at a bad moment.

Elation wasn't total as we left, hope of another grand uplift didn't, this time, quite materialise. As we made our way home in the early hours, Dave was devising plans for how to keep Andy awake, *all* the way home. Highly convoluted and bonkers tactics were conceived in an attempt to keep my eyes open, none of which had a hope in hell of succeeding. Until Jamie suggested, "Do you know any jokes, Andy, other than all those you've already told us at least twice?"

"Well, I know a very long joke."

"That'll do."

"A very, very, long joke."

"That's ideal."

"It's called 'The Pink Gorilla'."

It was a gag I'd learned from Fergie (not a tractor) at Cavenham Club one night in 1966. He was the singer in my first group and high on Greene King Pale Ale at the time.

"OK, Andy, does it need any harmonies?" said John.

"Well, if they're as bad as they usually are, I'll never get any sleep."

Dave made a note of that for the future.

"So what's this about a Pink Gorilla?" John asked.

"There was this Pink Gorilla..."

Really!

"It was green."

PROLONGED SILENCE.

"Is that it?!"

"Yeah."

"Ha-bloody-ha ha! We've only travelled five yards from beginning to end.

"No, just joking. That was the start of the beginning of the end before the beginning," my enigmatic response. "There was a man who had heard about a strange beast locked away in a massively fortified fortress..."

After the first few lines everyone was captivated and wide awake.

After twenty minutes the novelty began to wear thin.

After thirty minutes Dave was asleep.

After thirty-five minutes everyone except me was asleep.

After over two hours I was still wide awake, we were back home, and I still hadn't got to the end where the Pink Gorilla.....

Crawling out of the van, Dave, John and Jamie were in a trance. "The next instalment is tomorrow at midnight," I said as they departed.

Then I had to get myself the four miles home. Sliding door wide open to the December chill. Cold air torture. Worked perfectly.

Ray left a message to call him on Monday. I telephoned at lunchtime the next day. Mr Balaam answered. It was that deep, commanding, baritone voice again.

"Yes?"

"Is Ray there, please?"

"No, he's at lunch, who's calling?"

"Andy."

"Andy who?"

"Andy R."

"That Andy. What do you want him for?"

"Ow, doesn't matter, I'll speak to him some other time," I said, in haste.

"Before you go, he mentioned you were interested in the record department job."

"Oh! – well – yes – I am."

"Good. You'd better come in and see me tomorrow."

"Err, I'm working!"

"Can't you come in your lunch hour?"

"Well, it'll be a bit tight."

"Do you want the job or not!!"

"I'll come in my lunch hour, but I can't guarantee the state I'll be in and I can't be late back."

"That's no good, I can't interview you with a timer in my hand!"

"What about after work, say, five o'clock?"

"Shan't be here. You'd better come to my house on Barton Hill. It's the fruit farm."

"What time?"

"Six o'clock sharp. Today!"

"What, today?!"

"Yes, today. Is that a problem?!"

"Oh, OK, I'll be there."

By good fortune, or perhaps not, we were not out performing that night. It was straight home from work, into the bath – thank god Mum had kept the home fire burning, the water was hot – out again to Barton Hill. At two minutes past six, Mrs Balaam answered the door.

"Is Mr Balaam here?"

"Yes, he's expecting you. Come in, Andy." Nice lady.

Mr Balaam was sitting behind a table. "So you want the job in the record department?"

"Well, I suppose so, yes."

"What do you mean, suppose? Do you want it or not?!!"

"Errr – yes."

"Ray speaks highly of you. I expect good time-keeping, honesty and smart dress, tie included!"

Tie? I'd vowed I'd never wear one again after that court débâcle.

"The pay is nine pounds a week, hours nine to five-thirty, Monday to Saturday, with the exception of Thursday half-day closing at one so you get the afternoon off."

"Is there a lunch break?"

"Half-hour."

There was an exaggerated pause. Five and a half days a week, finishing an hour later than I did at present for £3 less a week? I hadn't paid any attention whatsoever to all of this.

"When would you want me to start?"

"Monday the fourth of January."

"OK, I'll take it."

"See Ray, nine o'clock sharp on the fourth."

I found my way home in a complete state of confusion. What had I agreed to? Once again the reality started to kick in far too late. I had been on a mission of debt reduction for the past six weeks. Spend nothing, on a wafer thin budget with money to spare near invisible. Do nothing involving commitment to cost other than work and the group. A drop of 25% in wages would hurt, and more hours and days at work not conducive with what was happening with the group. The more I thought about Mr Balaam the more I shuddered at the thought of working for him; uncompromising, blunt, grumpy even.

So it was all negative. What were you doing, agreeing to take the job?! I know! Because when he was running through the so-called conditions of employment, the only thing going through my scrambled brain was the desperation to avoid rubbish in my shoes, hair, pockets, and down my trousers. A pay cut was almost a blessing in comparison.

So I tried to look at the positives. The working environment couldn't possibly be as bad, I would save some cost in petrol as it wasn't so far to travel, and I wouldn't need to get up so early. I could prepare for bookings before going to work, and if needs be not go home. The thought of working in musically enhanced surroundings was appealing, and working with Ray a blessing. There was also the weird notion, whyever did Mr Balaam offer me the job so readily? I couldn't possibly have been his favourite customer; if anything I must have been his most loathed customer. Or was it Ray had explained the momentous effort made to address the HP arrears, and underneath that cold outward personality he had a modicum of admiration. Or, was it purely commercial, who knows.

The next morning I still hadn't decided, but I was barely at work for an hour down that pit again when I downed tools and went on the hunt for the plant manager.

"I'd like to hand in my notice, from Friday this week."

"Oh, yes. Why's that then?" he asked.

"Got another job."

"Oh, where's that?"

"Rather not say."

"Shame, you've been doing a good job."

"Well, thanks, I just need to work where there's a level of enjoyment attached."

"Yeah, I can see that. So Friday week, January 1st will be your last working day?"

"Yes."

"Can you put that in writing so I can pass that to Mr Casson?"

"Yeah, can you thank Mr Casson for me. He did after all offer me a job at a time when no one else was prepared to take the risk." Court conviction, sackings and all, I was thinking.

I sat in the station waiting room that lunch time wondering, *am I jumping out of a Rolls Royce into a Reliant Robin?* I knew nothing about retailing. Did I have the personality to work in a record store? Was I able to keep sales buoyant? Well, Mr Balaam hadn't given me a clue of what to expect. I wasn't getting paid a lot so surely there wouldn't be that much pressure.

Or was there a river in torrent to navigate before I took the plunge?

The marvelous thing about a lack of planning is that failure comes as a complete and utter surprise.

Peter Green

Chapter 21
A Psychedelic Stumble

Christmas Eve

IF MAN COULD land on the moon then Julius Pam could surely arrive in Norwich that evening. Over Christmas we had the two most important bookings so far on our odyssey, The Melody Rooms and headlining The Royal Links Pavilion, Cromer. Well, according to Beevis that is. First, I had a day's work to negotiate before euphoria, but sometimes we are blessed. The plant closed down at 2 p.m. Buying presents for Christmas hadn't crossed my radar, as normally I would have been paid too late in the day. Leaving early changed that. I wasn't that dirty either, all the bad jobs had been done the day before, so with cash in hand it was time to escape the shackles of Ebenezer's fiscal prudence and take my riches to town.

I wandered aimlessly around the shops on the Cornhill and beyond without a single inspiration passing by until, there before my wide eyes in the Quality House Store window, the gift that would change my parents' lives forever: an electric blanket. With no central heating at home, frost formed on the inside of the windows. Hot water bottles didn't even tickle the cold on some nights. I just had to get it. Couldn't afford it but that didn't matter, the luxury would be heart-warming for them. If this made a difference to their lives, however small, it would in some tiny way repay all the love and care they gave their children year after year.

What to buy my sister? I hadn't a clue. I was nineteen years old, it was just too much pressure. Mandy loved music… I spent some time wandering aimlessly from shop to shop and finally found inspiration inside number 77 St Johns Street. On a shelf at shoulder height, a toy grand piano, quite well made but not expensive. I wondered if she would play with it. A rush of sentiment engulfed my eyes; love of your sister is a love never broken. Mrs Rogers served my needs and the riches were reduced to small change after the wrapping paper, but I didn't give it a thought.

The joy of Christmas, the beauty of family love.

Time was on my side and I was early collecting Dave from Tollgate Lane. No prompt needed to visit Lake Avenue, Gertrude knew the way. Much had been arranged for that night. John was working late to accommodate those last-minute shoppers. Jamie, Clive, Richard and John were to meet us in Oak Street no later than 6 p.m. We were all aware this was to be a special Christmas for us and expectation was running high. Dave and I were in good time and unloaded before the others arrived; we were eager to set up and be ready. Fisher, active and smart, spoke with meaningful clarity. There was an air of elation as the clock ticked down toward our entrance.

I had been less connected to the other members of the group before our opening set, instead out in the audience hoping Leslie had received my letter and travelled to see us that night, but sadly there was no sign of her. When I returned to the dressing room the call came. Richard and Clive were leaving to enjoy the attention of the girls on the dance floor. John and Jamie appeared a little incoherent, not that it seemed to matter as we walked down the stairs and onto the stage. The dance hall was filled with hats and high spirits, streamers and a party atmosphere. Our audience, close, excited, crowded with anticipation, as I plugged the Strat into the stack. My mind was racing. *Is this the moment of aspiration in 1958 when I strummed that Tommy Steele plastic guitar for the first time at Christmas.*

The place was brim-full and buzzing, the tension searing as I counted us in. We came alive and pounded through the opening bars…

But! It was short — and fatal.

We stumbled, and stumbled again, down and downward to an incoherent, heaving standstill. Shock and fear thundered through my soul. Try again, it didn't last, I was near trembling as we fell from grace and into the arms of embarrassment. The audience was agasp with tantalising intrigue as Fisher rushed to the scene.

What's going on here?"

I looked to the others. Dave seemed dumbstruck, Jamie

and John clearly incapacitated. It was for me to answer.

"A couple of us aren't too well."

"What's wrong with them?"

"I don't know."

Jamie mumbled, barely audible, "I think… we need… just a little time."

Fisher ordered, "Get up to the dressing room and get yourselves sorted out. I'll get the other group back on."

Richard and Clive helped Jamie and John to mount those stairs. As we sat there, stunned, the door swung open and Fisher charged in.

"So what's happening then?!"

"Can you give us some more time? Hopefully they'll be OK."

"What's the problem?!"

"Something they've eaten, I think."

Thirty minutes passed, very few words were spoken. I was numbed, without feeling. John and Jamie appeared to revive and the decision was made to try and make amends. Fisher was informed and we found our places again on stage. I wasn't confident.

The same introduction ended with the same result. I was cast down. The embarrassment was beyond embarrassment and I was about to feel the magnitude of Fisher's anger as I sat, head in hands, in the dressing room. He charged in, intense with rage.

"What the hell is going on? There's rumour this is about drugs!!"

I knew by then, but I was in a semi state of tremble; shock was taking its toll. "I don't know," my apathetic answer.

Anger was riveted to his face. "The f——g press are here tonight, it'll be all over the newspapers on Boxing Day! Next thing you'll know we'll have the police here!"

I didn't know or comprehend the implications right then.

He demanded, "Were these supplied by anyone within this building tonight?"

Clive reply was short and unsympathetic. "NO." He was more concerned about John and Jamie's health.

Fisher stormed out of the room and we heard nothing more from him that evening. All the months of positivity faded into oblivion. Would we ever recover from this? In my mind we had almost certainly blown it with Norwich Artistes.

John was in a state of complete suspension, mind-blown and travelling with tunnel vision. He was helped outside for air but seemed to have no comprehension of time or place, trapped in the psychedelic void. He and Jamie did eventually emerge from their trip, but it was too late. Richard and Clive were loading the van, Dave disappearing with Angie. Somehow Jamie encountered another young woman and wandered off with her. The rest of us travelled home in Gertrude in sombre mood.

"They were supposed to be recreational pills, just to give a little uplift, that's all," said Clive.

"I dread the thought of any reaction to the real stuff," my caustic response.

I was in despair; the work and effort put into finding our feet may have been sacrificed on a recreational altar. I didn't want to listen to any mitigating circumstances or alternate outcomes.

We arrived home at around 1.45am, dejected, and the weather was turning colder.

When Jamie came round on Christmas morning he found himself in the young woman's flat, completely oblivious of what had gone before. As he walked to the Herald some streets away his head was still full with psychedelia, sparkling multi coloured snow spinning his sensational vision in a landscape of peace and love. Those pick-me-up for fun pills were more like LSD. Some idiot had either supplied totally the wrong prescription or was having a laugh. That was the first and last time Jamie and John ventured into the world of mind-bending.

MELODY ROOMS
and DISCOTHEQUE

TOMORROW
THURSDAY, DEC. 24th

Christmas Eve
Party Night

with two great Groups

Julius Pam

Mister Toad

D.J. HOWARD PLATT
GUEST D.J.s
HATS — BALLOONS
STREAMERS

Doors Open 7.00 p.m.   Bars
Dancing till 11.45 p.m.
Admission Only 8/-
Tonight — Disc Data with H.P.

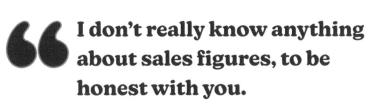

> **I don't really know anything about sales figures, to be honest with you.**
> Jimmy Page

Chapter 22
Christmas Comfort

Christmas Day

SNOW COVERED THE ground, the first truly White Christmas since 1964. The peace and purity of it. I was in tranquil surroundings with the people I love. What happened, happened, yesterday was best forgotten, today at least.

Christmas is for joy.

The electric blanket went down a storm with Mum. Dad, well, he took some convincing, telling us repeatedly, "It'll catch fire," but they were still using it ten years later.

"We just couldn't do without it now," they would often say in the depth of winter. Mandy and I had so much fun with that little piano. So my seven weeks of pulverising purgatory left me with these heart-warming memories. It was so worthwhile.

The snow lasted all day. People came, we visited others. There was laughter, fun, singing around the piano; nothing could have been more comforting. I made no mention of The Melody Rooms. It didn't seem the honourable or righteous thing to do.

Boxing Day

Snow still covered the ground that morning. Since July my whole reason for being was the group, but now it didn't seem to matter. This was the time and space I needed. But the respite was short lived. Mum's voice echoed up the stairs. "Andy, there's a John Fisher on the phone for you." Fisher? I had never spoken to him at home before, it was always Beevis.

I approached the phone with caution. "Hello, Mr Fisher."

"Andy!" He sounded curt. "Look, after what happened at The Melody Rooms we're taking you out of Cromer tonight!"

I was speechless – again.

"I will not have my clubs exposed to drug abuse in whatever form. Understood?!"

"Yes, understood."

"We have a reputation to uphold and there's no way I will have it compromised." This must have meant my worst fears had been realised.

He continued, "Julius Pam will not work at The Melody Rooms for at least the next three months and not appear under that name in Norwich until I see fit. If I had my way, you wouldn't be working at all tonight, but we need a replacement and you'll appear at Club America tonight instead. The group due to play there will go to Cromer Links."

I could not articulate a coherent reply.

"And make sure you do a good job. No drugs!"

He slammed the phone down.

There was much to consider from his call. He didn't infer this was the end for us and Norwich Artistes, just on probation, perhaps. There was no mention of the run of bookings from now until January 3rd. Maybe they were compromised, probably unable to find acts to replace us in that volume at such short notice. Whatever it was, it was severe punishment for our misdemeanour, and I was downcast knowing we were banished from The Royal Links Pavilion on their most cherished night of the year.

So we were on hold, still alive but in semi-suspension, not in favour but not jettisoned to mediocrity. Well, that had to be less painful than I imagined, and although a bitter disappointment, at least we were still working that night.

I telephoned John and explained the call from Fisher. "Can you let the others know? I'm not in the mood."

I had time to ponder. Could I just brush this under the carpet, forget it? No, probably not. The phone box incident, Germany and now this! I started out on this helter skelter fundamentally to address HP debt; before we had time to draw breath we were hurtling towards Christmas oblivious of any real dangers. It just all went to well, too quickly. But what happened really came from a lack of true guidance, a figurehead, a manager perhaps, in whom we could trust to navigate every hurdle and lead us to the Holy Grail.

Whatever the remedy, yet again my perception of the group had changed.

Snow was still plentiful in the landscape as I made my way with no heating to Club America that night, alone. A strange affair; for the first time I didn't collect anyone on the way and almost felt an outsider. Dave was in Norwich with Angie, everyone else came with Jamie. The night went well, it was still Christmas after all. One rainbow moment did raise my spirits. A very smartly dressed gentleman and tie came with well-spoken verse as he referred to the whimsical 'Good King Wenceslas'. "That's Fun. You should record that reggae version and release it next Christmas." Who was he, I wondered?

As everyone left, a young lady offered an invite to her flat, but as sure as night follows day, although we had sex it wasn't dreamland. Maybe I was too preoccupied, still in trauma mode maybe, or was it I hadn't yet fully understood what it was all about?

We returned to USAF Lakenheath the next day, Sunday, our fourth visit there. On Monday I was back to work in the snow and cold, full of dread, but at least there was a glorious horizon approaching in just five days. Bookings came and went in production line fashion, but concerns were stoking a potential storm.

Payments from Norwich Artistes for October and November had not as yet been forthcoming and December's bookings would add considerably to the amount outstanding. John had pursued Beevis but so far without response. As we were in uncertain times with our agency there was elevated concern should they decide to terminate our exclusive arrangement, we may have difficulty prising the outstanding money from them. We knew Fisher held the agency purse strings and any pursuit of monies owed would require a chase to his door. So we called at his house!

31st December 1970. The day The Beatles break.

We saw in the New Year at RAF Swanton Morley and all that goes with gay abandon, a late, late finish and mistletoe with a passion. After a crash landing on the bed at 5 a.m., by 8 I was on the pulverizing conveyor belt for the very last time. I said goodbye to Welnetham as Gertrude drifted down Station Hill in near dark and leftover snow.

On our way to a booking that evening, the van, full with six personnel, made a stop outside a private residence. John and I marched with stoic resolve to Fisher's front door. His Mum answered.

"Is John in?"

"No, he's out for the evening."

In the circumstances there was absolutely no answer to that one! We departed without a bean, and our quest for financial parity was thwarted.

On Saturday we travelled into deepest fenland for the Station Hotel, March, and then back again to Lakenheath on Sunday, another seven bookings in nine days. We had been on an extended express ride for the last seven weeks.

And what of Gertrude? Well, I must pay a romantic tribute her. She had carried our heavy load another 3000 miles in that time, in freezing cold, snow, fog and torrential rain, across country, through cities and home again, without protest or failure. A faithful and maternal devotion we rarely repaid. Despite little time or money spent in care of her needs, she just continued serving us with the loyalty demanded of a queen. It was 2 a.m. on that cold lonely road, four of us oblivious and sleeping. The night watchman, Jamie, was drifting off on the front seat as she purred contently, cruising back home, almost as though she was looking out for our welfare, determined not to let us down.

So what had come from the last ten days? Perhaps, in a negative way, a sense of modest division. Dave's relationship with Angie was growing, the friendship between Jamie, Richard and Clive was emerging, and John had also found a level of social connection with them. Me, well, I was about to start yet another employment, the fifth in three and a half years.

Monday 4th January 1971

As I stepped out of Gertrude in Risbygate Street at 8.45a.m., Badge was playing in my dreamlike head, every note from Clapton's captivating guitar part way through the song ringing clear in my sky blue mind, silencing the sound of traffic as I walked up the street to my new assignment. I reached that door, just as I had on 21st July five months before. Push to enter. It wouldn't budge, locked, no one there to greet me. So I waited, and there was time for my mind to wander. How different now am I from Friday last. Jacket, tie, jeans, moccasins, and those white socks. It was all a dream. No, it wasn't! It's real! How will my life change when I walk through that door?

Ray greeted me as he walked up the street. "Andy, *mon ami, bonjour*." He's turning French!

"Ray! Tractors are blue, violets have an engine."

"That must be the most bizarre greeting ever. How are you?"

"Fine thanks. All the better for meeting you here."

A large bunch of keys emerged and we entered, Ron close on our heels. "So, Andy, you've come to join us then?" Ron's eloquent and genteel greeting.

"Yes, from client to servant. All I need now is a new title."

"Well it's nice to have you here with us Andy, and long

may it last."

I felt at home already. Ray gathered the essentials for the day. "I'll meet you upstairs shortly, Andy."

Mounting that old Georgian staircase as an employee induced a warm spinal shiver. I was uncertain but pleased to be here. Never before in my working career had a storage heater come with the job. All of what went before was manual labour, in cold, wet, heatwave or snow. No longer being at the mercy of the elements was a luxury well worth a 25% cut in pay, as I'm sure you'd agree. I toured the modest room with a curious sense of pleasure as I awaited Ray's arrival.

"Well, what do you think?" asked Ray.

"Not sure where to start really."

"I'll show you the till, that's the most important bit."

Ray did the ensemble tutorial, which seemed pretty simplistic even for me.

"Must get on, you won't be too busy, just hold the fort. If you need help, there's the internal phone."

He didn't leave me with any immediate task other than to serve customers if they got this far. I stood against the heater, warming myself, and warming myself, staring at the ceiling, thumbing through the stock, scratching my ear, waiting, waiting, playing the odd record.

Suddenly, footsteps were mounting the stairs. *God, it's a customer!*

It was Ray, and 11 o'clock.

"All alright?"

"Er, yeah. Not very busy though, is it?"

"Cup of tea?"

"Yes, please."

"Come down and get one."

"So when's the mad rush?"

"I'll show you how to order stock later in the week. Mondays are generally quiet."

Lunchtime came and went, along with one non-paying visitor.

I spoke to Ray on one more occasion at afternoon tea when he explained "Albert insists on cashing up. If he's not here it's my commission to add up the day's takings and lock up."

It was twenty-five past five; and those footsteps on the stairs again. "Well, Andy, how's your first day?" enquired that emotionally void baritone.

"I can't give you anything positive in terms of takings; two paying customers, Mr Balaam."

He cashed up, total takings £2 precisely for the day. There was no reaction, not even a frown, almost as though this was nothing outside of the usual.

Anyway I have navigated the first day, I thought as I jollied down the road homewards. What a stark contrast to where I was a week ago. I didn't even need to have a bath! The only downside I could think of, if the pace remained this slow I'd have nothing to stimulate my imaginative heredity. There were plenty of positive vibrations trembling my inner sanctum, including: from rubbish-pulverizing lead guitarist to modern music salesman, with Strat. Prestigious, must grow my hair longer.

As Tuesday progressed it was barely a miniscule busier. I still had time on my hands. The highlight of the week so far was John coming across the street from the jeweller's, a bringer of good news. Norwich Artistes had at last sent us a cheque in payment of all outstanding fees until the end of November. My honest response was joy and relief.

John was apologetic. "No rehearsals this week, Dave

can't make it."

"I have no new material anyway," I replied.

"That's OK, our only remaining booking this week is Queen's Hall, Watton, on Saturday. But can you make meeting up on Friday evening at The Griffin (Ingham), 8 o'clock?"

"Do you want me to bring anyone along?"

"Dave and me if you can?

"Yep, I'll call around seven-thirty."

The respite was a blessing in recharge terms. Space was at a premium in December and we needed a break from our collective company. I personally needed three evenings away from the hustle, bustle and tumble of Julius Pam. But I couldn't leave the Strat in the van. A change of direction was following my shadow, all this pop was burning my fingers. The race to Christmas allowed no time for a vision of musical identity, and inspiration was virtually non-existent from within us. Covers upon covers were unlikely to take Julius far beyond where we were at that moment. I sat with the Strat in the one room in our house where solitude reigned supreme. Inspiration only strikes when it chooses. Nothing truly emerged that night.

I was gifted that real individual rock sound purely by an accidental marriage between a Mayfair fuzz-box, an old Strat with one weak pick up and pickguard controls that were unaware of their purpose. The union was perfect. Bertha Dorn was never void of creativity. I seemed to have lost that with Julius. The self-taught heavy riffs I had perfected came from hour upon hour of working with Bertha and within that room of perfect seclusion. I badly needed something to nudge my imagination. The words of that stylish gent on Boxing Night drifted into the vacant space. I couldn't find any other meaningful inspiration, so

Good King Wenceslas provided an opportunity to play around with what we had so hastily thrown together.

What transpired was a raunchy reggae version with outlandish keyboard and guitar instrumental solos, vocals in dictatorial mode returning to bizarre normality after that wild interlude with that first and only verse. Of course it was totally impossible to imagine us on *Top of the Pops* with this. Hang on a minute, though, if Beevis had anything to do with it he wouldn't let go until a slot was booked. So what if we found ourselves in front of a TV camera? There seemed something wonderfully certifiable in an image of three longhaired convicted offenders, plus a perfectly cool drummer, appearing as downtrodden sullen-faced rock musicians dressed in RAF greatcoats, pumping out a weird up tempo reggae version of 'Good King Wencesluslusalasus'. I put that idea, along with the rehashed Wenceslas remake, in my old zip-up school satchel, amongst all the 1960s song sheets that had accumulated in pre-Julius days, with the thought of perhaps resurrecting it close to next Christmas.

The routine in the record department on Thursday was much the same as the first three days, quiet and unchallenging. The limited number of tasks for the day I could clear up in an hour or so in the morning, leaving nothing much other than the odd customer appearing and disappearing without straining his or her finances. A small box had been delivered, but before I had an opportunity to break it open the internal phone buzzed. It was Ray.

"Andy, I have Phil Beevis on the phone, do you want to speak to him?"

"Oh, god, really? Yeah, can you put him through?" The surprise was total.

"Phil, how did you know I was working here?"

"Hello, Andy, long time no speak. I was just talking to Ray and he mentioned you had started work there so I asked if I could have a quick word."

"By some good fortune, yes, I'm in debt to Ray for that one."

"So how are you and the group?"

"Recovering from 1970. How's John (Fisher) by the way, after what happened on Christmas Eve?"

"The last thing he wants is anything that alienates the parents of the young who go to The Melody Rooms for enjoyment week in, week out. He feels he has a responsibility to maintain high standards within the club."

"Yes, I can fully understand that. I guess we've created some self-inflicted wounds Phil."

"Well, not so many as you may imagine. I think we look at it as a cooling off period, treading water you could say. In a couple of months' time let's look at it again and see where we are then. John may be a little more accommodating by that time."

"I'm curious, why did Fisher call me on Boxing Day? He's never called me before."

"Well, I'm sure he wanted to express his feelings. I would have called you in normal circumstances but Linda and I were married just before Christmas."

"What! Nobody told us. Congratulations! Here's wishing you a long and happy life together."

"Yeah, thanks. Now it's back to reality and rocky groups! Did you know we moved the Norwich Artistes offices to the Prince of Wales Road back in December? A bit more space and looks more official."

"No I didn't! Blimey, moving the office, getting married, Christmas, all in the same month. You're always full of surprises."

"That's another story."

"So what about bookings in the meantime, Phil?"

"Well, there's a number already through to mid-February – not as many as you have been accustomed to lately but this time of year is less demanding generally. There will be more to come; I have a few in the pipeline at the moment."

"We were due to appear again at Club America on the thirtieth of January. Are we likely to lose that?"

"I'm not sure. You did a good job on Boxing Night, that hasn't gone unnoticed, particularly as it was immediately after The Melody Rooms disaster. I don't know if you realised John was there briefly that night? Up on the balcony."

"No, I didn't! Checking up on us then?"

"It's possible you will appear there again, but most likely not under your own name," Beevis explained.

"Thanks, Phil, at least that implants some sense of security."

"Yeah, come March things will probably be back to normal. Have to rush. Good to catch up, Andy."

So we weren't ejected, but the momentum had undoubtedly been lost. Pity. Still, it was a delight to connect with Phil again. A level of sanity had returned, I had no doubt we would talk regularly in the future and the OTT rhetoric would flood the conversation again, and I looked forward to it.

That mystery package, once opened, revealed a few copies of Badfinger's 'No Matter What'. An edition of the Top Fifty chart for that week sellotaped to the wall revealed this new single had arrived at Number 35 in its first week in the charts. 'Grandad' was at Number 1. No comment. Determined not to lose sight of Beevis's preference for chart-listed pop without unduly compromising us musically, I decided the Badfinger song fitted the brief, and made my first purchase from Albert Balaam's as an employee of Albert Balaam that morning. It had swelled the takings enormously when Ray cashed up at lunchtime before half-day closing. At home I got the whole arrangement off that afternoon; the vocals suited my tonal range and I didn't have to change the key.

Friday 8th January

The Griffin, as it was known back then, in Ingham, was a typical Suffolk roadside inn-cum- public house with two separate bars. One for the local yokels if you like, with dartboard, dominoes, cribbage and, yes, a new-fangled jukebox. The lounge catered for the more refined, sedate, slightly upmarket clientele with jacket, tie and influence, perhaps.

Richard, who was a local, shuffled us all in among the numerous yokels, along with smoke, chatter, the high smell of beer and the sound of crunching crisps. He obviously had a modest opinion of our stature, but the main purpose was to save the tuppence a pint charged to the upmarket clientele in the lounge. This was much to do with a social gathering more than the group, but John did come with purpose and resolve. We squeezed in around an old battered pub table, Richard and Clive in particular revelling in the sounds of rich Suffolk dialect as a hotly contested darts match was in full flow. Cord blast!

John began, "I thought I'd update you all on the state of our finances. We've a fair bit of money in the piggy bank at the moment. Any suggestions what we should do with it?"

Other than "err", "um", burp, there was a stunned silence.

"I thought it was about time we had something for our hard work," John continued, in his accountant's mode.

"What… money?" said Dave, looking more animated

than he had in a while.

"Yes, we can afford about a hundred each."

A hundred pounds… That was eleven weeks' wages! I could completely clear my debts and then some, I fantasised.

"I may get my own amp for the keyboard instead of going through the PA. That should stop you moaning about that, Andy," John said with a level of satisfaction.

However, like a Ransome's Thresher driven by an out of control Burrell traction engine, the energy of Suffolk banter, passion and volume around the bar room was multiplying. Jamie was trying to talk over the noise with a raised voice. "I've always regretted selling my kit. Would be good to buy a new full set, Premier maybe. Then we can return Rick's kit to him!" he announced at level eight.

Dave, in vocal pain, added, "I've always fancied a Gibson."

Jamie, this time louder than Robert Plant: "It'll have to be a female model then."

The bar suddenly flooded with vigorous rapture in celebration of the arrow that won the match, and that was 'suffen exsoytun'.

"So, it's agreed, a hundred each then?" We couldn't hear him— John, that is. Everyone grunted, and then nodded.

"Well, I thought there would be total agreement, so I've brought along four envelopes. There was a sudden quiet lull around the room as the banter bombed. John was still shouting. "Do what you will with it." Everyone in the room heard that. He passed them around. A warm ripple of satisfaction flowed over that table.

"If you get a stack, John, we'll never get it in Gertrude," was my next concern.

"Thought of that! You're always on about the transits at Beefy's (Norwich). There'll still be enough in the kitty to get ourselves a tranny for around two hundred and fifty quid. Should be plenty of room then."

The prestige of having a Julius Pam transit figurehead appealed to us all, and the motion was carried without protest. We didn't pay Richard or Clive anything, other than buy them half a pint each. Important not to contravene their terms of employment.

Everyone was clearly uplifted, and to a degree this unexpected payment pushed thoughts of Christmas Eve into the background. This was another significant milestone, one that should have been expected perhaps but nevertheless a solid achievement. I was suffering a certain melancholy at the thought Gertrude would finally find honourable retirement, but that would only happen under strict conditions. She certainly wasn't going to end up in that demonic scrapyard amongst those bloodthirsty Rottweilers.

I spent years laughing at Harry Secombe's singing until somebody told me that it wasn't a joke.
Spike Milligan

Chapter 23
Undecorated Boston Glitter

Saturday 9th January

IT WAS BACK to work that morning with a spring in my step. Finally I was on the cusp of financial freedom, with the means to clear those three debts and, for the first time since I left school, in employment that didn't bring on an overwhelming sense of loathing. My first working Saturday at the Music Centre was revealing; not at all busy, but not mind-numbingly underused perhaps. What was strikingly evident were the Disco DJs who came hunting for records that day. I was completely unaware of the growing attraction of this form of entertainment, having never been in conversation with a DJ before, not even out there at the venues we were playing. It hadn't occurred to me this blossoming phenomenon was anything more than a way of filling in the time before the main event, live music. But the real joy that morning was conversation, the immense pleasure in sharing my lifelong passion for music with like-minded young DJs who appeared to find my enthusiasm appealing. I was handed business cards and made connection with a few Disc Jockeys that day, but there were two more memorable moments far above all that had gone before.

My mother visited me at work for the first time in my life, just before lunch.

Her expression radiated joy; could it be she was hoping at long last I may have found my true vocation? She could see my frame of mind had lifted markedly from the week before, and the downtrodden air that was so evident whenever I left for, and came home from, work was completely undetectable.

"Just calling in to see how you are getting on Andy."

A customer interrupted. She wandered around, curious, awaiting my attention.

"Thanks for coming to see me, Mum. Can I interest you in twenty-nine copies of Pink Floyd's 'Ummagumma', or something?"

She giggled. "Is there anything you need?"

"Thanks, Mum, that's OK."

"I won't keep you then. See you when you get home."

It was short, but so very, very sweet.

So to lunch, and the truly meaningful mission I awoke to that morning. Out into the street, I strode with purpose to the traffic lights, across St Andrews Street into Ron's Café, to be greeted immediately by Ralph. He looked almost surprised. Unusual, nothing ever seemed to stir him.

"Ralph, here's the thirty pounds outstanding on the Strat."

"Oh! Good. Thanks!"

"Can you sign the receipt?"

"Just a minute, I'll get a pen."

He signed and marked it: 'Paid £30.00 balance 0.00'.

"Thanks, Ralph. There were times when I thought I would never fully own this guitar."

We had an extended conversation; he was genuinely interested in how things were going. In Bertha days he did find us a few bookings while trying to set up his Tempo Entertainments Agency.

I left elated. At last, after 14 months of struggle, the Fender Stratocaster was safe from repossession, no longer a burden. I could finally fully express myself with her, a freedom I couldn't totally enjoy until that moment.

Mr Balaam's end-of-day accounting revealed a total of £16 2s 4d; not exactly inspirational. Other than a cantankerous, "Put all the notes the same way round in the till and make sure you switch all the lights off before you leave," there were no other expressions of opinion or criticism.

Renewed vitality had found its way to my soul that evening on our way to the Queen's Hall, Watton. Needs were not wanting and my life had changed for the better. Dave mentioned going to London on a day off work to look for a Gibson. Much talk surrounded a replacement for Gertrude and the one advertised in the *Bury Free Press* with a Great Barton telephone number.

We were 'The Main Attraction' that night, as Beevis

explained, supported by Sweeney's Fantasy of Sound Disco. But I paid much more attention to the 'fill in'. I began to wonder if, instead of the odd hand-operated flashing light and projector along with poor sound reproduction, there were spectacular light shows and special effects, quality sound and a not-so- self-indulgent DJ. Could this be dance halls in the not too distant future? Trying to recall our performance that night and how we were received leaves me vacant, so I assume it wasn't playing a tune of jubilation in my head.

Sunday 10th January

Desperate to unload the final two chains of insolvency from that dark day back in July, I drove to Bob's home out at Wickhambrook with unclouded mind. He was expecting me after I had telephoned earlier, but not yet aware of my new found riches. With probable anticipation I would be paying another instalment, he opened with, "I did wonder when you were coming again." He hadn't seen me since before Christmas. I sensed an expectation of brow beating and poverty reigns supreme.

"I have enough now to clear all that I owe you."

"Oh, good!" he said with a level of disbelief. "So what's happened then?"

"Can we settle this first and then I'll explain?"

"Fine, I'll get the signed paper."

He returned with the 'official' loan agreement typed on a small 8 x 5-inch sheet of notepaper covering fifteen words and figures. It was dated November 1969 and a fourpenny stamp was oversigned by me and a witness. With a feeling of release I handed Bob the outstanding balance. He signed it off, 'Paid with thanks'.

"Would you like a drink and a chat?"

I was almost desperate to depart and make haste to

Dick's house in Barrow, but I agreed. We talked for over an hour. He seemed captivated by all that had transpired since 1969 and sincere in his good luck wishes as I left. That was the last time I saw him.

Then cross-country to Barrow where, by chance, Dick was at home. So that final debt was settled, and with liberation jangling I decided to call in to see Jamie unannounced. We had an in-depth conversation that fortified my belief of his good-natured demeanour. He was upbeat, explaining his visit to see Ray at the Music Centre at lunchtime on Saturday and ordering a brand new Premier kit, partly on HP, using some of the monies we had received as a deposit. So much was happening and changing, I wondered again where this all would lead. In an optimistic direction, I hoped.

On Monday I returned to work at The Music Centre, to settle in and attempt to keep occupied on those almost barren weekdays. It was difficult, the time dragged, and I became ever-more aware the selection of records on view were predominantly unsaleable. Singles represented over half of all the very modest sales, but prices were not competitive. In my uneducated opinion the record department was a last resort for those unable to find what they wanted elsewhere. Unfortunately, I so often couldn't offer the small number of customers who did mount those stairs what they were looking for. But at least I was not burning energy, and it was good to be in a place that reflected my most fervent interests, along with those gentle staff, so accommodating.

Tuesday's rehearsal saw the introduction of 'No Matter What', the first chart song introduced to our playlist since November. We were short of any upcoming material. Although three songs added before Christmas were still at 2, 3 and 4 in the charts respectively, everything else was quickly becoming old hat. 'Black Night' had become an established classic, which I was reluctant to jettison, but I was determined that any new material should suit a musical identity I was trying to create for the group. Some songs, although popular in the charts, just didn't work for us and never would, and 'everything and anything' wasn't where I wanted to be. I was almost wracked with a rigid fear at the thought of one day having to sing 'Grandad'.

Wednesday 13th January

After partially recovering from that dreadful thought there was that second-hand Transit van to consider. But before I do, what can I say about Gertrude, our loyal servant? It was impossible to get her to put on weight; there wasn't room, plodding was her forte and devotion was in her oil, but expansion, totally alien. She creaked a little as John and I set out early Wednesday evening to Mere Farms Ltd., Great Barton. Perhaps it was a cry of sadness as she was no longer to be our leading light. She stood silent and forlorn as we gave her rival admiration worthy of a king. Blue, spacious, hinged opening front doors, and! a sliding side door. Back doors you could drive a Bubble Car through, space for Jamie's much larger drum kit and more, but the seats were like concrete compared to Gertrude's padded leather. It was a done deal and we arranged to collect it the next day, early afternoon. Gertie always did have a slightly sad expression, but at that moment I couldn't help but notice she looked broken-hearted.

On Thursday, someone, I can't remember who, drove John and I to Great Barton to collect our hard earned prize. Mr Ward presented an official bill of sale.

Transit van ECF 997D, (born 1966), 4 years younger than Gertie. Paid cash £205. 0. 0d, Taxed, MOT'd.

We both returned to Risby and transfered the equipment and whatever else we needed for the journey to RAF Coltishall, our third visit there. All six of us piled into the Transit for the first time that night. There seemed far less sentiment for this new servant, much more of a practical status symbol than a faithful companion. His masculine form cruised faster and effortlessly toward Norwich and beyond. Gertrude heartlessly left empty and abandoned in the dark between two garage sheds. The Twilight of a God, very sad. Don't cry, please.

We returned to Coltishall for the fourth time just 14 days later.

Saturday 15th January

Risbygate Street had become our assembly point par excellence. The image of four young long-haired pop musicians and their two roadies, piling into a Transit van in a car park next to the cattle market in sleepy old Bury St Edmunds, has an evocative feel, don't you think? Well I do anyway. It was 1971 after all.

We were on our second outing to the wilds of Lincolnshire, this time to the Aquarius Club in the heart of Lincoln City. John and I had left work at 4.00pm, with Ray, almost paternal, arranging covert cover for me. At 7.15 we arrived at 305 High Street, parking outside a tall red-brick Victorian building just down the road from Woolworths. The ground floor appeared totally severed from the world of late-night revelry, drink and high adrenaline. But how do we get in?

The whole building looked to be in total darkness, and to make things worse, it was dark outside. Dave asked, "Is this the right place? Where's the entrance?"

"Round the back?"

"Where's round the back?"

"Round the back!

After getting lost and nearly jammed down an alleyway we eventually found 'round the back', round the back. There was a door leading to two flights of stairs up to the first floor and into the large main room, an enclosed space. I don't recall any seating; it was almost sparse and dimly lit, dark even. The stage was high, and the room behind it overlooking the high street was our dressing room. From there a door led to another narrow and darkened flight of stairs providing 'servants only' access to the third floor lounge bar. A space that appeared to be more suited to a sedate cabaret entertainer maybe. We hauled our equipment up those torturous stairs to the main room. Four hours after leaving home the craving for intoxicants was overwhelming.

After a few drinks our march to the stage heralded "let's make a job of this!" Reggae was the popular flavour in that one hour spot along with anything holding a black America content. We came off with curiosity pinned between our ears and a venture to the second floor revealed Three Bees, another act, in full flow on that modest stage. Even more drink was vital, and we had time to indulge ourselves in the interval, but before long the call came and a final set leading to that crescendo ending. Another show, another shilling.

Dave disappeared for a while with an attractive blonde. I had no idea what the rest of them were up to; I was knackered. It had been seventeen hours since falling out of bed this morning to prepare for work and then drive to Lincoln. John was in the same condition, I knew.

Toil and tears saw the equipment back down that mountain and into the Transit. Homeward was calling. The mammoth task of keeping me awake was confronted with cunning imagination and meticulous skill, all carried out with great determination and fortitude. The resolve had to be foolproof; under no circumstances could they afford to fail. About twenty minutes into the journey, after lengthy negotiations between Dave, Jamie, Clive and Richard, an agreement was finalised.

"LET'S SING 'SHERRY BABY'!"

Would this be the torture of my worst nightmares? Could it possibly be the horriblest, most ghastly rendition of Frankie Valli in the entire history of mankind?

"1-2-3… SHER-ER-ER-ER-ER-ER-ER-RRY BA-A-BY SHERRY B-A-BY SHER-ER-ER-ER-ER-ER-ER-RRY BA-A-BY SHERRY BABY"…

It was hideous! Unspeakable! Frightening! Ear-splitting! The most gruesome harmony I had ever heard. My ears developed white flags and my eyeballs were protruding beyond the windscreen. I couldn't possibly endure this agony, torment, persecution, all the way home.

"For Christ's sake, can't you do a recital of 'Hev Yew Gotta Loight, Boyee' or something a bit more soothing?!"

It was like showing a bull your rear end. They launched into the most bizarre transmitification of the Singing Postman that has ever graced the halls of Norwich Castle. Nor Folk were under siege from the most terrifying lyrics conceived in the annals of Norfolk Turkeys, and they were 100 miles away.

But I did think, *what a brilliant idea*. Play around with this and see what we come up with; so we did. Out came a frantic 12-bar-style rendition of heavy species, bizarre tank-like keyboard, Dave playing as many noots out of tune as possible, Jamie smashing a relentless thundering beat, knocking hell out of his brand new kit, vocals in Norfolk dialect, almost completely indiscernible, and me playing a *Trumpton*-style melody line.

It was a brilliant innovation. Well, we thought so. The lyrics were terribly risqué though in places, so I won't reproduce them for the benefit of your sanity, but if you give me a call I'll recite them over the phone under the pseudonym Arffur Royt Zackly.

But it's with great regret that our reworking of that Norfolk classic never got beyond the interior of the van. Shame.

The plan worked perfectly. John slept through it without a murmur, I had nightmares for a week, Dave, Richard and Clive left their tonsils in the back of the van, and Jamie thought it was all normal, as we arrived back in Risbygate Street before dawn. Twenty-two hours after staggering down stairs I floundered upward, crawled onto the bed and awoke at 2 p.m. that Sunday afternoon.

Why the hell didn't you share the driving? I expect you're wondering. Good question. Maybe it's time to explain. Prior to November this wasn't an issue since I wasn't working and could start out in the evening feeling fresh. John didn't have a driver's licence, only a bike, nor did the two Clives. In the interest of poverty, the van insurance was third-party only and covering its commercial use, with one named driver only, me. A collective share had never been given consideration, and continued financial prudence along with other events in the future maintained that line. Besides, I enjoyed driving the van, even when I was in a semi-comatose state.

That following week all carried on as before in the record department: near-paralysing boredom for long periods, broken by the occasional spurt of a single customer calling in followed by a cup of tea. Making use of the time was extremely challenging, but on the other hand it did offer the opportunity to open my mind to album tracks I had never had the pleasure, time or money to indulge in. Some would say what a great job, in amongst a rack of musical gems with no real stress or hardship. I was blessed, I guess, but I needed a true challenge. Perhaps finding a buyer for that dog-eared copy of Andwella's Dream's 'Love and Poetry' would be a sizable conquest. But it was early days after all.

Jamie mounted the stairs on Wednesday lunchtime. "Got the kit!" he announced.

I had nothing new that night to add to our rehearsal list, still determined to feature only music that I thought suited us. Jamie indulged his most treasured fantasies with his new purchase. It was a superb complete kit, far beyond the mix-and-match set he had been making do with. It added new power and depth to our sonic collective. An opportunity then to exercise ourselves with familiar material for two hours, which had our 'through the looking glass' onlookers dancing in the haze.

Thursday 21st January

Mum's mission that morning: an announcement!

"Your dad and I are coming to watch you play tonight. Dad's friend Winkie and his wife are coming with us."

Parents coming to watch their son at a pop dance full of the virile and flirtatious!! This could be embarrassing, but it did produce a warm glow. After all, they had gone through those years of struggle; perhaps they saw, at last, all seemed to be worthwhile. And so close to home, there might not be another opportunity sometime soon. But I couldn't possibly let on my mum and dad would be in the audience, could I?

This was the closest to home we were to appear at a British venue. Lakenheath, USAF America, the next closest, didn't throw its doors open to the locals. Odd though, when I think about it now – were we a Bury St Edmunds group that was unknown in Bury St Edmunds and never seen performing live there, the only exclusive being at the Centa rehearsals? Were we outcasts or something?

RAF Honington, of former Vulcan and Valiant fame, and by now home to The Buccaneer bomber. Oh, and of course, The Suffolk Punch Club, our venue. Popular for the well-known acts it attracted. I felt privileged to appear here, although this would be the first time I breached its threshold, socially or otherwise. Buses were laid on to ferry the young and enthusiastic from Bury St Edmunds, Thetford and outlying villages, and it was Richard's established stomping ground, just ten minutes from his front door in Ingham. (A Suffolk Punch is a horse, incidentally, or, if you prefer, an act of violence).

We entered this manicured RAF aerodrome through the smart entrance and made a brief ID visit to the guardroom. Then upward to The Suffolk Punch, a classic British Air Force building of the fifties era perhaps, with a spacious dance hall and separate NAAFI bar area accessed through an entrance on the left. John and I wandered in together and were confronted by the poster announcing tonight's line-up.

JUST BACK FROM their Tour of Germany –
the Fantastic Boston International Showband
with Paul Raven!
IN SUPPORT, EAST Anglia's Top Pop Group –
Julius Pam.

"Oh, that's not too bad, is it?"

"Never heard of them, John."

"Who – Julius Pam?"

"Perhaps they come from Boston, USA."

"Still never heard of them."

"Me neither."

We were granted a stage of our own, and Jamie's kit shone like a beacon in the midst of us. The acoustics were less than perfect, but we managed well and performed as expected of a lead-in act before the main event.

I was curiously focused on the headlining singer when Paul Raven appeared, larger than life, almost wild-looking. But he didn't hit the high notes for me; it was the band that held my attention. I watched intently. They were tight, professional, solid and complete. They radiated an air of well-travelled experience and confidence, appearing to be at least five years ahead of us in terms of experience. They had clearly been on the circuit in some form for many years.

So here lies the 'The embryonic beginnings of Glam Rock'. Much of where Glam Rock started came out of 1971; T.Rex as early as March that year displayed modest Glam tendencies, and many other acts followed, including this showman before me. Paul Raven metalicalized into Gary Glitter and the band became Glitter's backing band, the Glittermen; later, independent from Glitter, they named themselves The Glitterband. It was a modest education for me that night. In all honesty I didn't see them as the future, but the 'Just Back from their Tour of Germany' opening headline reminded me of the prestige Beevis placed on this title and how well the audience appeared to respond to their apparent status, even though they were relatively unknown at that time.

We ran through the best of our best in that final set, and the audience enthusiastically responded, a dance floor full of revelry and the carefree. A few girls from the Centa had made the bus to see us. At least we had some fans around that night, and we were invited to return four months later.

Mum and Dad sat with their friends amongst the audience over on the far side of the hall. I did go to see them just the once, but the volume of the main attraction overpowered our conversation.

From there it was homeward, but we had to pack away first. Our van was parked beside The Boston's transport and both were being loaded at the same time. As we were about to close the back doors, a confrontation with one of their road crew broke out.

"We're a cymbal missing," he said.

"Have you?"

"We think you've got it in the back of your van."

"No, we bloody well haven't!" It was an affront!

"Well, let's have a look then."

"Christ, what a bloody cheek! What would we want with one of your beat-up cymbals? Our drummer's got a brand new kit."

"Look, I could always go and get one of the Military Police, if you like."

"If you're so convinced go and bloody get him then!"

The conversation paused. "Look, it could have been a genuine mistake."

"Sorry, I didn't mean to accuse you of stealing it," mumbled the Boston's roadie.

The heat cooled. "Alright then," tongue in cheek, "perhaps we'll meet up again sometime in the future, but I assure you, you won't find anything. If it has been stolen, anyone could have taken it."

So we unloaded ninety percent, only to discover that blasted renegade cymbal! Humble Pie regurgitated in my mouth. "Yeah, sorry, it wasn't intentional, just one of those things. Could have been the other way round…"

"Yeah, sure" he replied, and walked off with a scowl.

It didn't bother me or any of us really, just one of those things that happens out on the road. But the bell of truth rang loud and clear on the way home. It wasn't an accident, it was deliberate! I can't really say much can I? Roadies, they do try to look after you, don't they?

There was a time, everything was fine. You got drunk on the day like it was wine.
Marc Bolan

Chapter 24
Hot Love Rules

AFTER THE POST-CHRISTMAS lull, bookings were starting to spiral upward despite Fisher's cooling off period. Beevis appeared keen still to promote us as best he could, and at the end of January five bookings came in eight days, the first of these at the TA Pad Leiston, close to the East Suffolk coast, home of Garrett Engineering and the Territorial Army.

There was a feeling of warmth that night, an embracing audience of the young and happy, full of the joys of song and dance, their glow flowing endlessly over us as we performed. The ease in all that we did was perfected from so much that followed us to where we were at that moment, and the nervous tension of those early days just a mere sideshow compared to the enthusiasm of our audience and their response.

That night the penny may have finally dropped for me. Current popular music was this young generation's expectation when out enjoying freedom and letting their hair down, many dancing, a few standing in curiosity. All of those elements came together that night. So, Julius Pam, what had we become there and then? 'A Pop Group', through and through, void of any true self-indulgence, and popular to those within. Were we then worthy of Beevis's mantel as 'East Anglia's Top Pop Group'? Based on that night's performance, perhaps we were, or was it there were no other East Anglian true pop acts to compete with, so no competition for the top spot? Whatever we were, Phil's sense of mammoth overstatement had raised and fixed us upon that summit he had created. As we were leaving the proudly displayed old union flag of far eastern WW2 conflict induced a feeling of honour and respect as we found our way home.

Tower Ballroom, Yarmouth, the following night should have been a reunion with Lesley, but nothing materialised. I was preoccupied, and it barely crossed my mind. If she was there she didn't come looking for me. Another one of those brief encounters that found no direction. Disappointing on many different levels, as a fan club would have been good and perhaps even lengthened this story, don't you think? Unless, of course, no one other than Lesley enrolled. On the way home I did wonder if she had received my reply.

Our return to Club America, after some uncertainty,

did materialise on the 30th January, but the *Evening News* didn't reveal our name that night. We returned again twice in February, once billed as Edentree and the second time again without any mention of us. So Fisher was true to his word: for the two months after Christmas we didn't appear in Norwich under our own name. Disappointing, but in reality it clearly portrayed the thin line between in favour and out of favour. We were fortunate that Beevis remained in favour.

By February 1971 we had six months' experience on the road. Dave found some time with that £100 plus some of his wages to head off into London with John and Jamie in the hunt for a Gibson. They took the train, made for Shaftesbury Avenue and all that epitomized the music scene in that area of London. The numerous music stores were frequented in abundance by platinum stars and so many that aspired to follow them. HP agreements were prolific, many often administered with draconian iron, and upstairs storerooms were filled with the spoils of reclaim awaiting court proceedings. But Dave was a rare animal, a musician with cash to splash. Would he outwit the con-man salesman who saw him coming? After a multitude of doors opening and closing and then opening again, and Jamie and John distracting his mission with Drum City and keyboards, a Gibson EB Cherry Red locked his senses into I'm not leaving without it.

"I've got cash, what about a discount? I'll give you a hundred and ten."

The salesman disappeared into the manager's office with a radiant smile, and returned, with an even more radiant smile. "Done." A shake of hands and the deal was sealed.

After coffee shops and famous faces, a journey back by train that Thursday evening prompted thoughts of a first outing with Gibson, an iconic name of stage and fame. Those three bookings that weekend were perfectly placed to air that deep Yankee thunder, and with a prophesy it would add a vigorous dimension to our sound.

Saturday 6th February

Regal surroundings passed in Wymondham that Friday, and then onward to Saturday and The Royal Links Pavilion, Cromer, as support to The John Mcflare Band, Brummies through and through. They were very good.

We were welcomed and shown respect, much of which gave heat and favour to Dave and Jamie's new found dimensions, and in my mind our maturing sound and selected musical content raised us a little higher. Perhaps that night the stage was less filled with pop but instead with identity and direction. Beevis's pop remit still rang loud in our ears, but much more of our choosing rather than anything goes.

Girls were all consuming at the end of the night. I just loved playing at this place, it was special, and the wider audience too. One pretty young lady had no inhibitions in introducing herself after our final set. John had already disappeared to the lighthouse with a female admirer. With those looks who wouldn't fancy him? Well, not me, for certain. I had no idea where Jamie was; Dave and Angie were locked in passion. Richard and Clive were missing (I learned later, apparently Clive was getting stung in the nettles, I'll leave the rest to your imagination). I disappeared without a by-your-leave, with Christine, for over two hours. So it was gone 2.30am as I wandered aimlessly back up Overstrand Road and that endless hill. I did wonder if the rest of the crew had left for home, completely overcome by explosive frustration. Well, I was right, they had left!

I was only about halfway up the mountain when a pair of blazing headlights on full beam appeared on that barren road. I couldn't see a damn thing as it came closer and closer, but it was slowing down and pulled up three inches from my big toe. What kind of driver is this, a mad version of Evil Knievil?! As it turned out he **was** mad. The driver's door opened and an extended raging lion in the form of Dave hollered, "Where the 'obscenity!' have you bin?" It **was** Dave.

"Sorry 'bout that, I got held up."

"What, was the train late?!"

"No, I got lost."

"Is that why your flies are down!" -- But they weren't!

Chastised, I jumped in the vacated driver's seat and made for home. But that wasn't the end of it.

"OK, we've all agreed." (But I hadn't). And the rulebook was born. The first entry: 'Thou shalt not 'P—S OFF for more than half an hour.' "Sign here!"

As I was the official and only named driver, I had a feeling this rule was explicitly and exclusively designed for me. What are your thoughts?

The weekend closed with our billing as Edentree at Club America and then back to the day jobs. I wasn't trusted to order stock as yet. Ray was always given the task, probably due to Mr Balaam's ultra-grip on all things costly and every penny counts. Besides, he had a certain lack of trust, fear even, I would place orders of bank-breaking levels.

It wasn't busy for the group during the week, there were just two bookings at the weekend, but these marked the start of another run of seven appearances in nine days, the first being our premier at The Beachcomber Room, Clacton-on-Sea.

Just to let you know, if you're wondering what's happened to Jolly's Monday lunch, we didn't meet in such regimented form there by this time. Momentum had moved us on and perhaps there wasn't a need. Much had settled, considering how fraught finances were back in July, and that ball and chain had almost disappeared from view. Dave and Angie's love affair was continuing to blossom and he was starting to spend more time in Norwich. On some occasions we were collecting him from Angie's on the way to bookings.

On Wednesday morning at work I was introduced to one of the record company reps. We stood and chatted for some time about the music industry and all that was glamour to me. T.Rex was the main topic of conversation. As we parted he handed me a copy of their new single, 'Hot Love', on release that coming Friday, and to my almost overwhelming delight, a demo of Deep Purple's new single, 'Strange Kind of Woman'.

"You can have them. 'Hot Love' is gonna be big," he said.

"Hope Ray has ordered plenty then." He looked at me, puzzled. Big orders at Balaams? Never.

As he descended the stairs, I set this new acquisition on the turntable and cranked up the volume. Well, just a little really. Mr Balaam was due in any minute and I would get lambasted for disturbing the peace in the main showroom at anything above three notches. The reaction was instant. He was right, this was gonna be big. So infectious… and that outro – captivating! In a moment of total indiscipline, I rushed down the stairs, picked up an acoustic, rushed back, spent the next half hour or so getting the entire lead and bass work onto the fretboard and the lyrics down on paper and in my head, not one customer appearing until early afternoon. Rehearsal was that evening and I'd had nothing to offer until now. It was a godsend, and I was convinced this would find a place in our changing repertoire. I spent as much time as possible on 'Strange Kind of Woman'. It was perfect, and so much represented my vision of our identity. I was desperate to add this to rehearsal that night.

At the Centa the whole 'Hot Love' thing came together in just 15 minutes. Simplistic and hypnotic, we ran through one more time, banking it for the weekend. 'Strange Kind of Woman' took the rest of rehearsal time to perfect, but finally it was ready, and rapturous applause radiated through the looking glass wall. Were these new songs a window into our future?

I saw nothing more of everyone until Friday that week. Social outings were gathering but I was less involved, happy to find a level of social connection away from the group when time allowed. I felt refreshed then when we next met.

Saturday 13th February

It was seaside in winter, and only an hour and fifteen minutes journey time; this venue was a first for all of us. Clacton… a reminder of the old railway poster back in chapter eighteen, but this time for pleasure rather than pain. Historically Mods commanded the seafront in the sixties. Since then it had calmed, and peace had been restored. Well almost. The Beachcomber Room was part of Westcliffe Hotel along Marine Parade, looking out to sea, and our arrival in the dark wasn't greeted by fanfare. Pity. It was dry for the time of year and we were in high spirits.

Not knowing what to expect, the Beachcomber Room lived up to its name, dressed in everything tropical: wooden palm trees with a feel of calypso and colour. We left the winter outside. And what a joy it was, the young, vibrant audience once again fascinated by four young musicians playing what they wanted to hear. Well, most anyway. But the concept of a future Glam Rock cover that night opened a new world, and it went down a storm. God, I have tried, hard, not to overstate our reception at venues so far in this book, but a storm it was, and yet I was not sure everyone in the audience that night knew the song. I didn't introduce it as a T.Rex sensation; perhaps subconsciously this was deliberate. But what was uncanny, the silver stars Dave and I had plastered on our guitars, our extra-colourful shirts, John's high gold, Dave's shining emerald, Jamie's classy rich claret, and my own turquoise semi-gloss flared trousers, all glittering under the lights. 'Strange Kind of Woman', 'No Matter What' and all that we could perform in the style we aspired to, shone that night, and a feeling of elation embraced my whole persona as our last set came to a thundering end.

Imagine the atmosphere in the van homeward bound in the early hours that night. The conversation was electric. Very occasionally life gifts those special moments; certainly that was one of the few.

Sunday 14th February

We returned to Lakenheath for the sixth time that Sunday, Valentine's Day. Not our most cherished venue, a much different audience than the places we most enjoyed appearing at, but it was work, and so often on days that we were less likely to be in demand elsewhere. There were pluses. For instance, the loathed extended playing times, in front of a near-empty room, practically served as rehearsals whilst we awaited an expanding audience topped up with Schlitz and vodka. Much of that time allowed a freedom to ad lib, during twenty-minute-plus extensions of numbers that at times aroused the small scattering of GI's who hadn't yet felt the full effect of a few drinks. This free-for-all crafted an understanding and musical union that undoubtedly fortified our ability as a unit, and was reflected many times at rehearsals in the ease of adding new material to our set lists. I had become accustomed to the phrases 'YOU GUYS', 'GOD DANG', even 'YEE-HA'! Hospitality was often forthcoming in the form of drinks, and I rarely ever needed to buy any when blessed with an American audience, who were, if you were favored, very hospitable.

That night on-stage an attractive American woman… no, a very attractive American woman – appeared twice with a Budweiser gift, presented with a suggestive but classy smile. Another first for me and far more appealing than 'Heavy Duty' back in September.

Of course not everything was perfect when on-stage. We had our off days, maybe some venues just didn't suit us, maybe we were just off-colour, tired even, but when it worked it really did work and we became so aware of that.

Midnight breakfast was a gourmandize pastime after our performances at Lakenheath, sunny side up and all that, on a large scale, which didn't help the digestive hangover and lack of sleep on the way to work the next morning, unless like Clive you had an iron constitution.

Monday 15th February

I fumbled my way to the Music Centre that morning, glad and safe in the knowledge recovery was at hand in the form of boredom. But! it was **Decimalization Day.** I had totally forgotten, hadn't done any homework and was still completely void of pounds and pence. Shillings and ten bobs were a fixation I had failed to shake off. It was hairy stuff, and I dreaded the thought of a customer coming in and buying something. But I was blessed, not one customer appeared on the horizon until gone eleven, so I did some much needed homework on decimal coinage. I was absolutely convinced those weird-looking octagonal ten bobs would never catch on. The real highlight of the morning came early, at 9.30.

"It's Beevis again, Andy. Do you want me to put him through?"

"Yeah Ray, delighted… Phil, how's things?" How's things!! I must have had a total conversion course to Music Centre speak.

"Good, how did Clacton go?"

"Yeah, good, enjoyed it. Great audience."

"No problems?"

"Not that I know of."

"Gonna ring them this morning, Keep the line open, I'll get back to you."

What was that all about, I wondered.

A customer did come in at gone eleven, actually purchased something and gave me a real headache as the till still rang up in shillings. Anyway I muddled through with a little help from him. No sooner had I bagged up the goods than the phone buzzed again.

"It's a Mr Beevis for you, Andy."

Oh, Christ! That deep unmistakable baritone. Mr Balaam was taking calls for me.

"Er, right, yes. Put him through, please, thank you… Phil, can we try to make this short if possible?"

"Been on to The Westcliffe. They've re-booked for the sixth of March. Same price, same times."

"Ah, good, look forward to that."

"Incidentally, he mentioned a number you did called 'Woman of Gold' or something. Is that your own composition? Apparently it went down well."

"Hell, I wish!" I was crestfallen. "Sorry to disappoint, no, we only got it off last Wednesday. It's T.Rex's new single!"

"Orrrrh, pity, I was hoping you'd created a masterpiece. What's it called?"

"'Hot Love'. Look out for it, it's gonna be big. Can I sell you a copy?"

"Not likely! It's not in the charts yet, is it?"

"No, released on Friday."

"Julius Pam. Like Chalk and Cheese: easy to sell, but don't always please. Well, you did a great job in Clacton. I have a feeling you'll be back there several times, and take 'Hot Love' with you when you go."

He was right, we were booked to appear there again on five more occasions through to June, and his poetry rang true, a reminder not to sail close to the wind with Fisher again.

You're the finest, loveliest, tenderest, and most beautiful person I have ever know — and even that is an understatement.
F. Scott Fitzgerald

Chapter 25
Alana

SO ON WEDNESDAY it was on the road again for five days and back to RAF Lakenheath for thirty decimal pounds, our seventh visit there. A slightly different audience, but I was totally distracted by the same attractive American woman who'd briefly blessed me with her presence on Sunday. She appeared late into that night's performance. Sitting at a table to the left of our set up she was almost fixated and apparently on her own. As our final set ended I almost rushed to unload the Strat, determined to introduce myself before she left, but there was no need, she came to me.

As I turned she was already standing close, the fragrance of her perfume tantalizing. "Hello, I like you," was her opening line.

"You're very attractive," I said tentatively.

She gently laid both hands on my shoulders, whispering, "You're attracting me."

The chemistry between us was near-seismic and her body up close as she whispered in my ear: "I want you to make love to me. Tonight."

Hesitation rang loud. *The exclusive rule book! I'm committed.* A brief silence interrupted our powerful union.

"I have to drive everyone home, now. But I'd love to return and fulfill your wish. Would you like that?"

She smiled. "You can come to my place, my bed. Would *you* like *that?*"

I was completely entranced. She had an almost magical delivery.

"How do I find you?"

"Come." She took my hand and together we walked slowly beyond the club entrance and out into the cool midnight air.

"This is where I want you to come." She pressed a hand-written note into my jeans pocket. "It's halfway up the hill, on the right. There's a sign."

"Give me time. Ninety minutes maybe?"

"I'll be waiting. I want you." Her seductive kiss opened my senses even further as she held her leg high on mine. Passion was beyond restraint; she was sensual, hot, and infinitely desirable.

As she walked away in those high heels, pausing to look back, I started to wonder if I could live up to her expectations. I certainly wanted to try. As if she knew what

I was thinking, she smiled, leaned down and removed her most treasured underwear.

"I hope these are an incentive for you to make love to me. Return them later."

I walked almost at a sprint back into the club. How could I encourage them all to make haste for the journey home?

"Where's John?" I asked.

"Gone off with a sumptuous black girl."

"Where to?"

"No idea."

"Best get packed away and home," I said, randomly gathering up pieces of kit.

"What's the hurry?"

"Back to work in the morning, and we've a busy few days ahead."

There was little response and the pace frustratingly slow. Eventually, with everything packed into the Van with No Name, by some miracle of telepathy John appeared. Not an utterance from me of the experience that beckoned; discretion and concealment were my remit. After all, John was very coy about his escapade, other than a pool table and John Collins.

At 2.15a.m., that quiet and gentle hill halfway up in the dark revealed light from a single-storey window. No street lights, and I couldn't find the sign. Was this where she wanted me to come? Hesitantly, I knocked.

A gently opening door revealed the glory of her female form, dressed in a see-through negligee with auburn hair beyond her shoulders. Her beauty set my heart racing.

"You came! I'm so pleased."

The doorway embrace was charged with passion. She was my height, in her mid-twenties, an incredibly sexy female.

"Come to my bed."

She led me down a hallway into a room with a double bed. The mattress was covered by a single sheet scattered with pillows. Her bedroom was bathed in subtle red light from a shaded lamp, and colourful curtains hung open each side of the window.

"I won't be a minute," she whispered.

As I waited, I noticed a framed black and white family photograph standing on the bedside cabinet. There was a chest, and a few other personal items lying around. The only decoration on the plain walls was a large, framed, colourful image of a Balinese girl hanging over the bed head.

She returned, naked, and gently held her tender body close.

"What's your name?"

"Alana. And you?"

"Andy."

The lust was overwhelming as she stripped me naked. I had never experienced anything oral, ever; it was incredibly erotic as I stood in awe of her. She kissed her way up to my lips as I slowly ran my hands down her irresistible body.

"I want you to spank me," she whispered longingly. We kissed passionately again, and she nudged me onto the bed, gently laying herself over me, looking back, waiting. I caressed her beautiful form.

"Like this?"

"Harder – please," she said submissively.

"Like this, Alana?"

"Yes, please – Sir"

I could hardly contain myself. Unshackled sensations were racing through my soul. She was breathing heavily after every stroke, lifting me even higher.

I was craving to be inside her and she wanted me there, raising herself and pushing me onto the bed. "I want you badly," she said, and with unrestrained passion mounted me, riding with her hands on my torso. I had never experienced this position before; it was blissful, feeling her, watching her... but I had a craving to take control, rolling her over. Everything was so spontaneous, natural, easy, seamless. She was so wonderfully wet and warm. I could feel her body taught with sexual tension as she moaned in pleasure, her hands were gripping my back as she released a cascade of pent-up sexual energy, unable to hold back as I rode her to a monumental climax.

Never in my most vivid fancy could I dream of a night like this. At that moment I had come of age, like an inexperienced young male finding a new dawn. Alana was my saviour.

We lay together, gazing up at the ceiling, hands clasped. "Are all Englishmen like you?" she asked.

"I wouldn't know."

"Well, if they are, I'm moving to England."

She was playing with flattery, and I loved it. As she walked, naked, to the kitchen for drinks, I pulled her knickers from my jeans pocket. She returned with red wine.

"Were you looking for these?" I said suggestively.

She sighed and smiled. "God, I need you again."

In just one sip of that wine she had me hard once more and full of an energy I didn't know I possessed. She was incredible, and I didn't want this to end.

"Ride me from behind, please," she begged.

It was seductive, almost pornographic... and a new experience. I felt in total control of her as I pulled her shoulders towards me. Spanking her while we were coupled seemed to set her passion on fire as she delivered emotion with every motion. It lasted, she was leading and I followed to every position she suggested. I knew nothing of such heightened sensual experience until that night.

All wonders cease in time. Finally, exhausted, we slept, Alana lying with her head on my shoulder and one leg resting over mine. Her warmth against me soothing as we drifted off into a deep wonderland, oblivious of time.

The room was serene, tranquil, almost protective of our love making when I awoke. God, what was the time? It was dark through the open curtains. In the dim light I reached down to my watch on the floor: 6 a.m.

Peaceful and beautiful, Alana lay beside me. I lay thoughtful of her imaginative and intelligent personality and blessed to wake in her presence. Should I quietly dress and leave her to rest? But if I did, how could I arrange to see her again?

"Alana… Alana," I said quietly.

She stirred, her crystal blue eyes slowly opening.

"Andy – you're here."

"How could I leave without saying how much I enjoyed you?"

She rolled passionately onto my side. "Do you have to go?"

"I have work this morning. I need to go home and change to be ready."

"Can I have you for the next hour? Please."

"Do you want to make love?"

"Can we talk first and then make love?"

"Over drinks and something tasty perhaps."

"Me perhaps?" she said in fun. "OK, I'll go get something else to arouse you."

She walked to the kitchen, naked; my eyes following her, obsessed with her every movement. She returned with some newfangled Pringles and more wine.

We settled, sitting upright at the top of the bed. "Are all American women like you?"

"I wouldn't know." She smiled.

"I can't imagine there could possibly be anyone better," I said gently.

She caressed my most responsive hardware. "Would you like to try me again, maybe tonight?" she requested, optimistically.

"I'd love to. But we're out tonight and every night until Sunday. I could see you in the daytime then, or Monday evening."

There was disappointment owning her expression. With sadness in her voice, she said, "I'm returning to the States Friday."

"For how long!"

"Permanently."

A chill came over me. I was almost possessed by Alana. The thought of not seeing... not having her again, froze my senses.

"So you're not returning, ever?"

"I think it's unlikely."

I was devoid of words.

"I'm sorry, really sorry." I could see tears in her eyes. There was a long pause. "Do you want to shower before you go?"

"With you? Yes."

Passion was alive again as we bathed each other gently. The sex was emotional, filled with tenderness and feeling. My affection for her went beyond a one-night stand. There was so much synergy binding us. I needed her.

"Can I have your address?" she asked, and gave me pen and paper. "Write me back when you can. I'll always want you. If only I had found you sooner." She paused, then added softly, "I'll never forget this night."

We embraced at the door. As I was leaving, she held her arms so tightly around me.

"I will write back to you, I promise," I said.

"And I will have sex with you every night in my dreams," she whispered. There was a tear on her cheek as we parted.

I looked back as I closed the gate. She looked lonely. "'Bye," I said quietly, and turned to leave.

The walk to the van was almost heartbreaking. I sat with my head in hands for a moment. There were so many things I should have asked; perhaps I was still naïve when it came to women and didn't understand the complexities of emotion. It was 7.45, dawn was breaking, I had to get home for work. I should have been feeling exalted after a life-changing night with beauty personified. But instead I was tired and empty as I travelled along that long road lined with Breckland Pines, and feeling as lonely as I had ever felt at any time in my life. At work that morning I barely functioned. I was still full of Alana, pining to hold, to feel, to speak to her again.

Arriving home that afternoon, I fumbled through the pockets of my jeans. The address she gave me the night before was still there. I read it over again, on the flip-side a telephone number. A lifeline, perhaps. Was it her number? I had to try. There was no answer, but she was working today, I knew. I rang again just before leaving the house early that evening, still unsure.

This time the answer came. "Hello." Instantly, her voice summoned my emotions.

"Alana, it's Andy."

"Andy – I couldn't stop thinking of you." Her voice was broken.

"I'll try to come see you before you leave, if you want me to?"

There was a long pause and then she responded, "I'm to

be married when I return home."

Devastation was instant. I was crumbling in the fall.

"Are you still there, Andy?"

"Yes… I'm just….. Do you really want to get married?"

I could hear tears in her voice as she replied, "I'm not sure. I haven't been sure for a long time. But I do have to go back. I must."

"We have to stay in touch. You're so special."

"I want you so much, I'm craving for you right now," she said tenderly.

"We'll see each other again, I'm sure of that. I have to go now. Safe journey, Alana. Write to me and I'll write back. I must go."

Our call ended, and I stood in silence for a while. *Would I ever meet her again? I could only wish and hope.*

Our performance at RAF Bawdsey that night was a complete blank. I can't remember the venue or a thing that happened while we were there. I was totally preoccupied, solemn even. On the way home, though, there was a memorable moment as we travelled the narrow road beside the Orwell Estuary on our way to Woodbridge. Little conversation radiated, and what there was I was completely detached from. It was very dark, a low mist was drifting across the road off the estuary. There was an eerie calm outside.

Dave was in the front passenger seat. "You're quiet tonight, Andy. Anything wrong?"

"Just distracted at the moment."

Dave's remit was to keep me awake. "What about a joke then?"

"I couldn't find one even if I tried."

Suddenly, from nowhere, a voice yelled out from the

gloom. "A headless horseman, crossing the road… up there ahead, in the mist!"

There was disbelieving silence from the rest of us. Until! Jamie suggested. "Maybe he didn't want to be recognised!"

We didn't stop to see if he was alright, the headless horseman that is. It was spine-chilling.

Another six bookings came and went in regimental procession, without a thought or care. On the last day of the month we were back again at the Tower Ballroom, Yarmouth. I had felt under the weather during the day, and that evening was feverish with a sore throat. I managed to get through the night with minimal fuss and plenty of drink but vowed to visit my doctor the next day. I had a good idea what was wrong.

> **Live life, see it through.**
> **Carry on, it's all you can do.**
> Ray Davies

Chapter 26
Morris Jump Jet

Monday 1st March

THAT MORNING I rang Ray to let him know I was under the weather, seeing my doctor later and wouldn't be in that day. He was fine, "Let me know how you do" his passing words.

The appointment confirmed tonsillitis and the need for Penicillin for a week at least. A sick note was offered. I declined, as I wouldn't have got paid anyway, and simply stated the need to be back to normal by Wednesday. There were an upcoming four bookings in four days.

"I doubt you'll feel top of the world by then," doctor Green warned. "I'd advise you to lay low until you're fully recovered."

He knew I would reject that advice. Tonsillitis was the bane of my life when I was young, quinsies and all. I had been cheerfully free of any symptoms in recent years but not stunned by their return. I travelled to work the next day. The medication was having a fair-to-positive effect and I knew I wouldn't be stretched during working hours. No rehearsals were scheduled that week; we had been busy and ahead was the same.

A detour to visit Dave on the journey home from work that Tuesday demanded a social call, you could say. He was on the road in front of his home, standing by a Morris Traveller and radiating delight in my unannounced arrival.

"Andy," he called, "I've just bought a car!" It looked splendid, handsome, in green and wood. He melodiously magnified its attributes for a half an hour. "I can go visit Angie more often now and stay over." It delivered a new independence for him. He was undoubtedly pleased, and I was pleased for him, but it did add another, uncertain dimension. It didn't seem the best time to mention my health concerns.

Wednesday 3rd March

RAF Wittering, home of the Jump Jet, was our call that night, nearly two hours from home on the Great North Road. I was feeling confident I could get through without trauma and felt reasonably well after pumping myself with penicillin as we left. The six of us were greeted by the familiar promotional poster on entry, 'East Anglia's Top Pop Group', along with mention of the support act. Perhaps we were growing accustomed to this status and modestly confident we could go some way to living up to that billing.

On the dance floor everything was electrifying and sunny, particularly with the material we had. 'Hot Love' had still only reached 17 in the charts by then, that and 'Strange Kind of Woman' were so fresh and held us on a high. Girls in the audience were fascinated, fascinating and attractive, but I was totally focused on getting through the night. Relieved to unplug the Strat by the end, I was wondering if the aftershock of missing Alana was having a negative effect.

Five of us swiftly disappeared; I knew what delights had lassoed their attention. Exhausted, I sat just behind our stage equipment but in view of the main hall. I was desperate to sleep, but beauty is never far from reach. A pretty young true blonde, probably just taller than me, slim and about my age, walked up onto the stage and without hesitation or introduction mounted my lap, openly announcing what she would like me to do to her and what she was planning to do to me. Her fragrance was enticing. God, what temptation. Could I resist? Any other time there would have been no hesitation, she was very attractive. But I was low. "Could I just say, you are incredibly desirable but I'm not too well tonight. Maybe next time." She had a look of disappointment and walked away without comment. I was dejected but Alana was still filling my head and I just wanted to get home.

I had made it clear there should be no delay in making tracks that night, to at least give some chance of recovering enough for the next night's performance. After all, the rule book was in full operational demand by then. Jamie had disappeared with a girl in blonde by this time. I was not surprised girls were magnetically attracted to him. I discovered later he had a mission to complete as he was alcoholically disengaged, and to make amends had arranged to rendezvous with her 30 minutes northward the following night.

The statutory half-hour post-performance R&R had passed – and more. John reappeared first. "How are you feeling?" he asked.

"Not great."

"We'd better get packed away."

"I'll bring the covers from the van." I walked out into the clean night air, opening the sliding door on one side of the transit.

Shock and in awe!

Dave was with not one, but two, girls in the back on top of those covers. His sex-god status was permanently restored in my eyes. But my short comment was less than sympathetic. Without a word of warning he leapt out of the van like a raging tiger on top of my floundering stature and tried to beat the hell out of my unprepared frame. Fortunately, Clive and Richard arrived almost instantly and my integrity remained intact. I knew Dave was short-fused but that was completely unforeseen. A frost formed between us right there and then. We did try to make amends later, but although the ice was thin, it never thawed completely.

So our successful and colourful performance had turned a little grey. Pity.

Thursday 4th March

I arrived home at around 4 a.m. on Thursday, completely bushed. Mum appeared around my bedroom door at eight and reminded me of the time. I asked her to telephone Ray and explain I wouldn't be in that morning. Thursday was half-day anyway and usually near-devoid of any customers, so there would be no pay for Monday or today but I needed the rest. I spent the morning and early afternoon in bed sleeping, on and off, the journey with Alana reflected in those waking moments. Penicillin had all but cleared my head by late afternoon, and I rang John to confirm I was OK for Spitelgate that night.

We set off early on the two-and-a-half-hour journey to a different sort of RAF base, a Women's Royal Air Force Depot responsible for the recruitment and training of all non-commissioned females in the RAF. I'll leave the rest to your vivid imagination. Clive was overwhelmed by two Military Maidens from the Midlands. I lay low. God knows what the rest got up to, except for Jamie who'd completed his amorous mission with the girl from Wittering, looking totally sober and with that familiar cool smile on his return. There were two more bookings to complete that week and our return to Club America was the next day.

Friday 5th March

Two weeks had flown since that eternal night with Alana. Her personality and profile held my conscience without release. I just didn't want to let go, hoping a letter would appear from afar on the hall table as I passed every morning. Distractions however, were always close at hand.

Club America beckoned, our first time there on a Friday night. John, searching fervently through the *Evening News*, revealed Fisher's curfew had been lifted at last, our name appearing in a Norwich venue promotion within a Norwich newspaper for the first time since Christmas. But… Dave hadn't arrived. He was coming on his own in the Traveller.

The tension was rising as our opening raced closer. I was on edge and we discussed playing without him. Vic the manager anxiously appealed for us to start but there was still no sign of Dave. My main concern was our credibility.

We had only just surfaced from deep water with Fisher; how would this rebound? I had no doubt our favour would fall once again, and another lifeboat would be launched. By now Vic was giving me a hard time, so forty minutes beyond our curtain call we decided to go on without our bass player. But by some miracle of chance Dave appeared through the main entrance in the nick of time. He looked dishevelled, not to say a little dirty, his hands smeared with grease and usually well-groomed hair completely out of character. Having been exposed to a Spanish Inquisition-style ordeal by Vic, my greeting to our missing bassist was less than supportive.

"Where the heck have you been?"

"Bloody Morris broke down! I had to do some roadside repairs and get a jump start."

"Christ, we thought something drastic had happened. You could have rung and let us know."

"Haven't got the telephone number."

"Use the operator!"

I sensed he was less than impressed with my sentiments. We did get going, eventually, Dave still bearing remnants of his brush with mechanical mayhem. After we'd completed that night's performance I detected a touch of coolness in Vic's demeanor as we left. Julius Pam didn't appear at Club America again after that night; we never got to know the reason why. It could have been for letting Fisher down again, or possibly related to the number of times we had performed there in just over five months, some eight appearances. Maybe Fisher and Beevis considered we needed a sabbatical, who knows.

The potential and disconcerting outcome from all of this was I might have unintentionally driven the wedge between Dave and me a little deeper. I was learning of his sensitive character as time progressed. As it turned out we saw less of Dave after that. The new-found independence provided by the Morris probably contributed to this, and some rehearsals were missed as he was unavailable. Perhaps his enthusiasm was beginning to wane.

So could we have been losing favour with Norwich Artistes in general? Well it didn't appear so. We were still relatively busy, and whenever I spoke to Phil his enthusiasm remained unchanged. A return to The Beachcomer, Clacton the following night was an ideal antidote for any ailments that emerged from Club America.

Phil's call on Monday to John confirmed he hadn't lost faith, confirming two more dates at Clacton and further venues in April and May. My tenure in the record department was becoming accepted and I was beginning to take on a part-of-the-wallpaper reputation. I felt more confident and actually given the responsibility of ordering stock! However, there was a downside. The details were excruciatingly scrutinized and adjusted before the order forms were sanctioned by Mr B. Sales were on the up in the department and I do believe the sun was breaking through for me with Mr Balaam, or Albert as he was known in his absence. I was enjoying the work and challenge, but so far there was no reward for my endeavour other than keeping the job, and miraculously there was no sign of getting the sack. The truly fulfilling part of my work was when sales reps came in to reveal the new and on-the-horizon releases. I was learning at a rapid pace, there was so much to take in, and all without any tuition, other than Ray's occasional input. Record retailing was all about coming from a rubbish pulverizing background, it appears.

I was beginning to understand how the record industry

promoted anything and everything: the splendid, the terrible and the hideous, if you like. There were so many flops. The reduced-to-beyond-reduction box of totally unsaleable singles on the counter was evidence it takes more than poor production, void of any real play-me-again content, and just occasionally downright terrible musical ability, to succeed. All but one of those singles had the magic element missing somewhere; some made my eyes water, some were nearly but not quite. There were a number of Smoke's single, 'Dreams of Dreams', already in that box.

This was, in my eyes, one of those nearly-but-not-quite productions. Great drummer, good vocals and bass work, but the lead guitar element seemed to lack invention and creativity, devoid of the great sounds available from those tone-bender boxes that so many truly accomplished guitarists relied on during, in my opinion, the iconic age of rock guitar. The production too appeared a little lacking in depth. Record critic, Andy? Well, I'm sure I'm going to take a lot of flak for that, and the quality of my own guitar playing thrown to the dogs. But, remember, groups were often cuttingly critical of other groups and their peers. A classic example was a support group to The Kinks insisting the headliners were crap and boasting "we blew them off the stage". Despite such brazen self-regard, it's important to note they didn't make it. I think that probably added to my inward lack of self-confidence when a guitar was strapped over my shoulder, perhaps I was too sensitive. You had to be thick-skinned in those days. Or just thick, I guess.

But the one single on the Polydor label that stood out in that box of no sales, and that I had paid little attention to before, was by future Glam Rock giants Slade, titled, 'Know Who You Are'. I wondered why this had not at least charted; it was good enough and I was curious about who they were.

With no rehearsal again that week, conscious that no new material had been added to our stage set since early February, I went in search of potential upcoming blockbusters to vary our repertoire. Harrison's 'What Is Life' was given an outing during an earlier rehearsal, and although we got the complete song off, it didn't strike a chord, didn't gel – perhaps the first time ever we had a failure in our production line. A group I had never heard of, The Sweet, later to become icons of Glam Rock, appeared in the lower reaches of the chart that week. But 'Funny, Funny', written by Chinn and Chapman, failed to spark my Spangle or to fit my remit of the group's identity. Too poppy, too 'Sugar Sugar', by far. But hang on, perhaps we could do something with this… increase the tempo, a lot, give it a raw feel, delete those corny dabs on the keyboard, keep it basic, add singular heavy-fuzz downward strokes to each word in the 'Ah ah' bit and extend the break/pauses by a second or two. But the lyrics didn't fit the surgery so I decided to give it a miss for the time being. Perhaps just as well in view of what happens later in this story.

Friday 12th March

Another four bookings in four days. Oakington for the second time on Thursday, and then we were on our way to the Metro Club, Colchester for our third visit. It was the 12th March, my birthday, the first time any of us had celebrated a birthday during our journey. I was modestly cool about it all, apart from being accused of being ancient by John and Jamie, having left my teens by now and probably in need of a complete overhaul.

The club was on the High Street near Williams and Griffin, and underground. Richard and Clive were delighted – not! – to haul the equipment down a barrel ramp round the back and into the cellar. Despite the request for no alcohol, I was plied with drinks that night, never sure of the ingredients, but I did survive a very rare encounter on stage with delusions of grandeur. They certainly freed up my playing style and prompted a comment from John, "You're improving." 'Liberated' was probably a better definition.

As the club often had a military presence from the Garrison in town, we were offered a level protective assurance that should anything get out of hand the burly and menacing bouncer would step in and defend our quarter. The journey homeward that night was nothing less than extraordinarily exacerbated by my attempt at recovery from the 'splosh' I had been tanked with. The humour was at full throttle, and twice I couldn't drive for the pain of laughter and the sheer bonkers flow of madcap lyrics that Clive was particularly masterful at concocting. Dave, Jamie, John and Richard all adding bizarre, insane, nonsensical lines, which made the whole thing totally and absurdly Monty Python.

"There was once a big man with a mangle, who had a very big handle, he fell off the edge of a cliff, and came back with a very large quiff." Yes, I had the same problem; Richard got it in the end, but it took three months!

I guess I should butt in here with a warning: 'Don't drink and drive'! It's not good for your health. In those days it was commonplace, and many suffered the consequences.

Saturday 13th March

Thank god for sanity was jangling my conscious as I walked, knackered, into the shop that morning. Saturdays were busier by now, takings were up and stock slowly becoming more mass market. I loved this job and all that connected me with customers and the music scene. The challenge was inspiring, and Mr Balaam's excruciatingly modest, grunted approval on cashing up at least added in to feel-good factor as I was leaving.

RAF Sculthorpe, a USAF base, was our destination that night, our second visit there. Strange, so good to be working but I was disappointed not to be appearing at a more notable venue. There was a bonus however, the fee was higher than most on the native circuit. Not that we didn't have a good night, we did, but I never felt the jubilation I was getting accustomed to on the way home on many Saturday nights, and I think everyone else was of the same opinion. All seemed rather mundane. To instill a sense of euphoria before we travelled home, a unanimous localized election result demanded 'Castle Hill, we're starving'. John was busy again filling the pages of the biography he was to write if he reached ninety; his collection of posters and all that went with our appearances was growing weekly.

There was an imaginative and creative side to John that perhaps we hadn't fully tapped into. After all, he had once been part of a group whose members wore crazy make-up and thought nothing of brandishing naked flames on the stage. I had a strong feeling we needed to unleash qualities like that, in whatever form, if we were to stand out from so many others on the circuit with us.

Arriving at Beefy's in the dead of night, we were obliged to join the queue. Ahead was the banter of Brummie voices. Clearly another group. This one had a presence. But, you know, not all group musicians were openly friendly. They could be very aloof sometimes, but not on this occasion. The shortest of the group of four, standing at the front of the queue, greeted us with, "Where 'ave yow lot bin at tonight 'en?"

Jamie, in his usual all-friendly and laid back style, responded, "Oh, nowhere special, RAF Sculthorpe, entertaining Americans. Where have you been?"

"The Garla."

From there the conversation came alive. What a friendly bunch of Brummies they were, even if I wasn't totally sure what they were saying all the time. But none of us mentioned names, group or personal.

We parted amicably, and the tallest of the four said, "Mighbe we'll see yow agen sumtoime."

Our route out of Norwich took us past the Gala Ballroom on St Stephens Road. Curious, I pulled up outside and the poster read 'Saturday, Slade'. By pure coincidence, the single that had attracted my attention five days earlier now completed my vision of Slade, a group I had never heard of until then. Jamie was proving to be the most approachable of us all, very informal, and would make the perfect publican, I thought. A bit young though, at that time.

USAF Bentwaters on Sunday found us drifting home again in the early hours of Monday morning, and we were to return there again the following Friday. There was another busy mid-week ahead.

Home life by this time was good and the burden I had been to my family was lifting. I was in a job I enjoyed and my Mum and Dad approved of; this and the success of the group all married so well together. I probably had never felt happier in my life. Conversation around the table at meal times was so often full of laughter and happy talk. Gertrude remained abandoned between the sheds behind the house. I felt resigned to selling her. The ad was to appear the following week, but when the time came no one was interested and she stood forlorn and unwanted.

Poor Gertrude, an imposter had stolen her limelight.

Saturday 20th March

Eye Town Hall. Our second visit there, and it didn't disappoint. Another one of those venues it was great to be part of. The fun of all that surrounded the group at times was also great. Angie often coming with us in the van. And what fun she was, a lovely sense of humor and not a bad singing voice, joining in with the merrymaking and laughter that so often featured on the way home. The real transformation though was in our roadies. They had become confident, bold and hungry – for girls. Seeking out any who expressed interest or curiosity in the group during our performance, chatting them up and then disappearing. That night, opening the van before loading, a pair of knickers was evidence for the prosecution. No one owned up, someone claiming they "didn't wear those type of knickers", or colour. While we were slaving on-stage, good times were evidently rolling in the back of the van. It was blatantly obvious we were in competition with a pair of Randy Roadies. No wonder they were often too s—d to help pack away.

**You can't stay the same. If
you're a musician and a singer,
you have to change, that's how
it works.**
Van Morrison

Chapter 27
Horizontalitis

I'M GOING TO skip about two weeks, if that's ok. There is a lot to squeeze in and I'm running out of space.

In the first week in April, after a mid-week visit to an RAF camp, there were another three venues that weekend. A return to The Regal, Wymondham on Friday, The Melody Rooms, Norwich on Saturday 3rd and Clacton again on the Sunday. Our invitation to The Melody Rooms was the first since the psychedelic Christmas Eve incident. Fisher had raised the barrier to allow us in at last. This was our fourth visit there other than the audition.

Trevor aka Walter, his undercover name, a former school friend of Dave, had been coming to bookings occasionally when the van wasn't full, otherwise by Reliant Robin. We had by then elevated his official status to road manager. There were no real responsibilities involved but it meant he got free entry. That night we called on him to defend our equipment while we were on stage. The Rooms were busy and vibrant, the crowd much closer than had been before, almost claustrophobic. The truly stark difference though was the presence of Skinheads. Their over-enthusiasm threatened the integrity of our PA, and possibly ourselves, as they expelled their aggression, bouncing around, pushing forward, along with other crazed contortions. They were probably just enjoying themselves, and perhaps gorgonzised by the stuff we were blasting at them. "Oi! Play some Reggae." Or had they heard we were on drugs and decided to help us out? Do you know, I think it was actually fun, didn't pose any real threat and the majority of our audience loved it all. Rum ole job, enit?

I met 'The Girl from September' again that night. Normality. Blissful.

After our brush with a youth subculture, Fisher confirmed, "You handled that well, boys. A good night, got you down to return on May the first." We didn't know! This was a total transformation compared to the last verbal encounter. Knocked sideways by this reaction, celebration was afoot. We polished off Dave's wine and headed for Beefy's.

The journey home without Dave and Angie but with Walter instead was less bonkers than normal. Or was it? Outside was weird, and darker than black again, as we trundled towards Fornham St Martin with just four of us in the van by then. The verge was overgrown and I could see a strange object ahead, suspended motionless above the grass. Shivers were trembling my spine, and the others didn't look to well either.

"What the hell was that?!" The van pulled up twenty yards on.

"Better go look, had we?"

"Na, it's nothing."

"No, I'm going to have a look," Walter declared boldly.

All four of us, hesitantly silent, walked in perfect line abreast toward the frightening object in the murk. As we inched closer, a freakish growling noise followed by an eerie groan emanated from the 'Thing'. Dread was at its height as we crept even closer and its form started to clear. It was kind of a white mini coned spacecraft type-thing. Suddenly, out of nowhere, it discharged a strange barking sound.

Terror reigned supreme. We shuddered to a halt.

"It's a dog! Isn't it?"

We were all in shock. The thing had a mini Mexican hat on.

But!! Below it was a body!!!

"My god, it's a dog with a Mexican hat on, sitting on a body!!!!"

"You're right!"

"Christ, is he still alive?!!!!"

Just then that weird groan repeated, and again. The former alien rose up with the expansion of the body's chest.

"Christ he IS still alive!!"

"What do we do?"

The aroma of alcohol in a sudden breeze unmasked Horizontalitis, a condition only known to exist in Fornham.

"Got to call the police."

"OK who's going to stay?"

"Me I suppose," Jamie volunteered.

"Can you three stay with him? I'll go ring the police."

So I rode off into the distant black, leaving John, Jamie and Walter to fend for themselves in the dead of the dark… dark… night. The first phone box I floundered upon was out of order, smashed up, but by a miracle of chance a Panda (no, not a real Panda!) was coming towards the van as I reached Mildenhall Road. I was flashing to get attention. (No No, not that sort of flashing!!). The Panda pulled up beside me.

"What's the problem then?

"The other side of Fornham there's this old bloke and his spacecraft flat out on the verge."

"Ow, not 'im again! You lead, we'll follow."

Back at the UFO site the Mexican dog appeared to know them. "Come on you old codger, let's get you home then," said one Plod.

"Where have you been tonight, lads?" asked the other Plod.

"Norwich."

"Oh, that explains it." I'll leave it with you to work out what he meant.

I dropped Walter off around 3a.m. in Severn Road and made for my bed.

After that out-of-body experience, sanity beckoned the next day at one of our favourite venues, The Beachcomer, Clacton-on-Sea. Our third visit, and there was always an uplifted atmosphere on the way; no one wanted to miss out, Richard and Clive particularly. Just as we were about to open with our first set, two young maidens dressed in hot pants and without an ounce of inhibition mounted the stage and demanded 'Hot Love'!

"What, now?"

"Yes please!"

Nice, I thought. John and Jamie were clearly assigned to humour, Dave's expression unmoved with Angie in the wings.

By this time Marc Bolan had been at number 1 for three weeks and we were seven weeks into performing this song. It was a heart-warming night, particularly nice in early spring, and we left safe in the knowledge we were to return again in early May. On the journey homeward I had to mention what had been on my mind for some time.

"How about getting a singer front man."

"Oh no Andy, you're doing fine. We don't need a singer," the unanimous proclamation from the back of the van. I guess I should have been flattered, but seriously, I don't think flattery had anything to do with it, more to do with how many we could squeeze in the van. There were seven of us that night.

"Well, I definitely think we should be writing our own material."

"Yeah, OK. You can do that, can't you, Andy?"

Boy, sometimes this lot. I can't break them away from all the high jinks and fun.

In my opinion we needed to find a good charismatic singer with a strong voice, someone of around our age and ready to go. For some time I had been longing to hold the Strat without the distraction of singing lead, preferring to present my profile, mysterious in its presence, playing lead solos that caught the audience's attention. I never felt possessed with the talent to do both well simultaneously.

Monday 5th April

The Monday morning fatigue at work was more pronounced than normal. After the demands of the weekend I guess that was predictable, but it lasted longer. A package arrived containing two copies of Mott the Hoople's *Wildlife* album. I'd had the Island Records sampler *Nice Enough to Eat* since 1969. Mott's track from that LP, 'At the Crossroads', always held my attention. So in a quiet moment I listened to side one of their new album.

Hunter's lyrics on the second track, 'Angel of Eighth Avenue', were perfectly formed to play my emotions. The memory of Alana flooded in, and my head filled with flashbacks to our night together. Perhaps I needed some emotion. It was seven weeks since our lovemaking and there'd been no word from her. I'd thought I was beginning to put the memories aside, but realised now they were always there, barely beneath the surface.

My sentiment was broken by the buzz of the phone; it was mid-morning. "Phil, good morning."

"You had a good three nights over the weekend! Fisher has made space for you again at the Melody Rooms on the first of May."

"Yeah, he mentioned it."

"Got some more dates for May… Eye Town Hall, the fifteenth. They love you there."

"Must be something to do with girls, Phil? There was nothing mentioned about knickers, was there?"

"What!! No, but you'll have to tell me about it sometime. Anyway, where was I? Elms Pavilion on the fourteenth, Wreningham on the twenty-second. You did OK there back in March. Tower Ballroom the twenty-third, and The Links again on the twenty-ninth. I'll update John later. Before I go, have you ever thought of writing your own stuff?"

"I'm trying. Not exactly creative as yet though."

"Well, keep trying. If it's good I may be able to get you a recording opportunity."

After a little more banter he signed off. There was always something positive in Phil's delivery. Even when things were not going well, he found a way to assemble an optimistic perspective. I began to understand, respect and believe in him. He had taken us from nothing to something – and more, perhaps. Even when we didn't repay him, he never lost faith.

I sat in reflection for some time. Hunter's lyrics soon returned. Later that day I splashed out on *Wildlife*, asking Ray for a staff discount. "Don't mention it to Albert!" he replied.

At home that night, I spent some time creating a variant of 'Angel of Eighth Avenue'. Maybe I could sing this with some meaning. A copy of Ringo Starr's 'It Don't Come Easy', gifted by a rep, didn't quite fit my remit but was better than other available options. We hadn't rehearsed for three weeks and the last new additions were back in February, so I had to go with this to Wednesday's rehearsal.

Wednesday 7th April

We crafted our version of Ringo's classic with fair ease; the lead work was undemanding, and we upped the tempo just a little to add energy, if you like. '*It will soon be your tomorrow!*'

Most of the time that evening was spent with 'Angel of Eighth Avenue'. I didn't want this to be anything less than exceptional, hoping we could reproduce that Hoople intensity. Harmonies were vital, and Jamie's input needed to back me up. It wasn't perfect. My aspirations were demanding, so we agreed to look at it again the next week. I did think we could do this but needed time to work on it.

The next morning I rang Phil instead of him contacting me. "Phil, re. our conversation about original material... what about a cover as a compromise, for starters?"

"What are you thinking of?"

"There's a song on Mott the Hoople's new album I'd love us to record. 'Angel of Eighth Avenue'."

"Oh, really? Where can I get a copy of that?"

"You'll have to go buy one, or I can flog you one at

full retail."

"Hah! OK, well, I'll see if I can borrow a copy."

"You know, it's vital the production is top notch. I won't do it if it's anything less."

"I'll speak to you about it again next week, if you like?"

"OK. Incidentally, pity you couldn't have found us something special for this Easter Saturday."

"Why?!"

"If you remember, we're back at Lakenheath. Again."

"Well, that's a good one. Never heard you complain before. It should be a good night, and anyway you're with Raymond Froggat when they return to the Links in July and I've penciled you in to support Status Quo possible in September."

"Oh, I've got no answer to that one!"

"I'll be in touch next week."

"Have a good weekend."

That was the first time I had been openly forward with Phil. Work had always been gratefully received in whatever form. So was I becoming more expectant, with a desire to raise our profile a degree or two? Perhaps I was unconsciously sending a message in our conversation that after rejecting Germany were we serious now about stepping up in a true attempt to succeed.

Easter Weekend

It had been nearly five months since I'd seen her. When the phone rang that morning, just before I set off for work, I was surprised and charmed to hear a soft familiar voice.

"It's Emily here, how are you?"

"Emily – nice surprise! I'm fine, and you?"

"Yes, life is good. Daniel and I are to be married in May."

"Oh. Congratulations."

"So, tell me about your adventures."

We spoke for some time, more than I had time for, Emily explaining what had been happening in her life recently.

"We're planning to move abroad after the wedding, possibly to Italy. So I am to be married and entertainment is paramount at any wedding reception, don't you think?"

"I totally agree. I would, of course."

"What are you up to on Saturday the twenty-eighth of May?"

"Oh, just a sec, I'll get my diary." My euphoria plummeted. "Oh, we're already booked, Cromer Links. I am sorry."

"What a pity, I was so looking forward to the moment that you played our first dance." She wished me "Good luck in whatever you do, Andy. As my uncle once said, live life and be happy."

It was hugely disappointing, another chapter in my life closing. I never saw or was blessed to speak with Emily again.

USAF bases were an acquired taste, weekend dates usually more rewarding, and this was our first visit to Lakenheath since that February date with Alana. I felt a sharp jab of emotion as we pulled up at security, another reminder of how deep my feelings for her were. It was back to the Airman's Club where our Yankee journey had started in September. So, an Easter Saturday and an American audience with a will to celebrate; it turned out to be one of our enjoyable nights on stage entertaining overseas personnel. "It should be a good night," said Phil. He was right. They looked after us, and a late finish demanded midnight breakfast again. With no need to awake early that morning, we made a feast of it.

Easter Sunday

The Tower Ballroom, Great Yarmouth. This was our

fourth appearance there in four months and our fifth overall. A venue that was becoming familiar, and I suffered none of those intense nerves experienced on that first visit. 'It Don't Come Easy' by Ringo was received with rapturous applause and the place was lively with holiday weekend festivity.

So that quieter-than-normal April allowed space for creative thinking; the rehearsal had been cancelled that week, The Centa unavailable. Perfecting 'Angel of Eighth Avenue' again would have to wait until the following week, providing everyone was available. It was an ideal time for a pause. We had come so far but never found ourselves. Perhaps we should stop for a couple of months, find a meaningful stage presence and musical identity of our own, and then go out there again truly formed. After all, we were self-sufficient, no longer insolvent, not totally reliant on the income from bookings. Two months could be enough, but we'd need to convince Beevis this was worthwhile. If I detached myself from the distraction of the group, could I immerse myself in an attempt at writing good material?

I was sixteen on that warm summer's day in '67 as I wandered through the Abbey Gate and into a lost world, the breeze caressing my soul as a majestic blonde maiden walked towards me in the distance… Some memories never fade. Could I write a lyric about that moment? I spent a couple of nights that week playing around with ideas. It had to be good, with a magic that captivates and holds a lasting memory, provoking a longing to return and listen to the song, again and again. The best inspiration is always spontaneous.

We were back on the road on Friday, The Grafton Club, RAF Marham, and a return to The TA Pad, Leiston on Saturday; nothing too taxing in journey time, but still arriving home in the early hours, for whatever reason. That weekend I began to feel unusually fatigued after bookings, and slept for hours beyond normal on Sunday. I didn't put it down to anything concerning at that time.

Monday's guaranteed call from Phil came on time that morning. "Just spoken to John – I may change the dates on the seventh and eighth of May. You're currently at Pinebanks on the Friday and RAF Coltishall on the Saturday. Could send you to Birmingham on those dates… let you know as soon as. Also on the first – I'm changing that. You'll be headlining at the Gala, managed to get Status Quo for The Melody Rooms that night in a late change to their schedule."

"Oh. OK," spoken with a level of disappointment. Anyway, we hadn't played at the Gala before, so it was something new, I thought.

"Any more thoughts about a recording opportunity, Phil?"

"These date changes may have some influence on that, bear with me."

I felt weary and lethargic again a couple of times at work that week, on one occasion falling asleep at a quiet moment. When I came round I'd been out for around thirty minutes.

The Rolling Stones' 'Brown Sugar' had entered the charts that week. We just had to get this off, it was magical, spellbinding, and completely boxed for us at that moment. Rehearsals, on Wednesday centred on the Birmingham possibility and our need for new material. I also presented 'My Brother Jake', an unreleased single by Free, which I'd persuaded a Rep to 'lend' me. We spent all that night's rehearsal adding these to our set list. Great songs, both of them, so new and current. There was no time left to work on 'Angel of the Eighth Avenue' and no rush. Time and patience on this were much more important.

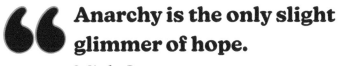

Anarchy is the only slight glimmer of hope.
Mick Jagger

Chapter 28
Sweet Pavilion

Friday 23th April
IPSWICH MANOR BALLROOM. We were under strict instruction to arrive no later than 6.30 p.m. and we did. Guess what? There was no one there. We tried the door twice, it was locked. Twice. The glazed cabinet outside at eye height, just to the right of the door, was adorned by the promo poster boldly proclaiming '**Julius Pam, East Anglia's Number 1 Pop Band**'. We had arrived, in Ipswich, for the first time. It was a dry, warm day. Walter, Dave and I stood outside wondering, we are expected but perhaps

they forgot? I was nervous of this venue, having heard a lot about those who had appeared there. Run by Nanda and Ron Lesley, The Bluesville Club in the 1960s entertained names to drool over: John Mayall, Rod Stewart, Christine Perfect, Cream, Eric Clapton!, Fleetwood Mac, Taste, Jethro Tull, Spencer Davis… the list was inspiring. And here we were, headlining there on a Friday. If we could get in, of course. Nanda and Ron moved in influential circles within the London music scene; I just hoped we'd live up to their expectations. I wondered what Beevis had been announcing to our hosts. Whatever it was it must have been more than our weight could carry. Surely. Or was it we were getting favourable feedback from his clientele and he felt confident in placing us in such educated surroundings?

Eventually someone emerged to unlock the door but, strangely, I have little recollection now of our night there other than the Caribbean flavour and the support disco having massive speakers, nearly as tall as a double-decker, pumping out reggae base, but little else. The vibrations were earth-shattering. I do remember the dance floor being full in front of us later on, and Walter and John in conversation with a lady, and that's about it. Sorry to disappoint if you were expecting a full rundown of the place and how we were received. I think we went home fairly content and I'm pretty sure we had nothing thrown at us.

Saturday 24th April

Another routine night at Cromer, Royal Links Pavilion – or so we thought! Beevis hadn't given us the lowdown on who we were supporting, but that didn't deter my mindset. As I've mentioned before, I loved this place. The first thing to catch my eye as we walked in was the poster proclaiming: 'Next Week Thin Lizzy'. Oh well, missed that one. The early bustle of preparation was evident as we entered the main hall. The group we were supporting were already on stage to the left and didn't appear to have any roadies. They were a striking-looking bunch but made no attempt at a greeting or introduction. In fact the atmosphere was decidedly cool; maybe that was something to do with tension before a performance. I didn't pay much attention, retreating to the dressing room and then off for a drink. On my way back to the stage, curious about who we were with that night, I tracked down the poster: so this was The Sweet. That song 'Funny Funny' I had rejected back in March had reached number 14 in the charts, and was the last record I'd sold before leaving for Cromer earlier. Coincidences, they are strange, aren't they?

The Pavilion was still quiet, as if anticipating a multitude. Just a scattering of staff around, Sweet, and us. I picked up the Strat to tune her in. Their lead guitarist (Andy Scott) was on-stage setting up at the same time. As always I plugged her in and set the Fuzz. She sounded just perfect in my eyes, a reflection of the many influences that had grabbed me over time.

Almost immediately, Andy Scott walked meaningfully over and candidly opened in rapid speak. "Do you wanna sell it?"

It caught me off guard. I was curt in reply. "No chance, I'd never part with her!"

"How old is it?"

"Sixty two." (1962)

"What's the fuzz?"

"Oh, it's just a Mayfair – really suits this old guitar."

"So you don't wanna sell it then?"

"Definitely not!"

He turned and walked away, short but not so Sweet.

"Speak later if you like?" I said, voice raised.

There was no reply. Their drummer (Mick Tucker) was running around his kit, so Scott probably didn't hear me. It wasn't the warmest, most embracing conversation I'd ever had, but musicians can be a strange bunch at times.

We kicked that night off with our established stuff. There was something about the sound up there on that Cromer stage, and judging by the mood of my band mates it always sounded good, but of course we hadn't a clue what it sounded like out there amongst the masses. As far as I know, Richard and Clive never complained.

There was always a good atmosphere at the Links. I have no doubt this was the case every week and not once were there any signs of a disturbance, well, at least when we were there. A punch-up appeared to be a collector's item. Pop music wasn't to the taste of everyone who regularly came to the Links, I guess, but actually much of our material by then had a leaning towards contemporary, so it did have cross-over appeal. There were undoubtedly more talented acts featured there, but maybe we were asked back because the young audience enjoyed dancing to what we presented them with. Whatever the reason, I always felt good when we came off-stage.

During our break, I joined Walter for a drink and watched Sweet perform. They were very solid and well-rehearsed. Mick Tucker was a driving force, Andy Scott a good lead, Brian Connolly an ideal front man. Their stage dress wasn't at that time anything special and they weren't wild on stage, polished perhaps, but didn't blow me away. It was their later Glam makeover that doubtless added the final magic ingredient. But the one thing that really did stand out, and Walter commented on, was Steve Priest's bass work. The depth of sound he contributed was significant and delivered a dimension Julius Pam hadn't, as yet, truly found.

The magic moment for me, though, came in the form of the pretty young teenager who confronted us, standing there with pen in hand and one of our photo-card flyers. "Can I have your autograph?" she asked politely.

This wasn't the first time either… but to establish a true perspective, there was only one other occasion, at Eye Town Hall. Fame just don't come easy.

"Yeah, of course."

"Can you sign it on the back, I don't want to spoil the photo."

She presented the reverse side. To my dismay I was not the first of her requests; John and Jamie's signatures were already there. Anyway, I was still honoured and at least third in line, unless of course Dave was nowhere to be found, so I was the only other alternative. The pretty teenager appeared delighted as she walked away.

So if you are reading this, remember that moment and still have those signatures, I would love to hear from you. Walter's grumpy comment: "You'll be insufferable for weeks."

By the time we reached Cromer that night, attraction to the opposite sex had become almost as important as our performance on stage to some, and a significant part of the reason we were out there. I could sense Sweet were singing from the same hymn sheet. Deeper into the night, as always, we all loosened up and were probably at our best by then, that new material having an impact. Richard and Clive were visibly preoccupied with anything of shapely form, no doubt planning some conquest beyond curtain fall. But Dave, well, he didn't look himself, and started to make signals to Richard, concerned about the whereabouts of Angie. The roadies both disappeared, a crisis perhaps. I didn't pay a lot of attention and neither did Jamie or John. Carry on, regardless! And the dance floor was packed.

As we came off-stage, Dave didn't follow us back to the dressing room. None of us knew what the distraction was. As it turned out, the next time I saw him he was with Angie, so crisis, what crisis? I watched Sweet's final set. Other than that one chart hit, their material was filled with reworked covers, including 'Born to be Wild', one we had ejected from big nights by then. I was hopeful to have a conversation with Andy Scott and take up where we left off without offering to sell him my Strat. It didn't happen. I didn't see him after that. Who knows what he was up to? With oppressing fatigue again after the rush of adrenalin faded, I returned to the dressing room, away from any distraction, tired as hell and not really ready to drive home.

Jamie and John, in the meantime, were in the bar with Brian Connolly and Mick Tucker. Jamie at his outgoing best asked Brian in conversation, "How do we get where you are?"

"You gotta keep out there, hopeful of being spotted, as we were. We've been around on the circuit for a while. How long have you been at it?"

"With this group, only around eight months. So what does it take to get a recording contract?"

"Luck really, being in the right place at the right time."

"So where are you next?"

"Er… next week Wolverhampton and then Liverpool, I think? What about you lot?"

"Tomorrow a USAF base, The Gala, Norwich, and Clacton next weekend. And there's talk of Birmingham for couple of nights the week after that."

The conversation went on for a while. In the meantime

Dave had been drinking. A lot. Of wine. I was still hopeful I could take a risk and ask him to drive if I felt overwhelmed by fatigue. But as it was, no chance, he was beyond a comeback. So I had to prepare to get us home one way or another. Maybe Jamie or Richard could step in if they were prepared to take a risk.

Time drifted; the place was emptying fast. Activity, nevertheless, was still rife in the entrance corridor by the cloaks. Jamie and Steve Priest were against the wall with two girls, locked in embrace, each couple a few feet apart.

One girl looked to the other and smugly announced, "I'm with Sweet's bass player."

"So what?" the other proudly declared, "I'm with the gorgeous drummer from Julius Pam."

They didn't appear to know each other. I actually felt quite warm about that when Jamie told me sometime later. Crikey, we go around battling without true fame, sometimes it's nice to have some recognition when fame is around, in whatever form.

I lumbered out of the dressing room onto the stage to pack away some of the leads and the Mayfair. Brian Connolly was sitting on his own directly in front of me, kicking his heels against the stage. He appeared preoccupied and quite detached. I did wonder should I speak, but thought better of it. Then I changed my mind.

"Good night wasn't it?"

He didn't reply.

"Everything alright?"

"Yeah, nothing I can't handle."

I didn't want to open that book. I had no idea what the text was about. I tried to keep the conversation going with a sycophantic statement.

"Loved that bass depth you've got."

"Where do you come from, then?"

"Local, Suffolk. Can I ask, Chinn and Chapman… how did they come into your life?"

"They were looking for a band to front 'Funny Funny' and chose us. Simple as that, really. That's about it."

He jumped down from the stage. "Gotta go, see you around."

"Yeah, hopefully."

He disappeared through the main entrance. I did think, was it as simple as that? Maybe for some.

The rest of the crew were returning from various crusades involving the wild Norfolk coastline; lucky them. Mrs Blow paid John, bless her.

"You're back again on May the twenty-ninth. See you again then, boys."

The van loaded, we headed for home, Walter leaving with the friend he came with. On the journey, I discovered that at some point during the night there was an altercation between Brian Connolly and Dave; Richard and Clive had intervened to keep them apart. Over what I am yet to discover. Maybe this was why Brian appeared preoccupied.

So what other intrigue surfaced. Nothing really, except:

"Hey, would you believe it, they've spelt the name wrong." John was scouring the Journal newspaper he had half inched from the office and found the Links add for that night.

"Who's name", Jamie enquired.

"Look, they've spelt Julius, Julias!"

"Assa problum, up ear ina Norfuk, A.E.I.O.U don't alluz cum inat orduh, doit," proclaimed Richard with a native Norfolk slant.

"I wonder if they've always spelt it wrong?"
It turned out they had!

Homeward bound the van engine was knocking. I had noticed something on the way there. Approaching Bury it worsened, not as bad as a knocking shop but improving. That helped keep me alert. Concerned about a possible breakdown I kept to milk float speed on the final leg.

The van with no name rolled to safety in front of my home at gone 3 a.m. My real concern was the fatigue. I began to realize this wasn't a passing ailment. I needed rest, and did think of going to the quack's on Monday if things didn't improve. We still had that day's venue to negotiate first. After leaving a message for my father about the van, I found just climbing the stairs a challenge. Mum woke me around 11.30. I felt better but not great.

The Resurrection of Gertrude
"It's the big ends," were Dad's ominous first words. "Engine out and bottom end needs sorting."

Hell, no van for today, and it's a Sunday! I rang John.

"What about Gertrude?" his response.

"She's been standing idle over three months."

"We haven't got a lot of time, have we?"

"I'll get back to you." It was already 12.30 and we had an afternoon engagement with American Teens.

Gertrude it was. There she had stood, forlorn, discarded, abandoned, forgotten. It was almost a joy to open her door again. The leather seats hadn't lost their aromatic appeal, and I felt a warmth from her very soul. She knew we needed her. Luckily, her heart had been revived in that attempted sale. Would she start again? The button fired life through her veins. She was hesitant, drowsy. Slowly but doggedly her motion came alive. A third attempt and she was free from slumber, awake and joyful of my presence. "Where to?" I could hear her say.

"We've missed you," I replied.

I've got tears in my eyes here; you'll have to give me a minute.

"Where's that box of tissues, Pat?"

"You used them all the last time you crashed."

Hell, we haven't got THAT much time! I left her running and charged to the phone.

"Gertrude's a goer!"

"Christ, that's a miracle!" John said in amazement.

"She *is* a miracle - and still taxed, until Friday!"

John said "We need to unload everything across from TVWNN."

"Can you all gather here by about one-ish?"

John signed off with "Leave it with me!"

Dad offered, "I'll ring the bloke from the insurance."

Gertrude was purring and a hoard descended on Quays Road well past one-ish. Within a fraction of a second the lot was in her warm embrace. The equipment that is. But she was loaded so badly there wasn't room for everyone. So there was a Herald for Jamie's taxi.

Better get some fuel. Dad had a gallon in the shed, and we were on our way by some miracle called Gertrude. She knew the way to USAF Lakenheath, not far, just twenty-five minutes.

Gerty had delivered us to thoroughly modern American Teens, high on Rock, and we could let our hair down a little. An enthusiastic teenage gathering very responsive to Deep Purple, Black Sabbath, The Stones, Free, and a resurrection from our early days, 'Born to be Wild'. It was good, and there was John, enjoying some adulation from a young American admirer, signing another of those photo cards. So our fame had acquired momentum. That was the fifth signature in five months! I'd be old and gnarled before we reached stardom at this rate, but it was always good for the soul to entertain a welcoming audience intent on enjoying themselves. These kinds of outings were a release in a way – less expectation. On this occasion our afternoon cruise allowed Gertrude to deliver us home early for once – a blessing for me as fatigue was threatening again.

My father had already started stripping the engine from the Transit, all done completely voluntarily and without any expectation from us. John and I had discussed how to pay for the repair. We still didn't have a great deal of money in our piggybank. Dad suggested to keep the cost down it might be possible to get the repair done at his works and said he would ask a favour of them on Monday. He and I spent that evening removing the engine. I realize now in my later years how much I owe my father. He never stopped believing.

Monday 26th April

There was still no joyous surprise awaiting in the morning when I passed the hall table where the post was left. The memory of Alana was fading a little, but only a little. I still longed for her touch, her presence, and wondered whether we would ever be together again.

Back at work, Phil's Monday morning call was perfectly on time as usual, but Mr Balaam was in early and intercepted it. "Who is this Phil Beevus?" he enquired with a grump when I answered the internal phone.

"Um... he's a customer, comes in a lot at weekends," I

replied, fingers crossed, biting tongue, hoping he wouldn't see through my deception.

"Well, don't be on the phone too long!" he demanded.

"Phil, we'll have to make this short and sweet. I'm getting it in the ear from Albert."

"Just tried John. He's busy at the moment so thought I'd catch up with you. Lots to update. Birmingham's on – put these dates in your diary. The Elbow Room on Friday, May the seventh, and The Belfry, Wishaw, Saturday the eighth."

"You'll have to let me know expectations at some time Phil."

"I'll try John again later and ring you at home this evening when you've got more time." The call ended.

The sound of Mr Balaam's slow-motion ascent up the stairs was daunting. "So who is this Beevus?"

"Must give our customers the best of attention."

"Well, he certainly gets a lot of that. He's something to do with your group, isn't he?"

My lack of response clearly answered that. "Well don't use the shop as an extension to your out of hours recreation!" He left disgusted.

I'd probably ignore that and find some covert way to counter Albert's command. I was already planning.

Getting through the busier mornings and clearing up from the weekend kept me preoccupied on Monday. Come the afternoon the exhaustion kicked in heavily, so much so I fell asleep in the chair for over an hour. By some miracle no one came in, or, if they did, felt sympathy, not wanting to disturb a lazy layabout who should by rights be administered the sack. When I arrived home, the van engine had gone, the engineers from Mann's having taken it at lunchtime.

Phil rang me with the details for Birmingham as promised. I was growing more and more respectful of him. In my experience a good and sincere man.

He began with, "The Elbow Room, a long-established nightclub in Aston, intimate, audience mainly older teens, twenties and thirties. It's well known, has had some big names appearing there."

"Big names?!" I said, inwardly concerned.

"Yeah, household names… Sabbath, Winwood, Move, Plant pre-Zeppelin," he said casually. "Oh, yes, and it's on the first floor."

"Oh, Christ! So we're OK for that one then, are we?"

"Yeah, yeah. You'll be fine. You had a good weekend, didn't you?"

"Suppose so. Who are we there with?"

"No one, you're on your own."

"Really!"

"The Belfry is another well-established venue in a hotel complex. Big names have been through there as well: Moody Blues, The Who, Procol Harum, Bee Gees, Move… oh, and Led Zeppelin were there a few weeks back."

"Well, that's alright, isn't it?" I enthused.

"You're there with The Bonzo Dog Doo-Dah Band."

"Oh! Well, that's – good, I guess." Sounding slightly disappointed.

"Other news though, Andy. I've been in contact with a song-writing team – Chinn and Chapman, heard of them?"

"Well, if I wasn't working in a record department, I wouldn't have," I said, a little dismissively.

"You'll know then that they wrote Sweet's 'Funny Funny'? who you were with on Saturday."

"Yeah. Jamie and I spoke to them about that."

"Did you?!"

"Yeah, nothing much said though. Right place, right time, comes to mind."

"Well, these writers are looking for potential acts to front other songs they have written or will write. I've put your name in front of them and they like the image."

"Well, that's flattering, but they haven't heard us yet."

"They might be at one of the venues in Birmingham."

"Oh, yeah, that sounds promising!"

"And finally, there's another chance to go to Germany, if things have changed since November?"

"Well, Jamie might be OK to go now but I'm still not sure about John. I guess we'll speak about it this week."

"I have mentioned this to him already," Phil replied.

We spoke for some time after that, and I mentioned I'd not been feeling too well recently. He signed off with, "Go and see your doctor."

All the world is birthday cake, so take a piece, but not too much.
George Harrison

Chapter 29
Dreams Give Me Strength

"IT COMES AND goes, sometimes I feel ok, other times just dead tired."

"You should go to the doctors," Mum's concerned reply.

"No, I'll just take it easy, should be ok by the weekend."

"You must look after yourself Andy. Perhaps you're doing too much."

"I'll be OK. Probably take the day off tomorrow. See how I am then, Mum."

"See you in the morning."

By ten o'clock that night I was out like a light. Slept like a brick. Twelve hours later, as I came round, the jingling travelling shop sounded like crackling fire. *Ray will be wondering why I'm not at work,* I thought. I felt strangely stiff as I got out of bed and walked to the landing.

"Don't worry, I rang him first thing this morning. Go back to bed," came Mum's reassuring voice from the bottom of the stairs.

I didn't. After food and drink there was some improvement. Stimulation opens the mind, so out came the Strat and most of that day was spent finishing what I'd started two weeks before, 'Madonna in the Park'.

My return to work for Wednesday, Thursday and Friday wasn't over-taxing. Back home on Friday, the restored engine stood by the transit. I was astonished by the speed of the repair, but Mann's had a very close-knit workforce and my father was a popular employee. No doubt this had a lot to do with its speedy return. Dad asked if I felt up to helping refit the engine. If not Uncle (ladder) Bob would help.

"No, I'm fine. Let's see if we can get it done for tomorrow." Three hours and it was back in.

"I haven't got to go in tomorrow. You go and get some rest, I'll do as much as I can tonight," Dad insisted.

I knew he would work into the late hours. By then I was not feeling too good again so called John to let him know. "Let's see how you are tomorrow," he replied.

Saturday 1st May

That morning I felt rough and a gravel throat had started to develop. I did go into work and by midday the rough had marginally subsided. Not wanting to let anyone down, my hope was to get through the weekend and see the doctor on

Monday. But come early evening, fatigue was oppressive and the gravel had turned to broken glass. By this time Dad had the transit going again with a test drive done, the lot. Thank goodness for faultless parental devotion. John came to the house around 6.00 p.m.

"Are you OK for tonight?" he asked.

"I don't think I can go, John. I feel pretty rough, seriously."

Mum was concerned. "He definitely shouldn't go out tonight!"

But John was quietly persuasive. "It's an important night. If you can get through it, Andy, we'll worry about Clacton tomorrow."

"Alright, I'll try, just for tonight."

"Oh, Andy, you really should stay at home and get well." I didn't heed my mother's advice.

The tightrope we walked at times with Norwich Artistes had already been tested. Letting them down again in their home town could be fatal as it was highly unlikely Beevis would be able to find a replacement so late in the day. The tax had run out on Gertie, everything had been loaded back into the transit. We were off to The Gala Ballroom, Norwich, me driving.

Much of that night was a blur beyond a blur. I did manage to struggle through the first set, stayed in the dressing room throughout the break and was plied with soft drinks and concern.

The second set I was all over the place. I'd difficulty hitting high notes and my throat was burning. I do remember some weird sensations, like looking at my fellow musicians and shaking my head. They were surrounded by a blue haze. At the start of 'It Don't Come Easy' I didn't seem to have any problems with the lead in but was looking out into complete blackness where earlier the spotlight glare had been overpowering. There was a lonely voice cheering me on from a great distance as I played the intro and it felt as if I was touching the ceiling with my head. The only memory after that was in the dressing room. Somehow we'd completed the set, as far as I was aware. Jamie mentioned I'd collapsed on-stage. Not surprisingly, I have no memory of that. Feeling feverish and absolutely drained, with blurred vision and sometimes incoherent, I sat slumped in a chair.

The advice from the management: take him to the Norfolk and Norwich Hospital, just a short distance down the road.

At midnight I was admitted via Casualty onto Ward 8. Boy, did I feel bad, drifting in and out of consciousness. A couple of male doctors came and went. I remember one of them standing side on at a desk, just beyond the end of my bed, with a black telephone receiver to his ear, saying, "Temperature is one hundred and five." His voice was pronounced but echoing. I definitely didn't want to be there.

There was an injection and fluids. After a time I asked could someone telephone my parents. The walls, the ceiling, the glare of the lights, appeared ultra bright in my hazy vision.

At 2.15 a.m. at home the telephone rang in the hall, for a long time. Mum answered. She was shocked. "We will come straight there." Nan came to look after my sister Mandy, Mum and Dad heading for Norwich around 3.00 a.m. Perhaps it's important to mention the anxiety my parents would have been experiencing on that small-hours journey. The memories of travel surrounding my brother's death at nineteen, my current age, would have been uppermost in their minds. Almost certainly my mother would have asked during that telephone call what was wrong. Mention of suspected septicemia and Glandular Fever would have raised her anxiety to a near unbearable level. Dad, he would have been very quiet and his thoughts concealed.

I have no recollection of seeing my parents when they arrived. I may have been asleep, or maybe since then the memory has faded. Sunday and Monday they visited religiously. During this time, with regular injections and a high level of care, my condition markedly improved and my vital signs were returning to normal. In fact, I felt better than I had for a long time and itching to get home, but the real incentive to leave hospital was the weekend ahead in Birmingham.

During those three days, events in the ward unearthed realities I had never been exposed to. The terrible cries of pain of a dying patient, the frantic activity of truly dedicated staff trying to revive him, and feeling powerless to help, all still live with me to this day.

On the third day I sat up in thought, writing the lyrics to a song I strangely titled 'Fantasy'. These are those lyrics from a piece of notepaper most likely given to me by a member of staff or another patient perhaps.

> Amber in the night, and I am falling
> Angel in white light, and I am calling
> There's nothing left to do, give all my life to you
> Angel in white light, and I am falling
>
> Dreams give me strength and I will follow
> She's fading from view, there's no tomorrow
> So little time to live, need more time to give
> Angel in white light, and I am falling

No time space or heart, I am drifting
No dark or light, feel my body lifting
I've lived my life it's true, time to give to you
Angel of my life I hear you calling
Angel of my life I hear you calling

Gentle haunting lead. Keyboard support

Bright lights I came alive, my eyes are weeping
You're with us now, don't cry, you have been sleeping
She's coming into view, so want to be with you
Amber in the night, and I am calling

Angel in white light, and you are fading
Amber in the night, and I am calling
Amber in the night, and I am calling

Fade repeat
Instrumental fade.

Reading these back now I can see the influence of Angel of Eighth Avenue, so perhaps in some ways not totally original, but pretty much reflects where my mind was and all that surrounded me at that time.

But, *'Gotta get outta this place'!* Like the Animals. It was driving me wild with frustration.

On Tuesday morning there were no signs they were going to let me out. After consultation I made a clear statement. I was leaving!

"We strongly advise against that. You need a little more time."

"No! I've got to get away."

"Well, we can't force you to stay, that's your decision. One of the doctors will talk to you before you go."

I dressed and rang home. "I'm coming home, Mum."

"Oh, I thought it'd be a few days yet."

"No, I'm coming out now. Can you pick me up?"

"Your dad won't be back till gone five… we'll come as soon as we can."

Later that day consultant doctor Oliver made an exclusive call. "We do encourage you to stay for a day or two, to give yourself a chance of better recovery. I have to advise you of that."

"No, I must go, there's things to do. Besides, it's driving me wild in here."

"At present we suspect this is a case of acute Glandular Fever. If so it does take time. It could take several weeks or more to recover from this type of illness. Your temperature was high when you came in and your white blood count considerably elevated. These have reduced to safer levels now, but in our opinion you are not fully recovered."

Countless thoughts raced through my head. I felt better than I had for some time. If I went home and there was a relapse, the hospital in Bury St Edmunds was close at hand.

"Thank you for your concern, I really do want to get home."

"Very well. With this thermometer and chart you must record your temperature frequently for a week, at least twice a day. If your temperature rises significantly or you feel unwell, you must seek medical advice, straight away, wherever you are."

"Thank you, I will." I'm not so sure how sincere that statement was.

"I've made an appointment at the clinic for you

Wednesday next week. Do be certain to come along. For your welfare, it's important."

By that evening, I was home, and glad to be, with an energy absent in recent weeks. Not perfectly restored but better, and I slept well. I hadn't spoken to anyone in the group since midnight on Saturday. They drove the van home without insurance that night, the first time we had truly gone illegal.

On Wednesday it was a joy to wake up in my own bed. My first mission was to ring John at the jeweller's. He was busy. "Call you back later, Andy."

I telephoned Ray at the Music Centre and confirmed I would be back at work the next day. He sounded concerned. "Don't rush back, we can manage. If you're up to it, come back next week." Bless him.

Beevis was who I most wanted to speak to, but he was not in the office when I called. I left a message.

I waited, deep in thought, feeling detached from all that had gone before. That void of three days with no contact, no interaction, had induced a feeling of starting over again. Negative thoughts intruded the landscape. Six years of making a noise and what had been achieved other than landing in hospital? That was all I could see at that moment. But there was Birmingham ahead, and numerous bookings beyond. My mother reminded me, Glandular Fever doesn't disappear overnight. I was young and indestructible, or so I thought, able to overcome any adversity and sail straight on to paradise.

'Never look back,' said the Lady in Black. The perfect philosophy for that searching moment!

No, the phone didn't ring immediately after that, so I backed Gertrude into her space, looking outward this time rather than her face in the hedge. *You may be needed again old girl*, I thought, walking away. She looked on anxiously.

Phil rang first, later that afternoon. We had a long conversation. He was very sympathetic, asked if I was OK for the coming weekend.

"Yeah, I think so. I'll try not to overdo it."

"Well good luck with that! Speak again next week sometime."

I had an odd feeling as I put the phone down. I couldn't see beyond that phone call. Mind playing tricks again?

John returned my call later that day. We had a short conversation; he was busy still. After explaining I was OK for the weekend, all was set for Friday and an overnight sleep in the van. Hell, that wouldn't exactly be good for my health!

"What happened with Clacton?" I asked.

"Beevis found a replacement, I reckon."

I made a conscious decision to do everything in a measured way, to conserve energy, not get involved in anything other than promoting the group's interests that coming weekend. Just getting through this and out the other side safely was the aim.

Friday 7th May

By midday we were outward bound toward Warwickshire, six within including a birthday celebration. The foreman at Boby's had a meltdown when three of his works staff disappeared without an alibi or *adios*. Some might call it absent without a care… but it was 1971, after all!

Jamie came with nineteen years to his name and full of the joys of spring. Celebrating his birthday in one way or another was a mission cunningly contrived by all but Jamie.

In those days, driving to industrial Birmingham from tractors in Suffolk was a navigational tangle, no motorways as such other than the joy of a short stretch on the M1 passing Northampton. We only had a 1940s map. The A45 would guide us into the heart of city and urban sprawl in transition, from antique and quaint to modern and stark. Ring roads driven through lives herded into high-rise. A strange uninviting landscape where concrete Leviathan stood by tiny Victorian terrace.

But before we made port there was a mission to fulfill. A not so affluent Coventry street with run down establishments selling cakes demanded a halt on the way. Richard, John, Clive and Dave disappeared through a small glazed Victorian shop front. I wondered if they had become lost, the wait was boring. After eighteen minutes of drift a large Corn Flakes box emerged, followed by three other persons. It was presented to Jamie with a rendition of 'Land of Hope and Glory'. He enthusiastically opened his gift and there in all its splendor sat a tiny cup cake with a minute candle burning. A momentous occasion, and it remains one of the defining moments of his life. What he has completely forgotten about is the horrendous choral version of 'Happy Birthday to You' after his speech. Who could blame him? It was fun and reminds me now of those times of carefree exuberance.

We were early into Birmingham, or Aston High Street, our destination. The weather was sunny and modestly warm as the van with no name came to a standstill outside the Elbow Room. But the surroundings were out of my comfort zone. A modern highway flanked by savagely stark architecture of higher than high-rise. On our side the old high street road of Victorian heritage, scattered still with structures of a discarded time. The modern Woolworths, just closed for the day, butting up against an unassuming building housing the Elbow Room on the first floor. On the ground floor, a shop beside a solitary entrance door that led up those stairs. There was no one around, all locked up and time to kill, food and drink was a need, so we went in search.

A director sends us back in time along a cobbled terraced street lined with dilapidated houses, many with boarded windows and doors. The neglect was somber, and demolition threatened obliteration. But we found that little forlorn shop front void of any display, and as I tried the door it opened to the sound of a quaint tiny bell. I could almost smell the dust on the bare floorboards. The room was gloomy, near vacant, except for two old wooden trestle tables with a meagre display of confectionary boxes supported by two bottles of Coca Cola. There was no feast.

Not wandering far, we loitered, past the Hippodrome with its old sign still fixed high on the side of the building, and Aston proudly displayed on the façade, a Mecca by that time. Across the road, The Barton Arms public house flanked by the High Street and Potters Lane. It captured mystique and charm, a superb old building with architecture a world away from the brutal trying to bully its downfall. Under request I telephoned home to confirm I was OK. The two telephone boxes marooned on a small triangular island in the middle of the road in front of the club were life threatening, but convenient.

Around 6.30pm, Elbow Room staff invited us up those wooden stairs and into a carpeted room tastefully dressed, the stage agreeably small off to the left, and a bar beyond the dance floor. Modest in size, perhaps it accommodated 200 or so pleasure-seekers. Phil was right, intimate it was. Stairs were a guaranteed challenge up or down in many of the clubs we played and always suppressed enthusiasm before the main event. Richard and Clive desperate to invade the bar after lugging the stuff upward, came over all queer when the barman politely demanded 4 shillings (old money) for two pints of Watneys Red Barrel. I'm confident they didn't fully recover from that, ever.

The whole festival was relaxed, I felt welcomed by our hosts and as the four of us prepared to colonize the stage, there were no feelings of nervous tension that often tormented the mind at the beginning of important performances. It was comfortable, and the acoustics were great in there, absorbing the sound beautifully, the low ceiling enclosing a warm atmosphere. With all that had gone before in this treasured place, we kept to a heavy blend of our most contemporary. I was feeling ok, and surprised; no fatigue and a voice without restriction. John, Jamie and Dave were clearly high on the moment, before an expanding audience intent on having a good time. Their close, friendly embrace, the magic of Midland accent and warmth, flowed over us as the night raced past. Bev Bevan (The Move, ELO) joined the party late, with some other apparent notable personalities. I wondered who they were; I didn't ask. I should have done. The last set we played with a dance floor full of revelry and joy, Jamie taking a singing lead part way through 'My Brother Jake', letting the frets of my Strat loose with Kossoff's magical lead work. The place was packed and I was almost disappointed, the ending, ended.

The set list for that second session:
'Black Night'
'Strange Kind of Woman'
'Evil Woman'
'No Matter What'
'It Don't Come Easy'
'Hot Love'

'Angel of Eighth Avenue'
'My Brother Jake'
'Brown Sugar'

Everything was so beautifully placed that night,. This was where our evolution had taken us, a repertoire that reflected the identity we aspired to, and in a place I felt so at home with. The only absentee, content of our own making.

When I look at the world I
wonder why. I got lost in a
maze of my own minds eye.
Truth is, the world is small,
but the mind is endless.

Chapter 30
A Message from Manhattan

"LEAVE THE EQUIPMENT here overnight if you like, collect it all in the morning." Our hosts were, as we found them, very accommodating. The thought of a night attempting to sleep in the van was chilling. Our budget hadn't extended to hotel bills, or sleazy backstreet one night bed and cockroach breakfasts. I have no idea what happened to Dave but I managed to get some broken sleep on the front seats while John lay flat out in the back. Thankfully it wasn't cold. But, unknown to us, Clive, Richard and Jamie had other objectives, crashing out on the floor in a flat occupied by a pair of female students not far from where the van was parked, but we had no idea where.

Morning came. Dave reappeared, and the three of us found somewhere to eat, then set out on a sight-seeing tour. But there wasn't anything inspiring on view. At a pre-arranged time back at the Elbow Room the equipment humped its way back into the van and the need to find the others was compelling. We had no idea where to start. Rather than using the Cromer formula we persuaded an Elbow Room member of staff to spill the beans after asking him politely. He was very accommodating, and even supplied free drinks.

It was a hot sunny afternoon by the time we discovered the flat was up another flight of stairs, where all was soon revealed. Far from being lost in a Bacchanalian orgy, our three deserters were transfixed by the Cup Final on the tele as we walked in, bottles and food wrappings strewn around and the whole dishevelled bunch of them watching Liverpool vs Charlie George. Apparently nothing controversial happened? I have to say I was vexed, with a top up of maddened. As always, don't rock the boat was the order, keeping a safe distance was better than taking the plunge.

So it was on to The Belfry, Wishaw, Sutton Coldfield, and our date with The Bonzo Dog Freaks. We were all spent after the night before and I was probably feeling the effects more than everyone else. After arriving early and lounging around in the parkland we were chaperoned to our station in the Mayfair Suite. It was an unconventional space for a music venue, the main stage completely open without wings and ours a kind of alcove with a sizeable transformer-type thing on the back wall. God knows what it was? But it was big. The dressing room was substantial, perhaps formerly a grand bedroom, with a screen down the middle to divide us, the Rabble, from the performing Royalty on the other side. The whole place was much more civilised than most of the venues we visited, and somewhere we could prepare ourselves and relax in relative comfort. Our first set was uneventful in that warm up role again – with one critical exception. Richard was out there sitting in the side-lines, sleeping like a log.

Jamie, John and I were in with the audience to watch Bonzo after our performance. They didn't disappoint; brilliantly bizarre at times, Viv Stanshall and Neil Innes amongst the clever and talented troupe on-stage. 'Entertains and held my attention' comes to mind, and their showpiece sketch about Jesus on a gig up North lodged in my brain for years. It was their sheer stage presence that impressed the most.

Back on stage our second set was going better than I had expected, a crowded audience gathered around in curiosity. Not quite the atmosphere of the previous night, even when The Bonzos were performing; even so we were making an impression. But! Like the devil rising from the depths, out of nowhere our sound equipment developed a disorienting *BUZZ*. Bulldozing through it, we soldiered on without remorse. However, I spotted one of the Bonzos with an abnormal hand-held device, lurking in a shady corner eating a Scotch egg.

Who knows what we sounded like out there in the audience? Anyway, it didn't seem to deter anyone, particularly when the *buzz* stopped. But when it returned with a vengeance at the end of 'Strange Kind of Woman', frustration mutated to "What the **** is that noise?!"

A voice from the crowd announced, "It's always happening."

Silently I thanked that guy, sincerely, for speaking up. We made it through without incarceration. As a night it didn't light my fire in the way the Elbow Room had, but on reflection we walked away with credibility intact, applauded at the end of our set. (That searing buzz, incidentally, was radiating from that dastardly alien transformer on the wall behind me.)

So the call came for home. Bonzo were the first to leave, and in thought provoking style they emerged from behind the stage in regimental single file, dressed in a mind-boggling array of eccentric garb, Stanshall leading, acting suave and weird, as they filed out by the front entrance, giving us a candid look as they passed by – and this was at least 30 minutes after the end of their show when most of the audience had found the exit. Showmen until the end of the end, quite brilliant.

The Bonzo Dog Doo-Dah Band

Home James, and don't bugger the engine. We drifted away from the Belfry and made our way back to the A45 and Coventry. Twilight was dawning and the M1 beckoning under a sunshine dawn. I was surprised to discover I was wide awake, like a second coming, and the silence within was deafening. Not a word or murmur from anyone, Dave on the front seat trying to stay wake to keep me awake. On the M1 there was barely a visible motion under a sun-blessed Sunday sky.

"Next stop, Watford Gap, anyone hungry?"

He was suddenly alert as the van drifted to a car park halt.

"Where–the–hell–is–this?" a voice in the background.

"We're lost."

"Somewhere in Wales."

"Pull the other one, it's got an alligator attached."

It was quite busy as we sauntered in at 5.30 a.m. before all sitting around one table, gladly filling ourselves with motorway mediocrity. After around 30 minutes Sweet appeared, looking dishevelled and worse for wear than we did. They had been performing at Oakengates Town Hall, Telford. Ideal, an opportunity to carry on where we'd left off at Cromer and collar Andy Scott about the Strat and other small talk, maybe. As they passed our table I greeted Brian with a nod and Jamie acknowledged their coming with a brief hello. But the response was cold as they sat at two tables' distance. Their presence almost immediately provoked an instantaneous aggressive reaction from Dave and was guaranteed to marshal a confrontation. His pent up emotion was clearly aimed at Brian Connolly. I was baffled; what was this all about? Richard and Clive, loyal subjects, kept any intensifying clash from truly emerging. We were not far from departing and encouraged Dave to "leave it".

I was disappointed and should have told him to go

wait in the van if he couldn't control his emotions, but as always, maintain the status quo was the call. I departed with everyone and our dignity remained intact; well, almost.

Out into the warm sunshine we left in unison as though nothing had happened. I remained mystified but eager to get home. The van with no name was happily cruising down the motorway under clear skies, playing nursemaid to weary faces, Jamie, the night watchman in the early morning, looking out for any signs of failure in my focus.

"Van's going well Andy," he commented.

"He's purring, running like a dream."

"They're all out in the back there already."

"You know, we should have a name for the old boy."

"Burt… what do you think?" Jamie suggested.

"A Van Called Burt. Well, it's novel. Or Burtrude, perhaps?"

Silence returned for two minutes. We were gliding without a rattle or bang. It was a glorious morning, the way ahead clear and unimpeded. Was it too good to be true?

"What's that strange noise?" I was brazenly unperturbed.

"Sounds like the engine Andy."

"Christ, not here, in the middle of a motorway. Surely." I was shockingly perturbed.

Burt began to flounder like the life was draining from his very sole. But he found new energy, spluttering forward, trying to overcome his failings. It wasn't to be. Slowly, to a grinding halt on a hardened shoulder he found sanctuary.

Jamie and I looked at each other. "Bugger."

Not a soul stirred in the back. We lifted the bonnet. From deep within came an eerie gurgerly, wobblizing, bubbleulating, as though Vesuvius was about to release the fires of Hades.

"What the hell's that?!"

I peered with foreboding down into the engine bay. The

gurgerly got louder… Jamie was holding open the bonnet, definitely looking perturbed.

Zogawongaoopolyyingaflobafffazomp! I jerked back. The oil cap took to the skies like a demented rocket soaring into the air vertically perfect. Caught by a breeze its momentum slowed, falling gracefully down beyond the fence and into an unsuspecting field with a cow in it.

Jamie and I looked at each other again, totally undiscombobulated. "Bugger."

Then a body fell from the driver's side door. It was John as I had never seen him before, beyond totally shattered.

"Wass happened then?"

"We've just had lift off."

"Should be fine, no problem."

"What about the oil cap?"

"Well, it wasn't very happy, was it? Probably better off without it."

The others were stirring as we tried to get him going again, but Burt was buggered and we were marooned. For a while, we sat brain dead.

"Sweet will probably be along in a minute; they'll stop and give us some help," said I with ultra-optimism.

In the sunshine, I stood leaning with back against the van in hope. Richard and Clive were trying to flag down the few passing vehicles with no response. Twenty minutes passed.

Yonder, a transit van the same size as Burt came hurtling towards us. It *was* Sweet. I parked in the middle of the carriageway arms aloft. *Christ, they're not slowing down!* I refused to retreat. The van sped up, careering across to the next lane with hands, arms and two fingers flailing out of open windows on both sides, voices hollering mockingly as they hurtled passed my left foot. *Bloody adolescence*, I thought, as they charged down the motorway, disappearing into the far yonder. If it were me, I would have stopped to help, Dave or no Dave, wouldn't I?

For a while we stood there, brain dead. The only alternative, to walk to the nearest junction and call for help. We had travelled some way from Watford Gap so the best option was Northampton services. Clive, Richard, Dave and John made for sanctity. Jamie and I stayed at the mercy of increasing traffic.

Of course there's no way a simple task of phoning for help would turn out to be a simple task. They landed up in a park somewhere in Northampton after buying a plastic football and playing a game without a referee. What can I say? The lot of us had prepared for work on Friday morning around 7 a.m., forty-eight hours before, and had averaged four hours sleep each by that time. Anyway, back at the van Jamie and I hadn't a clue what was going on. We just waited, and waited, and then waited beyond waiting.

At midday, fanfare! The cavalry arrived, in the form of a white Mann's of Saxham Class Combines van and a car loaded with the absentees, pulling up in front of Burt. It was my father, Mr Garratt driving, our neighbour from number three, and John's father, Ernie, in his car. With Jamie volunteering to keep me awake, we were hitched with a tow rope to the back of the van and hauled home closing on 100 miles, via country A-roads and town and city centres. The sleep deprivation was mind-numbing, but we made it home without crashing into the van in front, although it was excruciatingly close about twenty times as my eye lids failed to defy gravity. Everyone else had piled into the car with John's father and were kept awake the entire journey by Ernie's all-embracing chat.

So, back to my health… that escapade didn't help, I guess. Looking back, the wonders of youth seem to overpower the forces of oppression when adrenaline is flowing. Well, not always. There's a limit to endurance. Surprisingly I didn't feel desperately bad when I got home. I functioned OK, and the temperature chart didn't flag up anything sinister. I was hoping the hospital diagnosis was a misdiagnosis, and when returning to the Norfolk and Norwich on Wednesday I would receive a clean bill of health.

So I had time to reflect. We had played some notable, but not spectacularly notable, places, with some notable, if not spectacularly notable, acts of that time. Julius Pam was still only eight months old and Beevis had kept us busier than many pro bands. The apprenticeship was served; maybe it was time to find our true identity. After the hospital visit I decided to press Beevis for a recording slot in the hope of giving those songs an outing. Would everyone be in support?

But by Wednesday I wasn't feeling so good again, functional, but not good. Tests at the Norwich hospital confirmed I was not fully recovered. The Consultant's advice: "If you are serious about getting well you must respect your body. Burning the candle at both ends is not the medication I would advise. I will release you from our care today, but you will be under the supervision of your doctor and must arrange to see him in a week's time. I strongly advise you not to jeopardize your recovery by continuing doing what you have been doing."

Deep thought and reflection occupied my mind. There were three bookings that upcoming weekend and numerous beyond. How would I break the news of my decision to rest?

The door opened to home.

"Andy, there's a USA Airmail letter on the table, came in the post this morning."

My pulse raced. This could only be Alana! The opened envelope revealed a letter from a Manhattan address.

Dear Andy,

As Alana's mother and at her request it is with great sadness I write to you. Our darling daughter has died of injuries sustained in a car accident in early March. On the day before she died she handed me a note and requested this should be enclosed within this letter. Alana never mentioned your name before this, but I sensed when she returned home in February there was a change in her life. I hope one day we may meet or talk. Please do reply if you feel you can.

An Englishman forever in my heart.

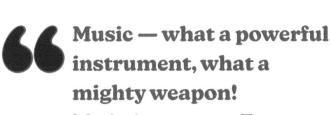

> **Music — what a powerful instrument, what a mighty weapon!**
>
> Maria August von Trapp

Postscript / Afterword

ANDY, YOU CAN'T end it like that! What happened next?

I am sorry. Sincerely. Julius Pam took six years to write. I just ran out of steam. There's a whole story still to tell, one that takes a new direction over the following ten years. The love of music continues, Mr Balaam carries his weight for a while, The Glitterband reappear, and Ray continues to have a positive influence. Black America and video emerge, there are new and old characters, highs and lows, and the wonder of children.

After all of that there's another ten years of adventure and an express journey through the world of a fast and demanding service industry.

I haven't started that new chapter yet. The house needs redecorating, the garden looks forlorn and I need a haircut. When I've overcome those challenges, in that order, I will, hopefully, sit down and once again put pen to paper.

Acknowledgements

BY GOLLY, HOW many of you can I thank, and where do I start?

Me! That's a good idea. Well, what can I say? I deserve a medal, six years, digging up all that stuff and never sure if it was right. Writing something and then discovering it's wrong after I'd had a telephone call from someone who said "I forgot to tell you", and then developing an instant vertical hair style as a result of having to rip up that chapter and start again. But! After that, there comes another phone call from someone who contradicts the first someone.

And! Very special thanks to the many who couldn't remember a thing. Three hours, six glasses of wine, only two words on the notepad, and then, suffering from tipsy-turvy, I couldn't stand up.

But this has been a very special journey. I was first to meet John in the jeweller's; nothing had changed after forty-five years. As I walked in he was still busy.

John, Dave, Jamie, Clive, Richard, Clive B, Angie, Wendy – I could write another book about how we reconnected after so many years. What an experience. There are so many on the fringes of this story I could mention whom I have spoken to and must express my thanks and appreciation to all.

I think the copy editing is absolutely brilliant. I did it. Myself. So if you can't understand half of it and can see my grammar and all the other stuff that goes with copy editing is almost terrible, fine, I'd even think that's great. But, actually, I did get help in editing from Lynn Curtis; her input and advice was immeasurable, bless her. But you wouldn't believe how much of a hard time I gave her. So if you're writing a book and need an editor, look her up, she comes highly recommended.

And I must express warm and special thanks to Rosalind Dickinson, Typo Terrier. What a joy it was to work with her at the proofreading stage. At my suggestion we took one chapter at a time. Her speed and efficiency was amazing, so much so I was getting completed proofs back before I sent them! I'm sure you've guessed I am only teasing, but it's a measure of how easy this was with Rosalind's help.

So on to the typesetting and design. I hadn't a clue how to navigate my way through all of this, but I didn't need to worry. Berenice Smith, Hello Lovely Design, was a fantastic guide. So much that I love about the design of this book comes from her all-important experience. There's something very special about how well organised, understanding and thoughtful Berenice was in the way she approached my less than conventional pre-requisite.

The cover design was an innovation from long chats with Kevin, K.W. Creative Graphic Design. A great listener, and he created this on the first pass. The fact he lived just up the road from me in Beyton had much to do with why I picked up the phone and chatted with him for about an hour that morning. I knew, there and then, we shared the same wave length; some things just seem to fall in place so naturally.

And Gill Robinson, Nexus Creative Print Production. Printing extraordinaire. Her infectious personality is not typically business, but it works perfectly. She guided me through this complex stage with ease. Thank you so much Gill.

And with honour I dedicate my final tribute and sincere thanks to Ray Broome. I couldn't find his telephone number so I wrote to him instead. He called me on one wet and overcast day and the surroundings lit up. It was like the thirty odd years since I'd last spoken to him hadn't passed. Special words could not describe the joyous conversations we've had. His memories were so invaluable.

It has been a tremendous experience. Thank you all, truly, for your patience.

Disclaimer

SOME DETAILS OF this narrative are a work of fiction, a figment of my imagination; I think that just about covers it all. In several cases I couldn't remember exactly what happened or what was said, so I've used inventive writing to fill in the gaps. To maintain anonymity, in some instances I have changed the names of characters and places to protect the privacy of the people involved. The depiction of characters is how I saw them, although this was part of my creative thinking back then. In some cases I have added people into events; in others I have made two people into one and in a few cases married two events together. Much of the timeline of the story comes from detail written at the time; diaries and booking lists were an ideal reference. But it is possible some of those events were incorrectly recorded.

Thank you for reading this book, and if this has been a perfect remedy for insomnia, it's all been worthwhile.